A New
Nuclear Century

A New Nuclear Century

Strategic Stability and Arms Control

Stephen J. Cimbala and
James Scouras

Westport, Connecticut
London

Library of Congress Cataloging-in-Publication Data

Cimbala, Stephen J.
  A new nuclear century : strategic stability and arms control / Stephen J. Cimbala and James Scouras.
    p. cm.
  Includes bibliographical references and index.
  ISBN 0-275-97061-2
  1. Deterrence (Strategy). 2. Nuclear arms control. 3. World politics—1989– I. Scouras, James. II. Title.
  U162.6.C58 2002
  327.1'747—dc21   2001058036

British Library Cataloguing in Publication Data is available.

Copyright © 2002 by Stephen J. Cimbala and James Scouras

All rights reserved. No portion of this book may be reproduced, by any process or technique, without the express written consent of the publisher.

Library of Congress Catalog Card Number: 2001058036
ISBN: 0-275-97061-2

First published in 2002

Praeger Publishers, 88 Post Road West, Westport, CT 06881
An imprint of Greenwood Publishing Group, Inc.
www.praeger.com

Printed in the United States of America

The paper used in this book complies with the Permanent Paper Standard issued by the National Information Standards Organization (Z39.48–1984).

10 9 8 7 6 5 4 3 2 1

CONTENTS

	Acknowledgments	vii
	Introduction	ix
1	First-Strike Stability Modeling: The Crazy Mathematics of the Cold War	1
2	Redefining Strategic Stability	25
3	Friction and Nuclear Deterrence	75
4	Triad and Tribulation: U.S. and Russian START Options	105
5	Proliferation in an Unstable World	127
	Conclusion	161
	Further Reading	181
	Index	183

ACKNOWLEDGMENTS

The authors gratefully acknowledge the following persons for comments and critiques on earlier drafts of parts of this study, or for their insights into the topics of deterrence, nuclear arms control, stability, and proliferation: Pavel Baev, Robert Batcher, Stephen Blank, Jerome Bracken, James Bradley, Michael Crutcher, Raymond Garthoff, Daniel Geller, David Glantz, Colin Gray, James Holcomb, Joanna Ingraham, Jerome Kahan, Jacob Kipp, David McGarvey, Wendell Nix, Fred Nyland, Keith Payne, Peter Pry, Thomas Scheber, and Brad Walker. We express special gratitude to Glenn A. Kent and David E. Thaler for their important efforts to address first-strike stability and subsequent impact on our thinking; our disagreements are intellectual, not personal.

We would also like to thank Dr. James Sabin of Greenwood Publishing Group for encouraging this project and Betty Pessagno for serving as senior production editor.

None of the above persons is responsible for any of the contents in this study. The views expressed in this book are those of the authors and do not necessarily represent those of any agency of the U.S. government or of the Pennsylvania State University.

INTRODUCTION

This study is the result of an informative collaboration between colleagues from very different professional worlds. One author resides in the academic community and is a political scientist. The other is a physicist who is also an arms control expert and a consultant to a number of institutions that deal with nuclear weapons issues. Our collaboration has involved a two-way exchange of perspectives on a number of important policy issues related to nuclear strategy and arms control. We intend to follow this study with others.

In this book we consider various issues related to nuclear weapons in the twenty-first century. The issues are both technically and policy oriented. Science and values are commingled. This means that arguments about nuclear strategy, arms control and proliferation are apt to be contentious. The first months of the George W. Bush administration in 2001 indicated that political controversy about nuclear weapons would not go away despite the end of the Cold War and the officially nonhostile relationship between the United States and Russia.

In Chapter 1, we discuss the "crazy" mathematics of first-strike stability that preoccupied analysts and policymakers during the Cold War. It is important to keep this effort in perspective. By "crazy mathematics" we do not mean to imply slipshod methods or deceptive approaches on the part of the investigators. Instead, we refer to crazy mathematics as limiting approaches that blinded analysts to the more subtle aspects of nuclear force modeling relevant to the question of first-strike stability. And first strike-stability was itself a limiting concept. As frequently used in the literature, it approached a tautological mathematics or formula-driven assessment that succeeded only by tautology. On the other hand, the first-strike stability theorists helped to provide a basis for later analysis to build upon.

The discussion of stability modeling in Chapter 1 is not merely an argument about method for its own sake. It helps to set up our discussion in Chapter 2. In this chapter, we argue for a more comprehensive definition of strategic stability and relate this more inclusive concept to the current relationship between the United States and Russia. Our assumption is that while the end of the Cold War terminated the politically hostile relationship between Washington and Moscow, the nuclear arsenals of the two sides remain poised in an uncertain posture of cooperation and competition. Cooperation is apparent in the U.S.–Russian discussions to reduce the strategic nuclear weapons of both states to levels below the 3,000–3,500 warheads permitted under the START II agreement. Competition remains implicit in the U.S.–Russian nuclear relationship as well; so long as the two states' arsenals are combat ready and mainly programmed to strike at targets in one another's national territories, stability remains a major concern for political leaders and military planners.

As Chapter 2 explains, a more nuanced concept of stability than that characteristic of many Cold War discussions leads to important insights about how we might better understand and measure the current and future U.S.–Russian nuclear relationship. We introduce the concepts of *generation stability* and *prompt launch stability* to show how the operational aspects of nuclear arms in a prewar crisis are as important as the calculus of nuclear warfighting. Of particular significance, the decision to place nuclear forces on high alert, or the willingness to launch retaliatory strikes on the basis of warning (instead of riding out the attack and then retaliating), can make it more difficult to avert an outbreak of war that both sides would have much preferred to avoid. However, measuring the relationship between alerting decisions or launch doctrines and stability is a challenge that calls for newer approaches and perspectives developed in this study.

In Chapter 3, we consider how the gap between theory and practice might influence nuclear force operations and arms control. For this purpose, we employ the concept of "friction" developed by the renowned Prussian theorist of war, Carl von Clausewitz. Friction is the difference between war on paper and real war—all of the things that can go wrong when the military machine is set in motion during times of peace, crisis, or war. Clausewitz's concept of friction sounds as if it is mechanistic. But it is more subtle than that: it also refers to the potential of each link in the chain of command, or each individual soldier in battle, to exercise an independent will that causes events to stray from prewar plans.

Friction has been a problem that U.S. and Soviet political leaders and military planners have had to deal with since the dawn of the nuclear age. In both Washington and in Moscow, important issues had to be thrashed out during the Cold War about how nuclear forces would be controlled in time of peace (in order to prevent accidental or inadvertent war) and about the management of nuclear force operations during crisis or time of war. Thankfully, there were no nuclear weapons fired in anger during the Cold War years, but there were dangerous nuclear crises, most notably the Cuban missile crisis of 1962.

Research has established that a number of things can go wrong not only in the mechanics of operating nuclear forces, but also in the relationship between policymakers and military operations, including operations with nuclear capable forces. Cold War experience showed that neither positive control (assurance that nuclear forces will be promptly responsive to duly authorized commands) nor negative control (assurance that nuclear weapons will not be fired accidentally or inadvertently) could be assumed without political and military leaders taking special precautions and insisting on careful monitoring of seemingly routine and insignificant activities. Our discussion considers some kinds of friction that might predispose American or Russian leaders to make decisions that were neither necessary for deterrence nor helpful for reassuring their opposite numbers of their nonhostile intentions.

We consider in Chapter 4 whether the United States might get by in the new century with fewer "legs" of its strategic nuclear triplet than weapons based on land, at sea, and in the air. The traditional Cold War "triad" was considered necessary on account of the diverse survivability it afforded against the large arsenal of Soviet missile and bomber weapons. The ICBM and bomber legs of the American nuclear triad were also thought to have a "synergistic survivability" because attacking both of these legs forced a choice of providing additional warning time for one or the other leg. Thus, it was assumed during the Cold War that platform redundancy contributed to force survivability and therefore to stability.

Notwithstanding the assumed validity of these arguments on behalf of the Cold War nuclear triad, the post–Cold War and twenty-first century worlds do not pose such a comprehensive threat to U.S. force survivability as the Soviet threat was thought to have done. It follows that the United States might get equally competent deterrence against any plausible nuclear attack or coercion by means of weapons deployed on fewer platforms, say, for example, on submarine launched missiles and bombers but without a land-based missile force. We consider some of the arguments pro and con for reducing U.S. forces to a "dyad" or even to a "monad," and we perform a stability analysis to assay what difference such a restructuring of forces might make.

In Chapter 5, the problem of nuclear weapons spread or "proliferation" is considered from the standpoint of both theory and policy. Although some highly regarded political scientists have argued that nuclear weapons spread can be controlled and is therefore not incompatible with arms race stability, we disagree. The theory marshaled in support of toleration for proliferation is simply wrong. It makes heroic assumptions about the motives of state actors and their leaders and ignores the latent potential for perfidy among self-regarding and threatened heads of state. We also discuss some of the current policy-related problems with regard to the spread of nuclear weapons along with ballistic missiles and other long-range delivery systems.

The spread of weapons of mass destruction (WMD) including nuclear, biological, and chemical weapons, along with ballistic missiles, is important in current policy debates. President George W. Bush had barely moved furniture into the Oval Office before his administration declared its intention to proceed with plans for a national missile defense (NMD) system. Missile defenses were necessary, according to Bush, to counter the imminent threat to the American homeland and to U.S. allies posed by the existence or potential availability to "rogue" states of weapons of mass destruction and ballistic missiles of various ranges.

A North Korean test missile launch over the Sea of Japan in 1998 and the "Rumsfeld Commission" report of the same year caused members of the U.S. Congress and others to question whether deterrence, old style, could still be counted on to prevent nuclear attacks against North America or against forward deploying American forces. Some favored missile defenses as insurance against rogue rage or accidental/mistaken launches, as from a rickety Russian early warning system. But critics of defenses cautioned that, even if the defenses worked against ballistic missile strikes, they left open the door to other means of attack: cruise missiles, or terrorist attacks with suitcase bombs or commandeered airplanes and other lethal devices. Defenses might even encourage additional nuclear weapons spread and, at the same time, prove to be less effective in the event of war than tests might suggest.

The United States and Russia have for some time been conducting Strategic Arms Reduction Talks (START) with the intent of reducing the size of their intercontinental nuclear forces on land, sea, and in the air. The Russian parliament finally ratified the START II Treaty shortly after the new millennium began, although with conditions that are unlikely to be acceptable to the United States. START II, if it enters into force, will reduce each side's deployed strategic nuclear warheads to a ceiling of 3,000–3,500 by the year 2007. Russia and the United States have also begun discussions toward further reductions by mutual agreement under a START III agreement. Interestingly enough, Presidents Bush and Putin recently declared that each side will engage in unilateral reductions whether START III is officially consummated or not. But further reductions in offensive weapons and progress with or without START III are tied to the development of missile defenses, which the United States values and Russia fears.

1

FIRST-STRIKE STABILITY MODELING: THE CRAZY MATHEMATICS OF THE COLD WAR

The term *crazy mathematics* (and its less sophisticated cousin, *crazy arithmetic*) appeared in public discourse of nuclear issues throughout the Cold War. It was applied, inter alia, in the late 1970s to a straightforward calculation that resulted in the assessment that there was enough nuclear explosive firepower in the arsenals of the Soviet Union and the United States to kill every man, woman, and child on earth many times over. The calculation went something like this: There are over 1,000 megatons in the arsenals of both countries, with each megaton the equivalent of one million tons of TNT. A few ounces of TNT, strategically placed, is a lethal amount. So, with the earth's population of approximately four billion, each person's allotment is some 500 pounds, more than enough to do the job. More than enough, that is, if only we could ignore the implicit assumptions that we could somehow divide each nuclear weapon into millions of micronuclear weapons and get the entire population of the earth to cooperate in the mass extinction of the human race.

As this example illustrates, crazy mathematics may be *calculationally* correct, but its misapplication to practical problems leads to unjustified, sometimes bizarre, conclusions. Of course, the point of this calculation was to dramatize the claim that the nuclear arms race had reached an irrational, even absurd level. Now, there may well have been far too many nuclear weapons on Earth during the Cold War. And, unleashed, they may indeed have destroyed every single person on the planet (although we were blithely unaware of the phenomenon of nuclear winter[1] at that time). This calculation, however, does not support either of these conclusions because it assumes *impossible conditions*.

Impossible conditions are not the only hallmark of crazy mathematics. The other salient feature is *unknowable or unquantifiable inputs*. Social scientists appear to be particularly susceptible to this affliction as they attempt to mimic the extraordinary success of physical scientists in developing and applying mathematical theories, but nuclear theorists are not too far behind. For example, can anyone reasonably defend assigning a numeric value to the probability of nuclear war? Or the "cost" of nuclear war? Many have tried, none have succeeded, but not all have recognized their failures.

While crazy mathematics wasn't invented by nuclear theorists, neither has the grave nature of nuclear warfare provided any relief. Indeed, as this chapter will demonstrate, Cold War nuclear theorists seem to have taken this phenomenon to a new level. And, although it has been over for more than a decade, modes of thinking ingrained during the Cold War are still very much with us today. That is why it is worth the trouble to critically examine these modes of thinking even in the aftermath of the Cold War. The challenge for the post–Cold War era is to reevaluate these modes of thinking to preserve those aspects that remain valuable while replacing others that are no longer relevant (or never were relevant) and, indeed, have become dangerous. This chapter addresses this challenge in the realm of first-strike stability by using one widely cited index of stability as a case study.

THE KENT/THALER FIRST-STRIKE STABILITY METHODOLGY

During the Cold War, deterrence and first-strike stability were the dominant concerns of national security strategists, nuclear war planners, and arms controllers. The cornerstone of both U.S. and then-Soviet (now Russian) national security strategies, deterrence has been based on the expectation—and the hope—that neither country will attack the other if the potential attacker anticipates a devastating retaliation. The logic of deterrence is rudimentary, but compelling in its crudity. It applies to the choice of initiating war or avoiding war. If initiating a nuclear war is under contemplation, the side that is considering initiating (striking first) can expect to suffer a retaliatory strike from the other side. If that retaliation is anticipated to be devastating enough, the deterrence will prevail and war will be avoided.

Unfortunately, in the context of a crisis that has risen to the level of nuclear threats, the perceived choice might not be to initiate or avoid war; rather it might be to strike first or strike second. The logic of deterrence does not apply to this choice. If nuclear war is perceived to be unavoidable, the critical issue for the side or sides with this perception is which side will strike first. The logical decision in this circumstance is to attempt to strike first because, no matter how devastating a retaliation is anticipated to be, an even more apocalyptic scenario would derive if the other side attacked first. To reiterate: if nuclear war appears to be unavoidable, it's better to strike first than be subject to a first strike by the other side. In a severe international crisis in which nuclear war appears probable or even just possible—*but not inevitable*—this logic leads to a grim choice: strike first or wait, with the possibility that waiting would allow the other side to strike first. This choice is the basis of first-strike stability considerations.

Based on much earlier work by Daniel Ellsberg, the Kent/Thaler index of stability was developed in the late 1980s at the Rand Corporation by Lieutenant General Glenn A. Kent (USAF, retired) with the assistance of David Thaler.[2] It had the singular objective of quantifying the impact of force structure and force posture on first-strike stability. By the time Kent and Thaler undertook this effort, the development of measures of stability had become something of a cottage industry in the United States. Every stability analyst seemed to have his or her own analytical approach. Many approaches were not well thought out, many were of limited scope, and none was universally accepted. Kent tried to bring order to this chaos.

During this period, one of us (Scouras) was also at Rand and had the opportunity to observe the development process closely and, more important, gauge the reactions of other analysts to the Kent/Thaler methodology. Most, including many at Rand, simply did not understand it. This was in large part because the methodology is complex; it takes time, concentration, and a certain level of mathematical sophistication to understand. Unless quantification of first-strike stability was an important professional concern, it just wasn't worth the bother. It was much easier to just nod politely in ostensible agreement and turn one's attention to other matters.

While a general comprehension of the Kent/Thaler methodology requires a substantial effort, a deeper understanding to the level necessary to critique the methodology requires even more effort as well as a background in nuclear exchange and stability calculations. Very few analysts accomplished this. Thus, the Kent/Thaler methodology, because of inherent flaws—its unnecessary complexity and overmathematization—escaped the rigorous peer review to which other methodologies were subject.

Although the Kent/Thaler methodology was never widely adopted, it has been erroneously *perceived* as widely adopted. Beyond insufficient peer review, this can be attributed to several additional factors. First, it was one of the few methodologies that were published in the professional literature. The second and more important factor is the vigor with which Kent made the defense and arms control communities aware of its existence. But *pub-*

lished and *well-known* do not mean *good* and *widely used*. In fact, the Kent/Thaler methodology seems to have sparked its own cottage industry of criticism and reactive development of alternative approaches.[3] One objective of this chapter is to dispel the myth that has grown around this measure, that it somehow is or should be the "accepted" standard methodology for stability analysis. This is important so that analysts and policymakers aren't saddled with this methodology as they turn their attention to post–Cold war concerns with multipolar stability. There is no easy way to do this, however, without lifting the hood to see what makes this methodology run.

OVERVIEW

The Kent/Thaler methodology envisions two and only two distinct types of targets for nuclear weapons—*counterforce* targets and *countervalue* (or, simply, *value*) targets. The defining characteristic of counterforce targets is that they can shoot back; that is, they contain the deployed strategic offensive forces of the other side. Such targets include submarine ports, bomber bases, mobile ICBM garrisons, and ICBM silos. They also include large areas in which weapons are thought to exist, but within which specific locations for individual weapons are unknown. Examples of this type of counterforce target are SSBN ocean transit and patrol areas, mobile ICBM deployment areas, and bomber flyout corridors and routes to target.

Countervalue targets are all other targets. For example, they can be nuclear targets that do not shoot back (e.g., storage depots for nuclear weapons), military targets not associated with nuclear weapons, leadership targets, and economic targets. And, despite the immorality and illegality associated with such targets, they can also be large urban areas.

Although some might criticize Kent and Thaler for oversimplifying the complexities of a realistic target set by using only two broad categories of targets, there are substantial advantages in such a simplification. It avoids myriad problems associated with making a detailed description of the countervalue portion of the target base. Because neither side presumably knows the targeting plans of the other, speculating on which combination of military, leadership, and economic targets represents the real countervalue target set is an analytically dubious endeavor. At the same time, this simplification preserves the essential distinction between targets that can harm the other country and those that cannot. Except perhaps for the distinction between civilian and military targets, there is probably no more important single defining characteristic of targets.

As illustrated by Step 1 in Figure 1.1, the underlying scenario of the Kent/Thaler methodology has one side striking first with *all* its weapons at a combination of *both counterforce and countervalue targets*. This is followed by a retaliation with *all remaining weapons* that is directed *solely at the countervalue targets* of the first striker (i.e., the retaliator does not attack the strategic forces of the first striker). It is important to recognize that, while this scenario has the first striker attacking both counterforce and countervalue targets, only the counterforce portion of the attack need be undertaken immediately. The first striker can withhold its strike against countervalue targets indefinitely, as can the second striker.

The methodology proceeds in Step 2 to determine the level of damage (percentage of total value destroyed) inflicted on the countervalue targets of both sides. Using these damages, Step 3 assesses the "costs" to both the first

Figure 1.1
Overview of the Kent/Thaler Methodology

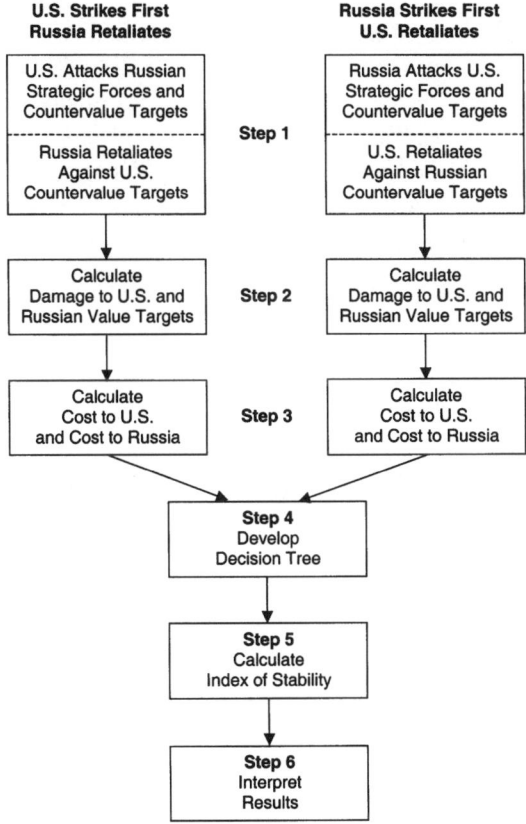

striker and retaliator of the nuclear exchange. Cost to a side is a function of both the damage inflicted on that side (which raises the cost) and damage inflicted on the other side (which lowers the cost). Then the methodology switches the roles of first striker and retaliator and repeats Steps 1 through 3 to calculate the costs to both sides of the alternative nuclear exchange in which the other side strikes first. That is, it calculates the cost to the United States and the cost to Russia[4] if the United States strikes first and the cost to each side if Russia strikes first.

In Step 4 two decision trees are developed, one for each side, which consider the consequences of each choice—strike first or wait. The key parameter in each side's decision tree is the perceived probability of the other side striking first. If this probability is small for a side, that side is generally better off waiting because it perceives little risk that the other side will strike first. However, the higher this perceived probability, the greater the relative advantage in striking first rather than risking the other side striking first. The value of this probability for which a side is indifferent to striking first or waiting is related in the Kent/Thaler methodology to the ratio of costs to that side of striking first to striking second. The methodology then multiplies these two ratios (one for each side striking first) in Step 5 to form an index of stability, which purports to be a measure of the lack of advantage in striking first. The final step, necessary for any analysis, is to interpret this index in terms appropriate to the broader question(s) under study.

With this brief overview, we now proceed to describe in detail the six basic steps involved in calculating the Kent/Thaler index of stability and the key assumptions and issues associated with each step.

STEP 1. DEVELOP DRAWDOWN CURVES

The first step in the Kent/Thaler methodology is to develop a set of what are commonly referred to as *drawdown curves*. A notional set of such curves is displayed in Figure 1.2. These curves are developed by the following procedure: We first determine how many weapons with which to conduct a nuclear exchange are available to each side. This requires postulating the alert state of both sides. Typically, the first striker is assumed to have, perhaps surreptitiously, placed its forces on generated alert (*increased combat readiness* in Russian parlance) while the retaliator is assumed to remain on day-to-day alert. The weapons that are initially available to each side with its postulated alert state define the common starting point of both drawdown curves. In Figure 1.2 this point is the large black dot in the upper right-hand corner of the graph.

Figure 1.2
Notional Counterforce Drawdown Curves

As indicated by the labels of the x and y axes of Figure 1.2, these weapons are available to attack the value targets of the other side. However, to the extent that the weapons of the first striker are used against the counterforce targets of the retaliator, fewer weapons are available on both sides to attack countervalue targets. Any weapon used by the first striker against a counterforce target is no longer useable against a countervalue target and any of the retaliator's weapons that were destroyed by this weapon also cannot be used against the first striker's countervalue targets. Each point on a drawdown curve corresponds to a potential stopping point for the first striker's counterforce attack. The coordinates of that stopping point are the weapons available to each side for countervalue attacks. An entire drawdown curve thus represents the locus of alternative allocations of both sides to countervalue targets as one side attacks the counterforce targets in a first strike on the other side. The choice of where to operate on the drawdown curve is the first striker's. He does this by deciding when to stop allocating weapons to counterforce targets and reserve remaining weapons for countervalue targets.

For example, consider the drawdown curve in Figure 1.2 labeled "Russian First Strike." We imagine that the Russian attack is directed at U.S. strategic nuclear forces and that counterforce targets are attacked in the order of most lucrative to least lucrative. In this case, Russia would first attack submarine bases to destroy the largest number of U.S. weapons for each Russian weapon expended in the attack, then attack in turn bomber bases, MIRVed ICBM silos, and single-warhead ICBM silos. Finally it would barrage broad ocean areas where it suspected U.S. SSBNs might be patrolling and airspace where it thought U.S. bombers might be in flight. This inefficient component of the counterforce attack is indicated by the dashed portion of the drawdown curves in Figure 1.2.

This order of attack—from most to least lucrative target in terms of weapons destroyed per weapon expended—determines the characteristic shape of most drawdown curves. Starting at the point with the maximum number of available weapons on both sides, they are generally very flat (steep for the drawdown curve with the other side striking first) initially as many weapons are destroyed per weapon expended, have a near 1-to-1 slope as single-warhead ICBM silos are attacked, then are very steep (flat for the other side's drawdown curve) as attacking weapons are directed at imprecisely located targets. Because drawdown curves usually have a sharp turning point, it is usually fairly obvious where the first striker will stop attacking the counterforce targets of the retaliator—near the turning point. This could be just before or, more likely, just after attacking single-warhead silos. Further attacking counterforce targets is usually very wasteful of attacking weapons and thus unlikely in practice. In Figure 1.2 these stopping points are labeled A (a_1, a_2) for the United States striking first and B (b_1, b_2) for Russia striking first. If the United States strikes first and stops its first strike counterforce attack at point A, it will have a_1 weapons remaining to attack value targets in Russia, while Russia will have a_2 weapons surviving with which to retaliate against U.S. value targets. Similarly, if Russia strikes first and stops its counterforce attack at point B, the United States will have b_1 weapons surviving to retaliate against value targets in Russia, while Russia will have b_2 weapons remaining with which to strike U.S. value targets. This terminology is summarized in Table 1.1.

Drawdown curves are a useful analytical tool, but care must be taken in using them. The assumptions used in generating drawdown curves are often driven more by the desire for analytical convenience rather than the requirement for realism. Three such assumptions, all representing potentially serious deviations from reality, are embedded in the

Table 1.1
Weapons Available to Attack Countervalue Targets

	U.S. Strikes First	Russia Strikes First
U.S. Weapons Available to Attack Russian Value Targets	a_1	b_1
Russian Weapons Available to Attack U.S. Value Targets	a_2	b_2

development of drawdown curves in the Kent/Thaler methodology. The most problematic of these assumptions is that *the retaliator does not attack counterforce targets*. One rationale for this assumption is that it would be wasteful for the retaliator to attack forces that have already been launched. However, in reality it is not at all clear that the retaliator would assume that all of the targetable strategic forces of the attacker have been launched and that none of these targets could be reloaded. Moreover, there is a plausible scenario in which limiting the retaliation to only *counterforce* targets may be prudent. The first striker might withhold the countervalue portion of the attack in the hope that the war might then be limited to counterforce targets. In that circumstance, it is not clear that the retaliator would wish to expand the war to include countervalue targets. In addition to not wanting to target only countervalue targets, the retaliator may not be able to do so. If the retaliation is prompt or disorganized, there may be little ability to execute a pure countervalue attack.

The other two problematic assumptions are not required by the Kent/Thaler methodology, but in practice, following the lead of Kent and Thaler, they are almost always made: *The first striker is on generated alert* and *the retaliator does not launch on tactical warning*. The rationale for the former of these dubious assumptions is that a first striker would be highly unlikely to launch an attack from a day-to-day alert posture because the first striker can mount a much larger attack from a state of generated alert. Since it is the first striker who determines when to attack, he can wait until he has generated his forces before doing so. However, this logic ignores a critical consideration. Any generation by the first striker—surreptitious or not—runs the risk of detection by the other side, with the possibility of the other side generating its own forces (or preemptively attacking) in response.

Thus, in reality a first striker might be much better off attacking from a day-to-day posture to ensure that the retaliator would also be on day-to-day alert. In addition, if the attack grew out of an erroneous tactical warning, such as occurred in the Norwegian missile incident of 1995,[5] clearly the first striker would not be on generated alert.

Finally, the assumption that the retaliator does not launch on tactical warning flies in the face of both U.S. and Russian nuclear doctrines. While it is possible that either side may choose to ride out an attack before retaliating or may not succeed in its attempt to launch its retaliation on tactical warning, it is also reasonable to conjecture that either side might launch its retaliation on tactical warning. In fact, it would be prudent for the first striker to assume so.

One might argue that these three assumptions are carefully crafted to enhance the assessments of first-strike instabilities of strategic force structures and postures. After all, the scenario in which the first striker is on generated alert, the retaliator rides out the first strike before retaliating, and retaliates only against countervalue targets may be implausible, but is not impossible. And if analysis of that scenario results in the worst assessment of first-strike stability, we might reasonably choose to focus on that scenario.[6] There is some merit to this argument, but it fails on two counts. First, only two of the assumptions tend to minimize the assessment of first-strike stability; the assumption that the retaliator attacks only the countervalue targets of the first striker has the opposite effect. Second, this argument fails to recognize that stability assessments tend to be comparative in nature. That is, we assess whether force structure A is more or less stable than force structure B. For comparative assessments, focusing on worst-case assumptions for both force structures negates any theoretical advantage to this type of analysis. To the extent that it is feasible, it would be far more satisfactory to model reality more closely to get a more accurate assessment of first-strike stability.

STEP 2. DETERMINE TARGET DAMAGE CURVES

With selection of reasonable stopping points on the drawdown curves, we have the number of weapons for each side that are available to attack the countervalue targets of the other side. For the first striker these are the weapons it chooses to not expend on counterforce targets; for the retaliating side these are the weapons that survive the first strike. The second step in the Kent/Thaler methodology is to determine the level of damage these weapons can inflict. To accomplish this, it is first necessary to decide which counterevalue targets to attack and then determine how damage accumulates as more of these targets are destroyed.

In general, countervalue targets include leadership, military (other than deployed strategic forces), and economic targets. Kent and Thaler, however, have included only theater projection forces, war supporting facilities, and possibly leadership in their countervalue target set. We will refer to this subset of targets collectively as power-projection forces, because Kent and Thaler thought that destroying the ability to project power beyond the Soviet Union's borders should be the principal objective of a U.S. retaliation. This was a questionable selection of value targets during the Cold War and is even more dubious today.

Notably absent from the Kent/Thaler target set are economic targets, despite the obvious fact that both countries clearly value economic targets. In fact, they almost certainly value these targets even more than power projection forces. Aren't cities, within which many economic targets lie, far more important to both nations than military bases? Cities are important not only for their economic value, but also for their cultural symbolism as was evident in the terrorist attacks of September 11, 2001, on New York and Washington, D.C. For the United States to focus on power projection targets is particularly unrealistic in the post–Cold War era. While during the Cold War the United States was greatly concerned with Russia's conventional military threat, especially to Western Europe, now that Russia's power projection capability is virtually nil there is little reason for the United States to focus on this target set.

In addition, Kent and Thaler make no provision for the inherent value of strategic forces in their methodology. Notwithstanding the useful distinction between counterforce and countervalue targets, we need to recognize that strategic nuclear forces are also valued targets. Their unique status as targets that can shoot back does not mean that they are not valued as much as other targets. In the post-Cold War era they are probably among the military targets *most* valuable to the Russian leadership.

Once the countervalue target sets for both sides are determined, the Kent/Thaler methodology requires determining how much damage will be done to those target sets as a function of the number of weapons allocated to attack them. That is, we need to determine *target damage functions*, such as those developed by Kent and Thaler for the United States and the Soviet Union and illustrated in Figure 1.3. With the Kent/Thaler methodology, this is accomplished in a two-step process. First, the analyst must determine the number of targets that, if destroyed, would result in a specific level of damage. Based on very little apparent analysis, Kent and Thaler assumed that for the United States the 2,000 most valuable power

Figure 1.3
U.S. and Russian Target Damage Curves

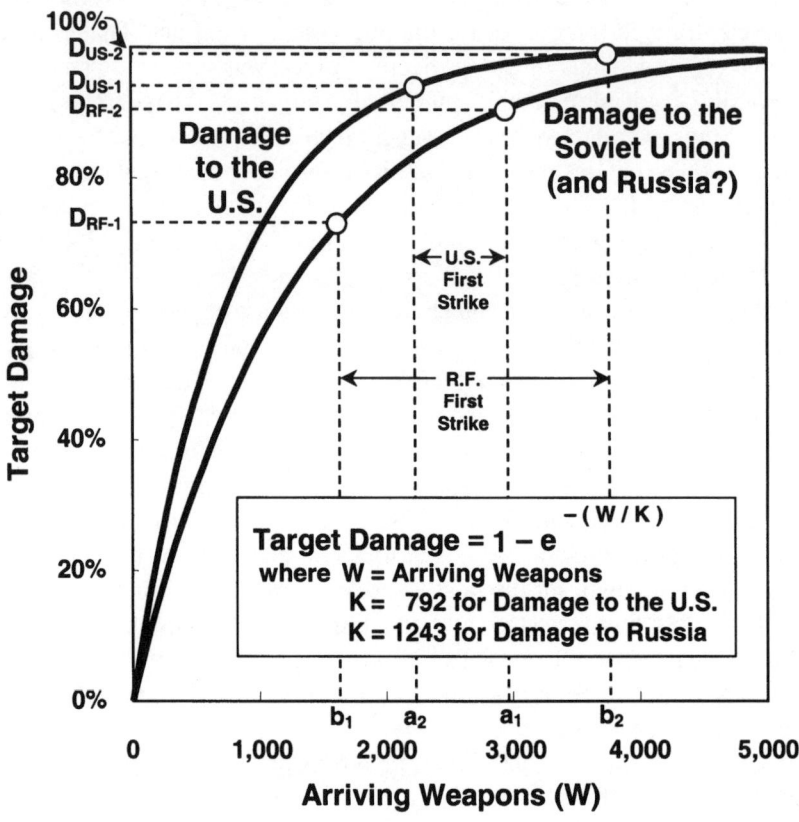

projection targets contain 80% of the value of all its power projection targets and, for the Soviet Union, 2,000 power projection targets contain 55% of such value. Because they recognized that these were controversial assumptions, Kent and Thaler also suggest an alternative set of assumptions: The first 2,000 power projection targets for the U.S. contain 92% of its power projection value and 80% for the Soviet Union. Since there are clearly fewer targets in Russia today than were in the Soviet Union when Kent and Thaler developed their methodology, we use this latter set of assumptions to develop the target damage curves of Figure 1.3 and treat these curves for illustrative purposes as *Russian* target damage curves, rather than Soviet damage curves.

For the second step of the process, we must recognize that some power projection targets are more valuable than others. The Kent/Thaler methodology assumes that, as power projection targets are destroyed in order of the most valuable to least valuable, damage accrues according to an exponential function:

Target Damage $= 1 - e^{(-W/K)}$

where **W** = **weapons attacking power projection forces**

K_{US} = **792 for the United States**

K_{SU} = **1,243 for the Soviet Union**

With zero attacking weapons, target damage is zero; with more and more attacking weapons damage approaches, but never reaches, 100%. Note that these values for K_{US} and K_{SU} are selected to result in target damages consistent with the estimation of the percent value (92% and 80%, respectively) found in the 2,000 most valuable power projection targets.

An advantage of the exponential accumulation of damage as targets are destroyed is that it reflects a decreasing marginal value of targets. But there is no particular reason to select the exponential function rather than other functions, such as the square root function,

Target Damage $= W^{1/2}$

which exhibit this same behavior.[7] This might seem like an esoteric concern, but the shape of the target damage function has an important effect on stability assessments. Because the exponential function rises quite rapidly, then becomes relatively flat, the difference between striking first and striking second is generally small unless the weapons available for the second strike fall below the "knee" in the curve.

Of course, now that the Soviet Union is no more, users of the Kent/Thaler methodology must come up with their own target selection and damage functions. This is where the mathematics of the Kent/Thaler methodology begins to get a little crazy. Just how is this to be accomplished? It is not unreasonable to assume value target sets that vary anywhere from some several tens to several thousands of targets. It's obvious that any such estimates are not much more than guesses. During the last few years of the Cold War, before the demise of the Soviet Union, analysts could always defer to the Kent/Thaler target base assumptions. However, that path of least resistance is no longer defensible. In the post–Cold War era, analysts and policy-makers differ widely on the targets that should be attacked, how that damage accumulates as more targets are destroyed, and the level of damage necessary for deterrence. Because it becomes necessary to make assumptions that are not widely held, the utility of the Kent/Thaler methodology as a universally accepted standard correspondingly diminishes.

In any event, carrying on with our calculations we have damages for the United States and Russia as summarized in Table 1.2. We hazard no guess as to what K_{US} and K_{RF} might be.

STEP 3. DETERMINE COSTS OF ALTERNATIVE NUCLEAR WARS

The third step in the Kent/Thaler methodology is to assess the cost of nuclear war. This is not just the damage done to the selected target sets of each side. Kent and Thaler view the cost of nuclear war to be a function of both damage incurred as well as damage goals not achieved. Lambda (λ) and mu (μ) are the factors used to weight damage goals not achieved compared to damage incurred. That is, for the United States and Russia respectively,

Cost to the U.S. = (Damage Incurred by the U.S.)^p
   + λ (1–Damage Inflicted by the U.S. ^{q})

Cost to Russia = (Damage Incurred by Russia)^r
   + μ (1–Damage Inflicted by Russia ^{s})

Cost can vary from zero to $(1 + \lambda)$ or zero to $(1 + \mu)$. Zero cost occurs when damage incurred is zero and damage inflicted is 100%. Maximum cost occurs when damage incurred is 1.0 and damage inflicted is zero.

Even if we accept the general form of the Kent/Thaler cost function, we are confronted with the problem of assigning values to its parameters. Lambda (λ) and mu (μ) are subjective assessments and once again, widely varying assessments exist.[8] In practice, Kent and Thaler use $\lambda = \mu = 0.3$ and, once again, other analysts have rarely deviated from these values. This is not because they think there are compelling reasons for this value, but be-

Table 1.2
U.S. and Russian Countervalue Target Damages

	U.S. Strikes First	Russia Strikes First
Russian Damage	$D_{RF-2} = 1 - e^{-(a_1/K_{RF})}$	$D_{RF-1} = 1 - e^{-(b_1/K_{RF})}$
U.S. Damage	$D_{US-1} = 1 - e^{-(a_2/K_{US})}$	$D_{US-2} = 1 - e^{-(b_2/K_{US})}$

cause they have no idea what the value should be. The easy choice is to follow the Kent/Thaler lead and press on. The exponents p, q, r, and s have the same problem. Kent and Thaler use $p = q = r = s = 0.75$, but there are no compelling reasons for these choices. These choices are intended to make costs deviate from otherwise linear dependencies on damages, but this implies a degree of subtlety in assessing the cost of nuclear war that is unjustified. This is another example of the overmathematization endemic to the Kent/Thaler methodology. Many analysts prefer to simply set $p = q = r = s = 1$.

Costs are defined for the United States and Russia for the alternative scenarios in which the United States strikes first and Russia strikes first. For the United States striking first,

C_{US-1} = Cost to the United States when the United States strikes first

$$= (1 - e^{-(a_2/K_{US})})^p + \lambda [1 - (1 - e^{-(a_1/K_{RF})})^q]$$

C_{RF-2} = Cost to Russia when Russia strikes second

$$= (1 - e^{-(a_1/K_{RF})})^r + \mu [1 - (1 - e^{-(a_2/K_{US})})^s]$$

For Russia striking first,

C_{RF-1} = Cost to Russia when Russia strikes first

$$= (1 - e^{-(b_1/K_{RF})})^r + \mu [1 - (1 - e^{-(b_2/K_{US})})^s]$$

C_{US-2} = Cost to the United States when the United States strikes second

$$= (1 - e^{-(b_2/K_{US})})^p + \lambda [1 - (1 - e^{-(b_1/K_{RF})})^q]$$

To understand these cost relationships, it is helpful to view lines of constant cost such as those plotted in Figure 1.4 for the United States. Each line represents a locus of alternative combinations of damage to the United States and Russia that result in a constant cost to the United States. For example, consider the line of 0.3 U.S. cost. All points on this line are equivalent in the Kent/Thaler methodology. Thus, according to Kent and Thaler, the United States should be equally satisfied with the outcome of zero damage on both sides and the outcome in which the United States' value target base is damaged 20% and the Russian's value target base is damaged 100%. It is unlikely that many policymakers, analysts, or citizens share this view.

Figure 1.4
Lines of Constant Cost to the United States

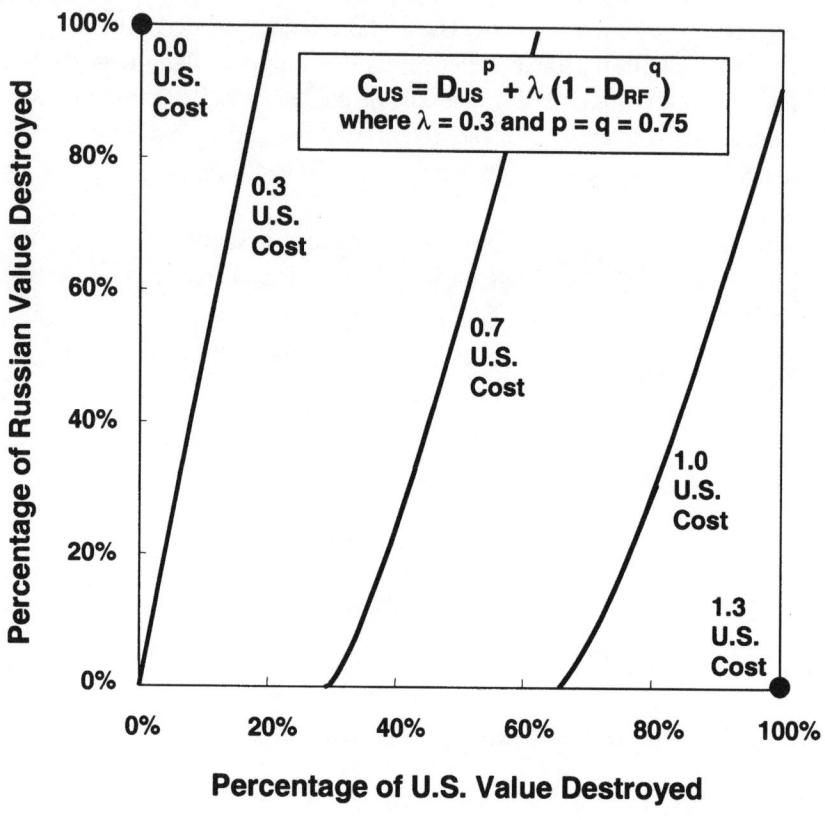

Consider also the point of zero U.S. cost. This occurs when the United States incurs no damage to its value targets and completely destroys Russia's value targets. Yet, if Russia struck first, the United States would have received numerous nuclear detonations on its territory, substantial damage to its counterforce targets, and undoubtedly many casualties from prompt effects and fallout. This is no damage?

Kent and Thaler present alternative possibilities for the cost of nuclear war, but all have the same problem—there is no convincing rationale for any of them and they all require the analyst to assign values to essentially unknowable parameters. And, unfortunately, the Kent/Thaler index of stability is highly sensitive to the cost function selected. So, in summary, the idea of quantifying the cost of nuclear war is dubious, quantification of the relative costs of alternative nuclear wars is highly subjective, the particular cost function used by Kent and Thaler is difficult to defend, and the sensitivity of

STEP 4. DEVELOP U.S. AND RUSSIAN DECISION TREES

Pressing on, with the four cost functions in hand, the next step is to consider the probability of nuclear war. Kent and Thaler do this using decision trees, as illustrated in Figure 1.5. As the United States, for example, contemplates its decision to strike first or wait, it considers the consequences of both choices. If the United States decides to strike first, the cost to the United States is C_{US-1}. Alternatively, if the United States decides to wait (not attack), either of two outcomes is possible. Russia may also wait or Russia may strike first. If Russia also waits, war is avoided and the cost to the United States is the cost of no war, C_{US-0}, which is defined to be zero. If Russia decides to attack, the cost to the United States is the cost of going second, C_{US-2}. The question for the United States is, given these alternative outcomes, what should it decide to do?

The answer depends on the United States' perception of the probability of Russia striking first if the United States doesn't. This probability is denoted p in Figure 1.5. If we weight the cost outcomes of the alternative branches by their respective probabilities, we have "expected" costs as follows:

Expected cost to the United States of waiting = $(1-p) * C_{US-0} + p * C_{US-2}$

Expected cost to the United States of striking first = C_{US-1}

If the United States were indifferent with respect to which branch it selected, these expected costs would be equal.

Mathematically, we have

$$(1-p) * C_{US-0} + p * C_{US-2} = C_{US-1}$$

Solving for p and remembering that $C_{US-0} = 0$, we have

$$p = C_{US-1} / C_{US-2}$$

This is the U.S. perception of the probability of Russia attacking such that the United States is indifferent between striking first and waiting. If the United States perceives that the probability of Russia attacking is greater than this, the United States would perceive an advantage in attacking first; if

Figure 1.5
The U.S. and R.F. First-Strike Decision Trees

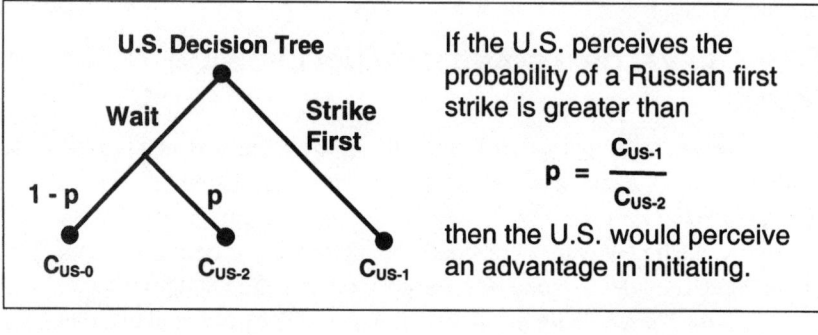

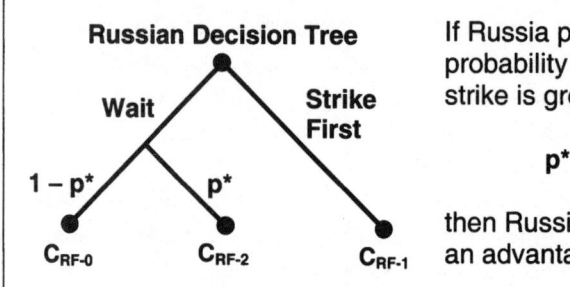

the United States perceives that the probability of Russia attacking is lower than this, the United States would perceive an advantage in waiting.

Of course, there is no reasonable way to assign a probability of the other side attacking with any degree of precision. Kent and Thaler avoid this problem in a clever way in the next step. Other problems with this decision-tree approach remain unsolved. Most important, it does not include important branches and it is based on an expected-value analysis of the branches. The choices are not only to wait or to attack. The option of generating one's forces is an important crisis decision option. Also, in a crisis the stark choice of strike-first-or-wait is clouded by the option of relying on launching a retaliation on warning. With respect to the expected-value approach, in the real world the choice of waiting will dominate any of this contrived mathematics. Waiting is the only option that can result in a satisfactory outcome—that of no war. So, unless the probability of the other side attacking is perceived to be an absolute certainty, waiting is the only sensible choice.

STEP 5. CALCULATE THE INDEX OF STABILITY

To (finally) calculate the Kent/Thaler index of stability, we consider all possible combinations of the U.S. perception of the Russian probability of attacking and the Russian perception of the U.S. probability of attacking. These probabilities define a *probability domain* as illustrated in Figure 1.6. The x axis is divided into two regions—one in which the U.S. perception of the Russian probability of attacking is below C_{US-1} / C_{US-2} and the other in which it is above that critical value. Similarly for Russia, the y axis is also divided into regions in which the Russian perception of the U.S. probability of attacking is below and above C_{RF-1} / C_{RF-2}. This divides the probability domain into four regions as shown in Figure 1.6. The bottom left region is the one in which both sides perceive an advantage in waiting. The top right

Figure 1.6
Calculating the Index of Stability

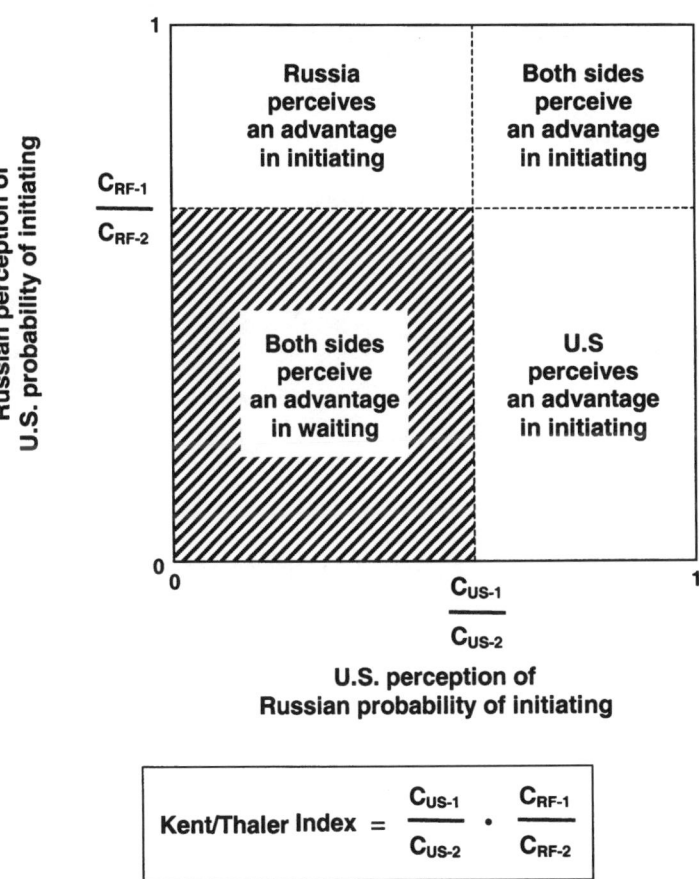

$$\text{Kent/Thaler Index} = \frac{C_{US-1}}{C_{US-2}} \cdot \frac{C_{RF-1}}{C_{RF-2}}$$

region is the one in which both sides perceive an advantage in attacking. The other two regions have one side perceiving an advantage in attacking while the other side perceives an advantage in waiting.

The Kent/Thaler index of stability is just the area of the probability domain for the region in which both sides perceive an advantage in waiting. That is,

Index of Stability = $(C_{US-1} / C_{US-2}) * (C_{RF-1} / C_{RF-2})$

This is the clever mechanism by which the perceived probabilities of the other side initiating a nuclear war are avoided in the definition of the index of stability. The problem with this step is that much valuable information is lost. Four important pieces of data are incorporated into a single measure. We lose the information as to which side—the United States or Russia—contributes most to an index of stability less than 1.0. The effect on the index of stability is the same whichever side has an advantage in initiating a nuclear war. Furthermore, whether one or both sides perceive an advantage in initiating also has the same effect on the index. Many analysts have partially solved this problem by calculating separate indices for the United States and Russia:

U.S. index of stability = (C_{US-1} / C_{US-2})

Russian index of stability = (C_{RF-1} / C_{RF-2})

STEP 6. INTERPRET RESULTS

A concrete example of the Kent/Thaler index of stability is illustrated in Figure 1.7. Here we plot the index of stability for four different force levels—1991, START I, and two START II levels (Phase I and Phase II).[9] The index is plotted as a function of target base size, because that is one of the more important and contentious inputs.[10]

Consideration of Figure 1.7 leads to a number of observations. First, the Kent/Thaler index of stability is unitless. There is no physical dimension (such as weapons) to it that could serve to provide an intuitive feeling for its magnitude. Second, the index is not linear. That is, for example, it is *not* the case that an index of stability of 0.6 represents a situation twice as stable as an index of 0.3. Thus, we have no way to judge whether we should be satisfied or dissatisfied with any particular level of this index. We could attempt to compare different force structures to determine whether one or the other was more stable according to this index. Unfortunately, the index does not consistently rank force structures, as can be seen by the crossings of lines

Figure 1.7
Kent/Thaler Index for Several Force Structures

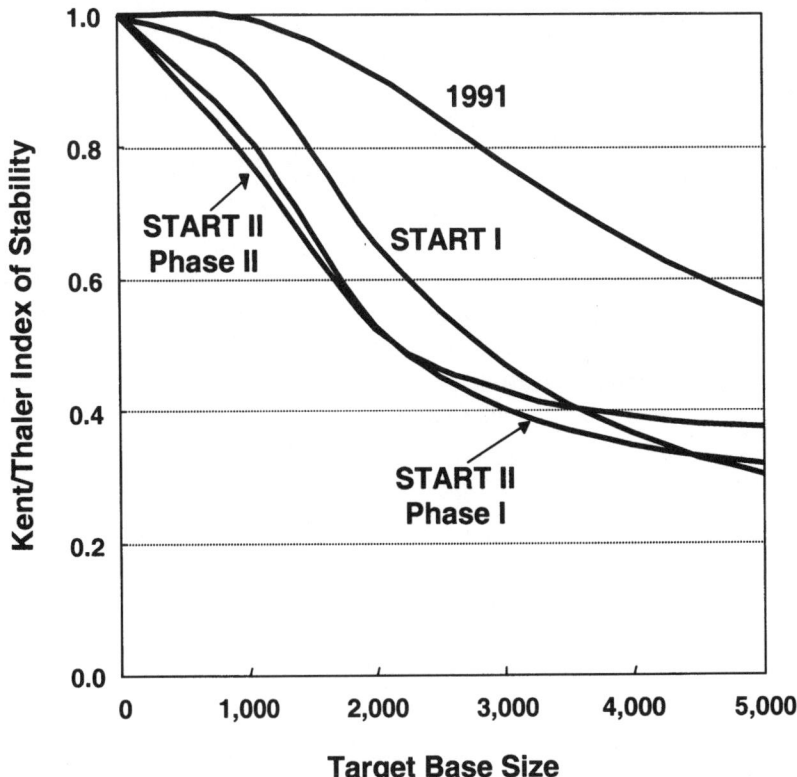

representing different force structures. Finally, if Figure 1.7 were extended to larger target base sizes, we would see that the Kent/Thaler index is not even monotonic in target base size. That is, as target base size decreases, the index also decreases up to a point, then eventually reverses slope and increases.[11]

CONCLUSIONS

Our review of the Kent/Thaler index of stability is not intended to disparage the credibility or the good intentions of its creators—they took a very useful step beyond previous work and encouraged students of nuclear arms control to be more rigorous in their analysis of stability. Despite these positive attributes, we dissected the Kent/Thaler methodology and we disagree with many assumptions, simplifications of reality, and mathematical modeling. The argument about the best method for measuring stability is not an excursion into academic irrelevancy. To the contrary: Kent/Thaler and many other stability assessment models were deliberately designed to influence the military strategy and policy debates of the Cold War, and that genre of thinking about stability has carried forward into the post–Cold War period.

The Kent/Thaler methodology was a gallant, if insufficient, attempt to address a potentially important chink in the armor of deterrence during the Cold War. Unfortunately, the philosophy upon which it is based—that neither analysts nor policymakers are to be trusted with the analysis of such an important problem—has led to a fatally flawed approach. All thinking is done mechanically by the model; users need only input inherently unknowable values for how much they prefer one outcome of nuclear war to an alternative outcome, how much more important it is to save one's own country's targets than it is to damage your enemy's targets, and other imponderables. And the nonmathematical policymaker, unfamiliar with the intricacies of the methodology, is even more likely than the policy analyst to accept this approach to measuring first-strike stability on faith alone. Our conclusion is that analysts and policymakers can and must do better. The next chapter illustrates a different and, we think, preferable, approach to understanding and measuring stability.

NOTES

1. Nuclear winter refers to the controversial theory that smoke generated by fires caused by nuclear explosions could spread around the globe and linger in the atmosphere for many months. Blocking of sunlight by this smoke could lower the overall temperature of the Earth by enough to threaten the food supplies of many species, including mankind. This theory was first introduced in Turco et al., *Science*, December 1983, pp. 1283 ff.

2. Daniel Ellsberg, *The Crude Analysis of Strategic Choices*, The RAND Corporation, P-2183, December 1960. The Kent/Thaler model is described in Glenn A. Kent and David E. Thaler, *First-Strike Stability: A Methodology for Evaluating Strategic Forces*, The RAND Corporation, R-3765–AF, August 1989. See also Glenn A. Kent, Randall J. DeValk, and David E. Thaler, *A Calculus of First-Strike Stability (A Criterion for Evaluating Strategic Forces)*, The RAND Corporation, N-2526-AF, June 1988, and Glenn A. Kent and David E. Thaler, *First-Strike Stability and Strategic Defenses: Part II of a Methodology for Evaluating Strategic Forces*, The RAND Corporation, R-3918-AF, October 1990.

3. Among the more thoughtful of these alternative approaches developed because of dissatisfaction with the Kent/Thaler methodology are Robert Batcher, *Incentive Based Indices of Nuclear Instability*, U.S. Department of State, unpublished manuscript, 2001, and Frederic S. Nyland, *The Index of Warhead First*

Strike Stability, U.S. Arms Control and Disarmament Agency, Washington, D.C, March 1998.

4. The Kent/Thaler methodology was developed before the fall of the Soviet Union. However, because analysis of U.S.–Soviet first-strike stability is only of historical interest, this chapter will refer to U.S.–Russian first-strike stability wherever possible.

5. See Peter Vincent Pry, *War Scare: Russia and America on the Nuclear Brink* (Westport, Conn.: Praeger, 1999) for a detailed account of this and other pre– and post–Cold War nuclear incidents.

6. One might conjecture that users of the Kent/Thaler methodology have a hidden agenda for invariably making the assumptions that the first striker is on generated alert and the retaliator rides out the attack before retaliating. If either or both of the alternative assumptions (the first striker is on day-to-day alert and/or the retaliator launches on warning) are made, the advantage in striking first would be much less. The Kent/Thaler methodology would then indicate high stability across a broad range of force structures. This rather inconsequential (i.e., boring) result may be more of a concern to policy analysts than stability itself.

7. The square root target damage function also has the desirable property that it is not artificially normalized (i.e., constrained to vary between zero and 100%). This eliminates the need to determine the absolute level of target damage associated with a particular level of attack.

8. Some argue, reasonably, even about the *sign* of lambda and mu. A negative lambda, for example, would correspond to increasing cost of nuclear war as more damage was inflicted on the United States by Russia or on Russia by the United States. That is, nuclear war costs increase no matter which side bears the brunt of it.

9. We do not provide data on these force structures because we are not interested in assessing their absolute or relative stabilities. Rather we are interested in difficulties in interpreting the Kent/Thaler index of stability. However, these results have been confirmed independently by Thaler.

10. Target base size is the number of targets that are assumed to have 92% and 80% of the total value of all countervalue targets for the United States and Russia, respectively.

11. As the target base size increases indefinitely, the index for all force structures approaches a value of 1.0.

2

REDEFINING STRATEGIC STABILITY

Enhancing strategic stability has been—and continues to be—the central motivation for engaging in nuclear arms control with the Soviet Union during the Cold War and the Russian Federation today.[1] The ABM Treaty, the INF Treaty, and the SALT and START treaties were all heavily influenced by this objective. The contribution to strategic stability comes from the treaty limitations themselves, and less tangibly from the associated verification regimes, implementation experiences, and increased mutual understanding achieved through the decades of negotiations that led to these treaties.

Notwithstanding its imminent demise in June 2002, the ABM Treaty's prohibition of a national missile defense made an incalculable contribution to strategic stability during the Cold War by averting an offense–defense arms race and by setting the stage for the SALT and START Treaties which first slowed, then reversed the strategic offensive arms buildup. By banning all intermediate-range nuclear missiles, the Intermediate Nuclear Forces (INF) Treaty allayed Soviet fears of surprise attack made feasible by short times of flight of Pershing II missiles based in Germany and similar Western European fears of Soviet SS-20 and other intermediate-range ballistic missiles. Data exchanges and onsite inspections associated with the INF Treaty instilled confidence that these missiles were in fact eliminated and no replacement missiles produced.[2]

The START I Treaty's major contributions to stability include a reduction by 50% of Soviet/Russian heavy ICBMs, accountability of mobile ICBMs, and greater predictability in strategic arms associated with its major limits and sublimits. START I's elaborate verification regime also broke new ground. Of particular importance was the advent of reentry vehicle onsite inspection (RVOSI), without which verifiable treaty limitations on warheads, rather than delivery vehicles, would not have been possible. If START II enters into force, it will further enhance strategic stability by eliminating all MIRVed ICBMs and all heavy ICBMs.[3]

These widely recognized contributions to strategic stability neither support nor refute the assertion that deeper reductions will further enhance strategic stability. Lower numbers per se are simply not necessarily more stable than higher numbers. In fact, there are strong arguments that deeper and deeper reductions will eventually undermine stability because destruction of the first striker by the retaliation of the second striker will no longer be assured. At what point this occurs depends heavily on the force structures, postures, and nuclear doctrines of both sides.[4] So, as we anticipate substantial cuts in Russian strategic forces brought about by economic imperatives and consider concomitant cuts in U.S. strategic forces brought about by either unilateral initiative as suggested by President Bush[5] or under the auspices of a future START III treaty, we should not assume that strategic stability will automatically be enhanced. This chapter explores this issue with a *quantitative* assessment of the impact of deep reductions on strategic stability. It also demonstrates a relatively transparent post–Cold War approach to strategic stability analysis based on a crisis decision-making perspective.

IS STRATEGIC STABILITY STILL RELEVANT?

A legitimate challenge can be raised as to the continued relevance of strategic stability in the post–Cold War period. After all, compared to the Cold War, it is now much more difficult to imagine a U.S./Russian crisis rising to the level of a nuclear confrontation. The most worrisome setting for nuclear war during the Cold War—the NATO/Warsaw Pact confrontation in central Europe—no longer exists. The emergence of other potential nuclear flashpoints seems unlikely because the expansionism that drove Soviet international policies is absent and because Russia's power projection capability has diminished to the point of near nonexistence. Nuclear alert levels have been reduced by reciprocal unilateral initiatives and nuclear forces have been reduced by the implementation of the START I Treaty. All this is reinforced by the significant, albeit imperfectly executed, strides Russia has made toward a market economy and a democratic political structure.

This optimistic assessment of the post–Cold War context for assessing the relevance of strategic stability fails to recognize that most, if not all, of these positive developments are fragile, even reversible. A new confrontation in Europe could emerge with further NATO enlargement, especially if it includes the Baltic states. Russia's economy is unlikely to remain a basket case forever and with its recovery may also come increased Russian interest in, and capability for, re-assimilation of the former Soviet republics. The START II Treaty appears unlikely to ever enter into force and START III negotiations are proving highly problematic. Although initial Russian reaction to the U.S. withdrawal from the ABM Treaty was muted, the long-term impact on the entire edifice of bilateral arms control agreements constructed over some three decades remains uncertain. And rather than approaching irrelevance as U.S. and Russian strategic nuclear weapons are being reduced in numbers, nuclear weapons are becoming increasingly important for Russia, China, India, Pakistan, and would-be proliferators, and therefore of continued vital importance to the United States as well. Finally, there is a growing body of evidence that Russian economic reform and democratization may be at risk under Putin, not to mention complete uncertainty as to the commitment of his unknown successors to these goals.

The existence and importance of nuclear weapons, the fragility of U.S./Russian relations, and the precarious state of arms control may be conditions necessary to support the continued relevance of strategic stability; however, they are not sufficient. To take strategic stability seriously it is also essential to be able to posit scenarios for nuclear war and have a healthy respect for the unpredictability and uncontrollability of crises. Unfortunately, there is no shortage of potential developments that, with a little additional bad luck, could precipitate into a U.S./Russian nuclear confrontation or war:

- A coup attempt in Russia
- Erroneous tactical warning
- A misinterpreted nuclear exercise
- An accidental or unauthorized missile launch, or an accidental nuclear detonation
- Civil war in Russia or the breakup of Russia with loss of central control over nuclear weapons
- A nuclear exchange between India and Pakistan that does not remain isolated to South Asia
- Conventional military operations on the periphery of Russia or on Russian territory that Russia responds to with tactical nuclear weapons
- A U.S./Chinese confrontation over Taiwan that expands to include other nations
- An attack or threat of attack on the United States by a so-called rogue nation[6] armed with weapons of mass destruction, especially if allied with or supported by Russia

- Nuclear preemption by the United States of an impending rogue-nation attack
- U.S. conventional attack on Russian nuclear forces

Although some of these potential future nuclear crises may be less likely than others, none should be dismissed as the product of an overactive imagination or paranoia. In fact, the first two on this list have already occurred since the end of the Cold War and the third during the Cold War.[7] Considered in sum, together with the realization that future crises that actually do occur may well be ones that were unforeseen,[8] these scenarios argue not just for the continued relevance of strategic stability as a national security objective, but for its paramount importance.

Supporting this view is the significant lip service[9] paid to the importance of strategic stability by both U.S. and Russian leaders. In particular, strategic arms treaties and negotiations seem compelled to mention strategic stability as a primary motivation:

> Recognizing that the interests of the Parties and the interests of international security require the strengthening of strategic stability.
> —Preamble to the START I Treaty, July 31, 1991

> Desiring to enhance strategic stability and predictability, and, in doing so, to reduce further strategic offensive arms.
> —Preamble to the START II Treaty, January 3, 1993

> President Clinton and President Yeltsin hereby reaffirm their commitment to take further concrete steps to reduce the nuclear danger and strengthen strategic stability and nuclear security.
> —*Joint Statement on Parameters on Future Reductions in Nuclear Forces*, March 21, 1997

A series of recent U.S./Russian joint statements also pays homage to strategic stability. In order to encourage unconditional Russian ratification of START II and to gain Russian cooperation in modifying the ABM Treaty by dangling the carrot of deeper START III reductions, the United States has engaged Russia in bilateral discussions on strategic arms control over the past few years. Although they have not achieved their original aims, these discussions have, inter alia, resulted in a series of joint statements on strategic stability. They break little new ground, but these statements affirm the importance of preserving strategic stability and provide some insight into how the leadership of both countries views strategic stability:

- The *Joint Statement Concerning Strategic Offensive and Defensive Arms and Further Strengthening of Stability* confirms both nations' "dedication to the cause of strengthening strategic stability." It then reaffirms their commitment to START III negotiations, transparency measures aimed at nuclear stockpiles and warhead elimination, and the irreversibility of deep reductions, and "to contribute through all this to the strengthening of strategic stability in the world."[10]

- The *Joint Statement on Principles of Strategic Stability* begins with the obligatory reaffirmation of the need to maintain strategic stability and the dedication of both sides to do so. It asserts the principle that both sides "agree that capability for deterrence has been and remains a key aspect of stability and predictability in the international security environment." The inclusion of this principle almost certainly reflects Russia's concern that U.S. plans for national missile defenses will undermine Russia's deterrent. The remainder of this Joint Statement focuses more explicitly on the ABM Treaty. Reading between the lines, there is a clear undertone of disagreement regarding the desirability of modifying the ABM Treaty. It somewhat schizophrenically characterizes the ABM Treaty as "essential to reductions in offensive forces" and—once more—as "a cornerstone of strategic stability" while suggesting the need to consider changes to address the emerging proliferation of ballistic missiles.[11]

- The *Joint Statement on Cooperation on Strategic Stability* emphasizes controlling ballistic missile proliferation, the Nonproliferation Treaty, and the Comprehensive Nuclear Test Ban Treaty. Additionally, it commits the United States and Russia to "strengthening stability" by creating a joint center for exchange of data from early warning systems and to a prelaunch notification agreement for missile launches. It closes by calling upon "all other nations of the world to unite their efforts to strengthen strategic stability."[12]

- Finally, the *Joint Statement/Strategic Stability Cooperation Initiative* defines some tangible, albeit small, steps toward implementing measures intended to enhance strategic stability. Each nation will brief the other on its assessment of the ballistic missile threat. Joint theater missile defense simulation and training exercises will be conducted in 2001 and 2002, with the possibility of reciprocal observation of test firings of TMD systems. Early agreement is anticipated on a prelaunch notification system for launches of ballistic missiles and space launch vehicles and initial operations of the Joint Data Exchange.[13]

So, what are we to make of this surfeit of joint statements on strategic stability? First, it is apparent that these statements are designed to impart an aura of progress (i.e., mask the lack of significant progress) and create the impression of a greater convergence of viewpoints than there really is. In fact, since the Clinton-Yeltsin summit in Helsinki in 1997[14] there has been very little progress on the central issues of missile defenses and strategic force reductions. Second, although both sides are quick to agree that strategic stability should be the consistent guiding principle and goal for arms control, there appears to have been little serious discussion of just what that term means. It is quite likely that difficulty in making progress can be traced to different perceptions of the meaning of strategic stability. Finally, even the limited agreement found in these statements, such as characterizing the ABM Treaty as "a cornerstone of strategic stability" is ephemeral. With Bush's withdrawal from the ABM Treaty, it is apparent that no such joint statements between Presidents Bush and Putin will repeat this phrase.

Our final piece of evidence of the continued importance of strategic stability is the National Defense Authorization Act (NDAA) for Fiscal Year 2000, which requires the Secretary of Defense in consultation with the Director of Central Intelligence to produce a report "on the stability of the future strategic nuclear posture of the United States for deterring the Russian Federation and other potential nuclear adversaries." The report is to address the deterrence objectives of the United States, the military requirements for U.S. nuclear forces, the force structures and capabilities necessary to meet those requirements, project U.S. and Russian nuclear forces, and assess whether strategic stability would be enhanced or diminished under START III.

One disturbing aspect of this NDAA is that it shouldn't—but it apparently does—take an act of Congress for the Department of Defense to perform a thorough and rigorous assessment of the strategic stability implications of START III. The bill can be seen as an attempt to force the Executive branch to get its analytical ducks in a row *before* it develops negotiating positions on START III and to engage the Congress on these issues. The NDAA also attempts to foster a broader public debate by calling "to the extent possible" for an unclassified report as well as a classified report. Unfortunately, as of this writing only a classified report is being produced.[15]

To sum up, we argue that strategic stability is not only relevant, but of critical importance in the formulation and assessment of U.S. national security and strategic arms control policies. Nuclear weapons continue to exist, nuclear war is still possible, and the consequences of any nuclear war remain unimaginably horrific. It is imperative that we continue to try to reduce the nuclear danger as much as humanly possible. Quantitative strategic stability analyses are one important facet of this endeavor.

DEFINING STRATEGIC STABILITY

Now that we have made the case for the importance of strategic stability, we somewhat belatedly ask the question, just what *is* strategic stability? Although the term *strategic stability* is widely used, it is not consistently applied throughout the arms control and national security communities. Quantitative analysts are predisposed to focus on the relationships between (1) force structures, force postures, force capabilities, nuclear doctrines, and target set characteristics and (2) the calculated outcomes of nuclear exchanges. Policymakers tend to consider a much broader array of factors that might upset the international equilibrium. Common to the diverse usages, however, is the central theme that strategic stability characterizes those states of U.S./Russian relations in which there is only an extremely remote possibility of nuclear war.

Although we adopt this broad common ground to define strategic stability, this analysis remains focused on the quantifiable impacts of force structure, force posture, and nuclear doctrine on strategic stability. It is important to recognize the limits inherent in such a quantitative assessment. In particular, many important factors such as perceptions, motivations, intentions, propensity for risk-taking, political costs of nuclear use, probabilities of future unlikely events, and unforeseen confluences of events, do not lend themselves to quantification. It is evident that quantifiable factors in strategic stability analyses may not be the most important factors, and, taken in isolation, may provide erroneous conclusions. In addition, quantitative analyses can be—and often are—confusing, misleading, or both. The philosophy here is to present a transparent analysis that cuts to the heart of the issues of strategic stability without unnecessary mathematical embellishments. Intricate scenarios and calculations are not appropriate for our purposes.

To develop a concept of strategic stability amenable to quantification we first briefly review Cold War characterizations of the elements of strategic stability, then define a more appropriate post–Cold War approach. Cold War analyses have generally parsed strategic stability according to the following taxonomy of elements:

- *Deterrence stability* (or, simply, *deterrence*) relates disincentive to initiate a nuclear exchange to the risk of unacceptable consequences to the initiator. This psychological construct is applicable to both crisis and noncrisis scenarios. Deterrence has been traditionally evaluated during the Cold War by assessing both the potential benefits of a first strike and the likely retaliatory consequences to the first striker.
- *First-strike stability* is the absence of pressure to strike first in a crisis due to fear that the other side is likely to attempt to do so. In a severe nuclear crisis the perceived choice of either or both sides might be to strike first or strike second, rather than war or peace. The concept of first-strike stability addresses this decision by comparing the consequences of striking first in a nuclear exchange to the consequences of striking second.
- *Crisis stability* is simply strategic stability in the context of a crisis. Since first-strike stability is also relevant only to crisis scenarios, crisis stability is often erroneously used as a synonym for first-strike stability. Crisis stability is a broader concept, however, encompassing the full range of motivations to take action that could further aggravate a crisis and potentially lead to nuclear war.

- *Arms race stability* is characterized by lack of growth in the quantity or improvement in the quality of nuclear arms due to real or perceived growth/improvement or plans for such in the nuclear arms of the other side. It is an element of strategic stability because arms race instability both reflects and fosters mistrust and uncertainty. It is less directly related to the issue of nuclear war initiation, however, than the other forms of stability discussed here.

Although these concepts have been widely used in Cold War stability analyses, a more relevant and insightful analysis can be achieved by utilizing a crisis decision-making perspective to define the elements of strategic stability.[16] That is, we will modify the Cold War approach to stability analysis to reflect more realistically a crisis context and achieve greater clarity in analysis. Our approach will result in focusing the concept of deterrence stability to consider only the level of retaliation that can be expected in response to a first strike and in replacing the Cold War calculus of first-strike stability with more transparent measures—generation stability and prompt launch stability. Finally, while we recognize that arms race stability remains a potentially important element of strategic stability, because Russia appears unable to race for the foreseeable future, this aspect of strategic stability will not be considered further in this study.

In a severe nuclear crisis, a number of major nuclear weapons-related decisions might be confronted, either by intent or by neglect. These include:

- Whether or not to place strategic forces in a state of generated alert or increased combat readiness (generate strategic forces),[17]
- Whether or not to launch a retaliatory nuclear strike upon receipt of tactical warning of an attack (launch on tactical warning) before attacking weapons impact on their targets, or to ride out the attack before retaliating,[18] and
- Whether or not to initiate nuclear war (strike first).

These three questions form the framework for the stability analysis developed in this study. Although these questions are interrelated, it is useful to attempt to isolate them by developing distinct quantitative metrics to separately evaluate the impact of force structure, posture, and nuclear doctrine on each of them.

Generation Stability

A decision to generate strategic forces could be taken because day-to-day alert strategic forces are deemed inadequate for deterrence during a crisis, to convey a message of resolve, in response to real or perceived strategic force generation by the other side, or as preparation for a preemptive strike. Unfortunately, distinguishing these quite different motivations is not a high-confidence endeavor. Depending on the detailed circumstances of the crisis, one side viewing the other generating could well regard it as preparatory to a first strike and thus be under great pressure to preemptively strike before the generation can be substantially accomplished. It could also feel pressure to respond in kind (similarly generate its strategic forces), thus increasing pressure on the side that first generated to preemptively attack. In short, whatever the motivation, the *act* of generating strategic forces in a crisis could be highly destabilizing.

Paradoxically, failure to generate strategic nuclear forces in a crisis could also be destabilizing, as day-to-day alert forces are more vulnerable to preemptive attack. In addition, failure to generate could increase reliance on launch on tactical warning, also potentially destabilizing for reasons discussed in the following paragraphs. So, while the act of generating can be destabilizing, being in a state of generated alert may be less so.

Clearly, the relationship between force generation and stability is complex and scenario-dependent. Nevertheless, it is apparent that the degree to which either side feels pressure to generate simply because of inadequacies in the day-to-day alert posture of its strategic forces is an important source of instability. *Generation stability* is thus defined as the lack of pressure to move strategic forces to a state of generated alert or increased combat readiness.

Prompt Launch Stability

The decision of whether or not to launch retaliatory forces upon receipt of tactical warning is also a focal point of strategic stability considerations. Unfortunately, data from tactical warning systems might not be of high quality; they could be erroneous, incomplete, or ambiguous. If a substantial portion of nuclear forces are in a "use or lose" situation, the interpretation of such data could force a decision to launch nuclear forces promptly, as soon as the first indications that an attack might be underway are received. Such reliance on promptly launching retaliatory forces is potentially destabilizing because it provides little time to assess or improve the quality of tactical warning and to make a considered decision on how to respond. *Prompt launch stability* is thus defined as the lack of pressure to promptly launch retaliatory forces before they are destroyed in a first strike by the other side.

Deterrence Stability

The third—and ultimate—crisis decision to be made is whether or not to initiate nuclear war. The United States maintains a first-use option in its nuclear doctrine. During the Cold War, the United States relied heavily on this option to deter Warsaw Pact conventional attack against our European NATO allies. Although this once-dominant threat has vanished with the dissolution of the Warsaw Pact, the breakup of the Soviet Union, and the withering of Russian power projection capability, the United States maintains a first-use option to preempt other threats, notably chemical and biological weapons of mass destruction, as well as any nuclear threats that might arise. Russia also maintains a first-use option. As its nuclear doctrine clearly indicates, Russia increasingly relies on the threat of first use to compensate for the weakness of its conventional military forces in the post–Cold War period.[19]

Assessments of deterrence during the Cold War have generally concluded that neither side initiated nuclear war because the anticipated "costs" greatly exceeded the anticipated "gains." Costs were damages incurred by your side; gains were damages inflicted on the other side. Both were typically measured in terms of the destruction of military, political, and economic targets. Notwithstanding the greatly decreased enmity between Russia and the United States, this logic of costs and gains is also theoretically applicable in the post–Cold War period. However, the concept of gains in a nuclear war appear to be less relevant in the post–Cold War period, with the United States and Russia neither friend nor foe, than during the Cold War when the two superpowers were engaged in a life-or-death competition. Simply put, it has become increasingly difficult to think of the destruction of targets in Russia as a gain to the United States. So, rather than compare costs to gains, to analyze deterrence stability we can now more straightforwardly focus on costs alone. The issue then becomes quite simple—are the anticipated costs unacceptable, whatever the perceived gains? Deterrence stability is thus defined as the cost that an aggressor could expect to incur for initiating a nuclear strike.

Note that we have intentionally excluded first-strike stability as a separate element of strategic stability, worthy of a separate metric, in this analysis. The essence of first-strike stability is the decision to strike first or wait. This decision depends heavily on the vulnerability of strategic forces, which in turn is primarily a function of both alert state and the ability/intention to launch on tactical warning. Since this study explicitly examines generation stability and prompt launch stability, first-strike stability becomes a redundant measurement that does not need to be independently addressed. Stated another way, since the principal source of first-strike *in*stability is the vulnerability of strategic forces to a first strike, and the principal means of increasing survivability are to (1) generate strategic forces (for U.S. SSBNs, Russian SSBNs not alert in port, and U.S. and Russian bombers), (2) launch on tactical warning (for U.S. and Russian silo-based ICBMs), or (3) either generate or launch on tactical warning (for Russian mobile ICBMs in garrison and Russian SSBNs alert in port), we find that generation stability and prompt launch stability are more direct and transparent concepts for addressing first-strike stability.

MEASURES OF EFFECTIVENESS

Assessing the impact of force structure, force posture, and nuclear doctrine on strategic stability is a complex undertaking. Physically characterizing nuclear forces in terms of quantity and quality can be relatively straightforward, although many variables—especially those describing Russian strategic forces—are imprecisely known. A far more difficult challenge lies in relating these physical descriptions to the psychology of strategic stability. This analysis was performed by developing simplified scenarios for nuclear use and assessing the consequences of such use. Although such connections are necessarily theoretical, it is useful to perform such analyses to gain as much insight as possible into this critical national security issue.

We begin with the recognition that nuclear forces can be counted according to various categories:

- *Total* strategic weapons include all *deployable* strategic nuclear weapons that are accountable under strategic arms control treaties. Deployable weapons are those for which there is an accountable strategic nuclear delivery vehicle to carry these weapons. Total strategic weapons thus include all warheads on ICBMs, all warheads on SLBMs, and all bombs and air-launched cruise missiles for which there are launch points on accountable strategic bombers. We do not count bombs and air-launched cruise missiles that might be reloaded on strategic bombers returning from previous missions.

- *On-line* strategic weapons, also sometimes referred to as *available* strategic weapons, are those weapons that could be used, either immediately or after some period of preparation, in a nuclear exchange. For purposes of this analysis, this category includes weapons that could be made ready within approximately several weeks of a decision to do so. Weapons that could not be made ready are defined as being *off-line* or *unavailable*. Off-line weapons include SSBNs undergoing major overhauls and bombers that are undergoing major maintenance procedures.[20]

- *Alert* strategic weapons are the subset of on-line weapons that can be used immediately. Two states of alert are recognized in this analysis: day-to-day alert and generated alert. On a day-to-day alert basis, both the United States and Russia maintain only a portion of their on-line strategic weapons in a readiness condition that would permit a rapid launch following a decision to do so. Generated alert is defined as the state in which essentially all on-line strategic weapons are ready to use. No scenarios of partial generation are modeled.

- *Surviving* strategic weapons are those weapons that, according to this analysis, would survive a first strike. Two scenarios are considered—one in which the retaliator launches on tactical warning (LOTW) and the other in which the retaliator rides out the attack (ROA) before retaliating. These represent the two extremes of a continuum of retaliatory launch possibilities. In the launch-on-tactical-warning scenario we assume that all weapons so launched escape before incoming warheads detonate. At the other extreme, in the ride-out-attack scenario we assume that no retaliatory weapons are launched before all incoming warheads detonate.[21]

- *Arriving* strategic weapons include only those surviving strategic weapons that are launched and, after some attrition due to reliability and possibly defenses, would arrive on target. The only defenses we model in our calculations are air defenses; our force projections do not include any national missile defenses for either the United States or Russian Federation. In addition, because the Moscow ABM system is limited in terms of its number of interceptors, it is not explicitly modeled.

Many nuclear exchange analyses go beyond arriving weapons to assess the damage done to a prescribed target set, to population, or both. However, to do so presumes knowledge of both the U.S. and Russian strategic targeting doctrines. Although both sides may know these for themselves today, they can only make educated guesses for each other. And for both nations it is problematic to project targeting doctrines even for themselves a decade into the future at significantly reduced force levels. For the purposes of this study, therefore, it is better to stop the quantitative analysis with arriving weapons, then proceed with a qualitative assessment of the implications of this quantitative analysis for strategic stability.

Before we proceed, it's worthwhile to consider the relative likelihoods of the four retaliation scenarios defined above and displayed in Table 2.1. We address *relative* likelihoods because it is impossible to assign an absolute probability to the future occurrence of nuclear war.[22] In particular, analysts can—and do—argue endlessly about the plausibility of the day-to-day alert, ride-out-attack scenario. It *seems* probable that if nuclear war were to occur it would have been preceded by a severe international crisis during which both sides would have had the opportunity to generate their strategic forces and also would have been prepared to launch on tactical warning. Therefore, many erroneously conclude that the generated-alert, launch-on-tactical-warning retaliation scenario (upper left box in Table 2.1) is most likely or, to reflect the assessment that none of the scenarios is likely, the least unlikely.

This reasoning is faulty on several counts. First, it is important to recognize that the day-to-day alert scenario is not inconsistent with a crisis. After all, because the first striker decides when and under what conditions to attack it's the first striker as least as much as the retaliator who decides the alert status of the retaliator. Since a first striker would obviously face a larger retaliation if the retaliator were on generated alert, it is clearly in the

Table 2.1
Strategic Warfare Planning Scenarios

		Retaliator Alert Scenario	
		Generated Alert	**Day-to-Day Alert**
Retaliator Launch Scenario	Launch on Tactical Warning (LOTW)	• Crisis scenario • Best case for retaliator • Often unjustifiably proclaimed least unlikely	• Not inconsistent with crisis • Failure to receive/respond to strategic warning
	Ride Out Attack (ROA)	• Crisis scenario • Failure to LOTW	• Not inconsistent with crisis • Failure to receive/respond to strategic warning and LOTW • Worst case for retaliator; often derided as "bolt from the blue"

first striker's interest to strike while the retaliator is on day-to-day alert. The attack could come if the first striker sees (correctly or erroneously) the other side in the initial stages of generating its forces or preparing a preemptive attack from day-to-day alert, in the (apparent) aftermath of a crisis after the retaliator or both sides have returned to a day-to-day alert state, or in any number of other circumstances. This logic generally applies whether or not the first striker has generated his strategic forces. In other words, a would-be first striker is almost always better off striking from a day-to-day alert posture if the retaliator is also on a day-to-day alert posture than waiting until both sides have moved to generated alert.

Second, crises need not follow the Cold War model of a two-sided crisis. The January 1995 Norwegian meteorological rocket launch, during which the Russian leadership briefly considered whether or not to respond based on erroneous tactical warning, was a one-sided crisis. The United States was completely unaware of the danger. The August 1991 coup attempt against Gorbachev, during which the Soviet Union placed its strategic forces on increased combat readiness, was also essentially a one-sided crisis. Although the coup leaders were concerned about possible U.S. interference, there was no international dispute. The United States was aware of the Russian move to increased combat readiness but, in order to not exacerbate the situation, kept its strategic forces on day-to-day alert. So, if this one-sided crisis somehow led to a Soviet attack, the United States might easily have been caught on day-to-day alert. The coup attempt against Gorbachev illustrates yet another reason to not dismiss the scenario in which the retaliator is on day-to-day alert. In an effort to maintain control over a potentially volatile crisis, one or both sides might *choose* to remain on day-to-day alert.[23]

These arguments that the retaliator might not be on generated alert also support the argument that the retaliator might also not launch on tactical warning. It does seem more plausible that a retaliator will launch on tactical warning if he has previously generated his strategic forces in the context of a crisis. But if no such crisis or generation occurs, it seems at least as plausible that he will ride out the attack before retaliating. And, since the United States is not overly dependent on launch on tactical warning, it could well decide to ride out an attack before retaliating. Moreover, due to the degradation in Russia's early warning system, Russia may not have the technical capability to launch on tactical warning, now or in the foreseeable future, even if it is theoretically much more dependent on this retaliatory strategy.

The conclusion of this thought exercise is that while the day-to-day alert, ride-out-attack scenario is often derided as an improbable "bolt from the blue," it may well be *more* likely than the other three scenarios. At the very least, we should be reticent to rank order these scenarios in terms of relative probability. None are so improbable that they can safely be ignored.

STRATEGIC FORCES

Every quantitative analysis makes assumptions to develop input data and relies on certain methodological practices. Without explicitly describing these particulars, it becomes difficult to assess the range of conditions under which the conclusions are valid. In addition, it becomes highly problematic for other analysts to knowledgeably critique the computations or understand why other analyses develop different results. This chapter in general and this section in particular therefore contain a fair amount of detailed descriptions of assumptions, data, methodology, and calculations.

Two key assumptions limit the scope of this analysis. First, because START III is anticipated to be a bilateral treaty, this analysis considers only the U.S./Russian Federation bilateral nuclear relationship; other nuclear nations are not included. Although every nation that can threaten the United States with even one nuclear weapon is of great national security concern, other nations' strategic arsenals are at least an order of magnitude lower than U.S. and Russian strategic arsenals will be under the prospective START III Treaty. In addition, a methodology appropriate for any multipolar analysis of the stability implications of the nuclear arsenals of these other nations would necessarily be quite different from that presented here. Second, within the context of the U.S./Russian nuclear relationship, the calculation of stability metrics for this study considers only strategic nuclear forces; nonstrategic (i.e., tactical) nuclear forces are not included in the calculations. While the implications for stability of nonstrategic nuclear forces are also of concern, this issue is best addressed in qualitative terms, not in the quantitative stability calculations.[24]

Even limited to only U.S. and Russian strategic nuclear forces, the variety of potential future force structures can lead to an unmanageable number of cases. To circumvent this problem, this analysis utilizes only a single representative force structure for each START treaty limit considered. We, therefore, attempt to develop more plausible force structures, rather than those that are possible, but less likely. We also use these treaty-compliant force structures to represent U.S. and Russian strategic forces if no START treaty is in force. For example, if the United States decides on unilateral reductions to some 3,500 weapons, we assume its force structure would be the same as if it were complying with the START II Treaty.

The U.S. strategic forces used in this analysis are presented in Table 2.2. Corresponding Soviet and Russian strategic forces are displayed in Tables 2.3 and 2.4, respectively. Strategic forces are shown for the year 1991, START I, START II, and two START III cases—one with an overall limit of 2,500 weapons [START III (2500)] and the other with an overall limit of 1,500 weapons [START III (1500)]. The year 1991 is selected as a point of reference because it was just prior to the end of the Cold War. More precisely, we have selected the point in time *before* the September 1991 unilateral initiative by President Bush that, inter alia, took all U.S. strategic bombers and all ICBMs scheduled for deactivation under START I off day-to-day alert.[25] At that time the United States had some 11,700 total strategic nuclear weapons and the Soviet Union nearly as many at some 10,800 weapons.[26] The Soviet Union's forces were dominated by ICBM warheads, while the United States held a more balanced—albeit somewhat SLBM heavy—triad of ICBM warheads, SLBM warheads, and bomber weapons.

All START cases are based on the year 2010 because we anticipate that is the earliest time by which a START III Treaty is likely to be fully implemented. In addition, while projections beyond a decade or more are possible, they naturally tend to be less accurate than shorter-term projections. For one of the START treaties to be in effect in 2010 implies one of the following alternatives:

- START III enters into force (and is fully implemented) by 2010, in which case START III would be the controlling treaty.
- START II enters into force (but START III does not) and an extension to START I is agreed upon, in which case START II would be the controlling treaty.[27]

Table 2.2
U.S. Strategic Forces

System	Loading	Delivery Vehicles / Weapons				
		1991	START I	START II	START III (2500)	START III (1500)
Minuteman II	1	450 / 450				
Minuteman III	3	500 / 1500	350 / 1050			
Minuteman III	1		150 / 150	500 / 500	500 / 500	300 / 300
Peacekeeper	10	50 / 500	50 / 500			
Total ICBM		1000 / 2450	550 / 1700	550 / 500	500 / 500	300 / 300
Poseidon C3	16x10	160 / 1600				
Poseidon C4	16x8	192 / 1536				
Trident C4	24x8	192 / 1536				
Trident D5	24x8	72 / 576	336 / 2688			
Trident D5	24x5			336 / 1680		
Trident D5	24x4				336 / 1344	
Trident D5	14x4					196 / 784
Total SLBM		616 / 5248	336 / 2688	336 / 1680	336 / 1344	196 / 784
B52G	12 ALCM	46 / 552				
B52H	20 mixed	55 / 1100				
B52H	20 ALCM	40 / 800	75 / 1500	33 / 660		
B52H	8 ALCM			42 / 336	62 / 496	32 / 256
B1B	16 bombs	97 / 1552				
B2	16 bombs		20 / 320	20 / 320		
B2	8 bombs				20 / 160	20 / 160
Total Bomber		238 / 4004	95 / 1820	95 / 1316	82 / 656	52 / 416
Total Triad		1854 / 11,702	981 / 6208	931 / 3496	918 / 2500	548 / 1500

- Neither START III nor START II enter into force, but an extension to START I is agreed upon, in which case START I would be the controlling treaty.[28]

Weapons shown in Tables 2.2 through 2.4 are *not* START-accountable weapons, but rather *actual* strategic nuclear weapons.[29] For example, the U.S. strategic forces shown under START I do not include B-1 bombers because, although they remain accountable under START I as nuclear bombers, they have been converted to a conventional-only role. In addition, the delivery vehicles displayed in Table 2.2 do not include two U.S. bombers (one B-2 and one B-52H) assumed to be declared as test vehicles under all START treaties.

No judgment by the authors is required to determine U.S. strategic forces under the START I Treaty; they have already been officially decided.[30] For U.S. START II strategic forces, the ICBM and SLBM legs of the triad have also been officially decided.[31] For U.S. bombers under START II, we assume the United States would keep all current strategic bombers and that these bombers would carry *at a minimum* their full internal loadings of weapons (sixteen gravity bombs for the B-2 and eight ALCMs[32] for the

Table 2.3
Soviet Strategic Forces in 1991

System	Loading	Delivery Vehicles	Weapons
SS-11	1	326	326
SS-13	1	40	40
SS-17	4	47	188
SS-18	10	308	3080
SS-19	6	300	1800
SS-24 silo	10	56	560
SS-24 rail	10	33	330
SS-25 mobile	1	288	288
Total ICBM		**1398**	**6612**
Yankee I (SS-N-6)	16x1	192	192
Delta I (SS-N-8)	12x1	216	216
Delta II (SS-N-8)	16x1	64	64
Yankee II (SS-N-17)	12x1	12	12
Delta III (SS-N-18)	16x3	224	672
Typhoon (SS-N-20)	20x10	120	1200
Delta IV (SS-N-23)	16x4	112	448
Total SLBM		**940**	**2804**
Bear A,B,G	2	63	126
Bear H6	6 ALCM	29	174
Bear H16	16 ALCM	57	912
Blackjack	12 ALCM	15	180
Total Bomber		**164**	**1392**
Total Triad		**2502**	**10,808**

B-52H). Some—not all—B52-Hs are also assumed to carry twelve external ALCMs as well. Application of this assumption, and further assuming the United States will deploy as many weapons as possible under the START II limit of 3,500, results in the breakout shown in Table 2.2 of 33 B-52H bombers loaded with 20 ALCMs and 42 B-52H bombers loaded with 8 ALCMs.[33]

To project U.S. START III (2500) and START III (1500) strategic forces, a significant amount of judgment is required. The first issue to address is what the START III Treaty provisions will be. According to the Clinton/Yeltsin Helsinki Agreement, START III negotiations will include:[34]

- Establishment . . . of lower aggregate levels of 2,000–2,500 strategic nuclear warheads for each of the parties.

Table 2.4
R.F. Strategic Forces Under START I, START II, and START III

System	Loading	Delivery Vehicles / Weapons	
		START I	START II, START III
SS-19	1		105 / 105
SS-19	6	105 / 630	
SS-25 mobile	1	251 / 251	251 / 251
SS-27 mobile	1		60 / 60
SS-27 mobile	3	60 / 180	
SS-27 silo-based	1		60 / 60
SS-27 silo-based	3	60 / 180	
Total ICBM		**476 / 1241**	**476 / 476**
Delta IV (SS-N-23) or equivalent	16x4	112 / 448	112 / 448
Total SLBM		**112 / 448**	**112 / 448**
Bear H	6 ALCM	66 / 396	66 / 396
Blackjack	12 ALCM	15 / 180	15 / 180
Total Bomber		**81 / 576**	**81 / 576**
Total Triad		**669 / 2265**	**669 / 1500**

- Measures relating to the transparency of strategic nuclear warhead inventories and the destruction of strategic nuclear warheads . . . to promote the irreversibility of deep reductions including prevention of a rapid increase in the number of warheads.
- Resolving issues related to the goal of making the current START treaties unlimited in duration.

The presidents also agreed to "explore, as separate issues, possible measures relating to nuclear long-range sea-launched cruise missiles and tactical nuclear systems, to include appropriate confidence-building and transparency measures" and "issues related to transparency in nuclear materials."[35]

Unfortunately, most of this is not particularly helpful for the purposes of this analysis. While we do analyze an overall limit of 2,500 strategic nuclear weapons, we also consider an overall limit of 1,500 weapons. We do not examine even lower levels because START III reductions below approximately 1,500 weapons seem highly improbable in the near term. Russian concern with the irreversibility of deep reductions (i.e., U.S. breakout) is reflected in our projection of Russia keeping all allowed downloaded SS-19s. We implicitly assume a START III treaty with a duration long enough that force structures are not influenced by the prospect of its expiration. We do not address SLCMs or tactical nuclear weapon systems. Essentially, we assume that START III will be similar to START II, but with a lower overall limit. In particular, we assume continuation of the START II ban on MIRVed mobile ICBMs. A reasonable variation that we do not consider would allow Russia some level of MIRVing of mobile ICBMs under a modified START II.

The second fundamental issue to address is whether or not the United States will maintain a triad of strategic forces. Fortunately, with current modernization/life-extension plans (in particular, continued procurement of Trident D-5 SLBM missiles, the life extension plan for the D-5, and replacement of guidance and propulsion systems on Minuteman ICBMs), none of the weapon systems composing the strategic triad will reach the end of its service life before the year 2020.[36] So, it is evident that while a triad may not be cost efficient at these levels, it is affordable. Fewer weapons simply cost less to maintain than more weapons, even if they would cost even less if they were all from only one or two legs of the triad. If we can afford a triad at START I or START II levels (which we evidently can), we certainly can afford one at START III levels. Since there are legitimate strategic reasons to maintain a triad and importance of a triad has been ingrained in the U.S. strategic culture over some four decades, we believe arguments against maintaining a triad based on cost effectiveness will not be persuasive. Thus, we project a triad of U.S. forces under both the START III (2500) and START III (1500) treaties.

For START III (2500) we employ the philosophy of keeping as many existing (i.e., START II) delivery vehicles as feasible. We thus project 500 single-warhead ICBMs and 14 Trident SSBNs, each with 24 missiles now downloaded to four warheads apiece. The 20 B-2 bombers are now assumed to be downloaded to carry only 8 bombs each. Since this is less than the B-2's internal carrying capacity, this loading will likely present serious—but probably not insurmountable—verification problems. B-52H bombers are assumed to be reduced in number to 62, each with a full internal loading of 8 ALCMs. Because of the nature of our methodology, however, our results are not dependent on the particular loadings of bomber weapons. That is, our results would be identical if we had assumed that more B-52 bombers carried fewer weapons each, as long as the total number of bomber weapons was not changed.

It's important to recognize that alternative strategic force structures under START III (2500) are also possible. In particular, the number of ICBMs could vary from 500 all the way down to zero, allowing for additional SLBM and/or bomber weapons. However, we believe that national security planners are more and more recognizing that the importance of single-warhead ICBMs will only increase as forces are reduced. A would-be first striker will either have to attack them with an unfavorable exchange ratio (i.e., fewer than one warhead would be destroyed with each warhead expended) or forgo attacking them with even worse consequences. In addition, the relatively large number of targets that 500 ICBM silos represents might require a would-be attacker to undergo some level of force generation before attacking. This would increase the risk of providing strategic warning and potentially thwart the advantages of a surprise attack.

For START III (1500), we finally have been compelled to abandon our goal of keeping all Minuteman ICBMs; we project only 300 Minuteman III ICBMs. Because of the cost of SSBNs and their central role in the U.S. deterrent, we project all 14 Trident SSBNs, but now with only 14, rather than 24, missiles, each carrying only four warheads. De-tubing will also present verification issues, but we presume they are resolvable. As with our START III (2500) force structure, B-2 bombers have been downloaded to carry only 8 bombs each. However, B-52s have been further reduced in number to 32, each still carrying 8 internal ALCMs.

Projecting Russian strategic forces with confidence is even more difficult. Other than the general uncertainty with respect to the Russian economy, there are additional uncertainties with respect to the ability of Russia to maintain existing systems beyond their planned service lives and priorities in Russian military modernization. We assume that Russia will be severely financially constrained, at least through 2010, in replacing current aging strategic weapons. We further assume that, to compensate for this, Russia will be willing to stretch the service lives of existing systems. This can be achieved in part by cannibalizing retiring systems, in part by reducing wear and tear on deployed systems by maintaining low (in-the-field or at-sea) alert levels for mobile systems, and in part by accepting reduced operational effectiveness.

For Russia, it turns out to be more convenient to first project strategic forces for START III, then address START II and START I in turn. Based on recent Russian proposals[37] for overall caps significantly below the Helsinki agreed limit of 2,000–2,500 weapons under START III, we project some 1,500 Russian strategic nuclear weapons independent of the overall START III limit. That is, we project Russia will have identical force structures under START III (2500) and START III (1500). Although Russia clearly will not be content with the disparity in U.S. and Russian strategic forces under START III (2500), it is not overwhelmingly large and it is at least partly counterbalanced by Russia's advantage in nonstrategic nuclear weapons. Russia can also use this disparity to its political advantage vis-à-vis the rest of the world and simultaneously work toward achieving parity as its economy improves. As shown in Table 2.4, we project a Russian triad at this force level, although now more evenly balanced among the three legs than in 1991.

The logic used to develop the START III Russian force structure is direct, but clearly not infallible. We start with the most recent START Treaty Memorandum of Understanding (MOU) data exchanged by the parties to the treaty.[38] This source shows that Russia currently has fifteen Blackjack and sixty-six Bear ALCM-carrying bombers. These bombers will not reach the ends of their service lives before 2010, so we project this same number of bombers in year 2010.[39] For loadings, we assume twelve ALCMs for the Blackjack and six ALCMs for the Bear.[40] For the SLBM leg of the Russian triad, the START I MOU shows seven Delta IV SSBNs with sixteen missiles per SSBN and four warheads per missile. We also assume that Russia will maintain this force through the year 2010, even though the Delta IVs may exceed their planned service lives. Equivalently for this analysis, if Russia replaces Delta IVs with a more modern submarine, we assume it will retire Delta IVs at the same rate.

For ICBMs, we start with the assumption that Russia will deploy a combination of existing and new systems to reach the overall level of 1,500 weapons. This will allow (or require) 476 single-warhead ICBMs, composed of some combination of existing SS-19s downloaded to one warhead, existing SS-25s, and existing/new SS-27s. For example, the START III ICBM force structure in Table 2.4 is based on the following assumptions. First, Russia will exploit the START II provision that allows up to 105 SS-19 ICBMs to be downloaded from six to one reentry vehicle each. Second, Russia will add to its existing inventory of 20 SS-27 ICBMs at a rate of 10 per year,[41] and that half of all SS-27 deployments will be silo-based and the other half will be road mobile. This will allow Russia to retire some older SS-25s to a level of 251 and keep within the overall limit of 1,500 warheads.

As with the U.S. START III force structures, variations of this projected Russian force structure are also possible. In particular, Russia could significantly increase the production rate of SS-27 ICBMs.[42] This would allow Russia to retire additional SS-25s and/or retire the SS-19 entirely and still remain close to the 1,500 weapon limit. The methodology employed in this analysis is insensitive to what particular combination of Russian silo-based ICBMs is assumed, and similarly insensitive to what particular combination of mobile ICBMs is assumed, provided the total number of silo-based ICBMs is not changed and the total number of mobile ICBMs is not changed.

As shown in Table 2.4, we assume this same Russian force structure under START II. Although Russia will chafe under the large disparity in U.S. and Russian forces (assuming the United States deploys forces close to the START II limit), there is little that Russia can do about it in the short term. One unlikely possibility would be to upload Bear bombers to carry sixteen, rather than six, ALCMs each. Since Russian bombers are not on constant combat readiness, however, this would do nothing to improve the day-to-day survivability of their forces. It would only divert scarce resources from more effective longer-term solutions.

Russian START I forces can exploit the lack of an overall ban on MIRVed ICBMs. We assume that Russia will thus maintain all 105 SS-19 ICBMs with 6 warheads each and upload all SS-27s to 3 warheads each.[43] As shown in Table 2.4, this results in an additional 765 ICBM warheads. Still, Russia's START I forces will be significantly below U.S. START I forces but, again, Russia has few options. Russia could begin production of a new, MIRVed missile. Although this is not likely by 2010, it is more probable in the farther term without agreement on deeper cuts in strategic forces.

Note that both the U.S. and Russian projected force structures in Tables 2.2 and 2.4 have substantial potential for uploading weapons. In theory, the United States could reconfigure its single-warhead Minuteman ICBMs back to 3 warheads, its Trident SSBNs back to 24 SLBMs, its SLBMs back to 8 warheads, and its B-2 and B-52H bombers back to 16 bombs and 20 ALCMs, respectively. Thus, the U.S. upload potential under START I, START II, START III (2500), and START III (1500) totals 300, 2512, 3554, and 3908 weapons, respectively. Not surprisingly, Russia is concerned with this upload potential; its own upload potential is not insignificant, but considerably less than that of the United States. The Russian START II and START III missile upload potential is represented by its START I force. In addition, if the 66 Bear H bombers were uploaded to 16 ALCMs each, this would provide an additional 660 bomber weapons. Thus, the grand total Russian upload potential under START II and START III is 1,425 weapons.[44]

This discussion has been based on the assumption that the force structures of both the United States and Russia in 2010 will be constrained by either the START I, START II, or a prospective START III Treaty. It is also possible that no strategic arms control treaty will be in force in 2010. If START I expires without a replacement treaty, we project Russia's force structure to closely resemble its START I structure as shown in Table 2.4. The United States, however, has a wider set of options. Recognizing Russia's rapid decline in strategic forces, the United States could elect to voluntarily reduce its own strategic forces. Reducing to START II levels, for example, would enable the United States to save money and might divert criticism of its withdrawal from the ABM Treaty to deploy a national missile defense, all while still maintaining a comfortable margin ahead of Russia in strategic force deployments. As Russia's forces continue to decline, the United States could even reduce to START III (2500) levels with the same benefits.

TOTAL STRATEGIC WEAPONS

The U.S. and Soviet/Russian total strategic force levels, broken out by triad leg, are displayed in Figure 2.1. Two points are evident from this figure. First, as can be seen from the U.S. force levels, each START treaty mandates a significant drop in total strategic forces. If START III comes to pass, limits on total strategic forces will be only one-fifth to one-seventh of Cold War levels. Beyond the quantitative analysis presented here, the broader implications of this large reduction deserve careful study. Second, under START I, START II, and START III (2500) the United States has a unique opportunity to maintain significantly more strategic weapons than Russia in the near term if it chooses to do so. There are both potential benefits and potential dangers in exploiting this opportunity.

On the benefit side of the ledger there are a number of apparent advantages.[45] Most significantly, lack of parity in strategic forces would seriously undermine the last vestige of Russia's claim to global power status. Since Russia cannot hope to match the United States in the foreseeable future in economic power, conventional military power, or in worldwide political and cultural influence, nuclear weapons remain its sole remaining claim to global power status. Second, a serious case can be made that having significantly more weapons than our principal adversary is potentially a very stable situation.[46] Russia would have little incentive to initiate a nuclear war if it knew that even if it were to strike first, and even if the United States was on day-to-day alert and failed to launch its retaliation on tactical warning, Russia would not only be subject to a devastating retaliation, but that retaliation would inflict greater damage on Russia than Russia's first strike would inflict on the United States. Finally, achieving a state of disparity could pave the way for multilateral strategic arms control not based on parity. This is because one of the biggest impediments to eventually including other nuclear nations in the strategic arms control process is facing the quandary of deciding what levels of nuclear arms each participant would be allowed. With Russia already at a level lower than the United States, the perpetuation of this disparity could be more acceptable to Russia. This, in turn, might make multilateral arms control more palatable to the United States.

Figure 2.1
Total Strategic Weapons

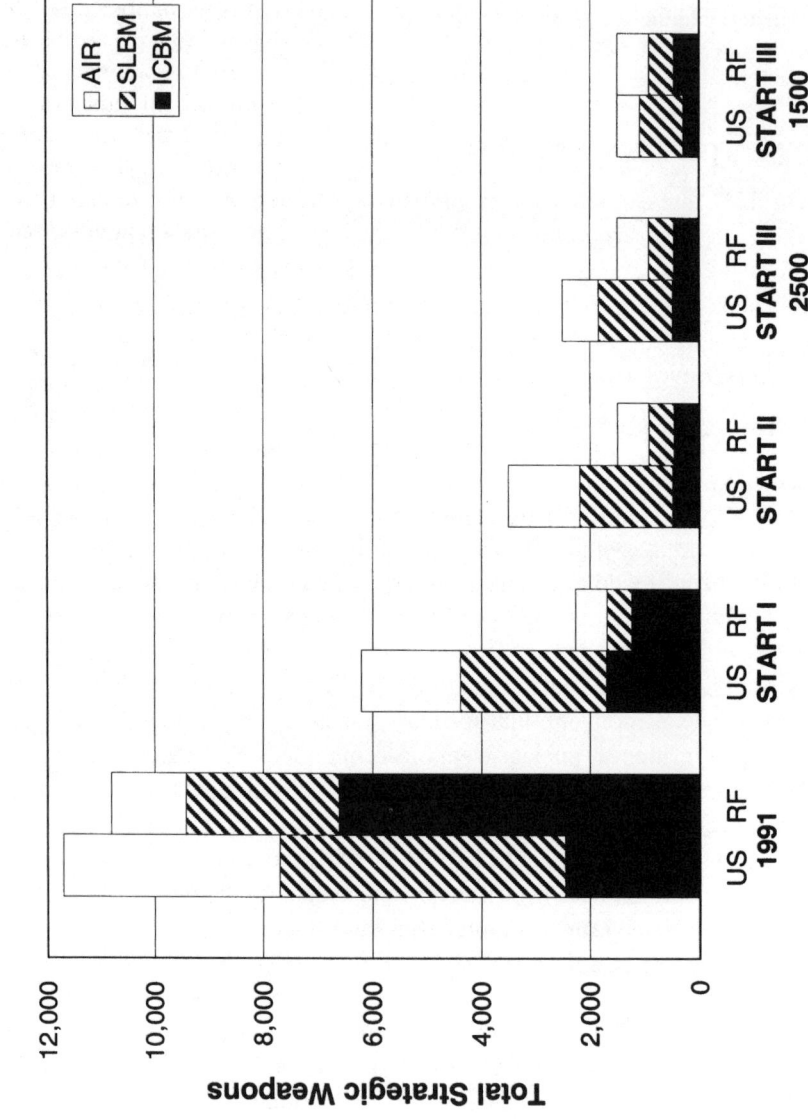

On the other hand, exploiting this opportunity could heighten Russian fears and cause unwelcome changes in Russian arms control policies. In particular, if the United States maintains a large disparity in strategic nuclear weapons, it will likely be very difficult, if not impossible, to get Russia to redress the large imbalance in its favor in nonstrategic nuclear forces. In fact, Russia could balk at any constraints on nonstrategic forces. And Russia may well let the START I Treaty lapse, even if it has no intentions of immediately deploying systems that would violate its provisions. There would also undoubtedly be a sustained negative reaction from much of the rest of the world for U.S. failure to fulfill its commitments under Article VI of the Nonproliferation Treaty.[47]

The bottom line is that while the United States can achieve an advantage over Russia in the numbers of strategic nuclear weapons, it could come at a significant cost. And any U.S. advantage is liable to be transitory. The United States is unlikely to maintain—nor Russia to acquiesce to—a large imbalance in strategic weapons over the long term. Probably the best strategy for the United States is to exploit the potential for an imbalance in strategic arms by pressuring Russia to redress the imbalance in its favor in nonstrategic nuclear arms and to gain other arms control concessions.

STRATEGIC WEAPON SYSTEM PLANNING FACTORS

Strategic weapon system planning factors used to determine the number of on-line, alert, surviving, and arriving weapons are shown in Table 2.5. *Fraction on-line* is the proportion of total weapons that are on-line. *Alert rate* is the fraction of on-line weapons that are on either day-to-day or generated alert. *Prelaunch survivability* is the proportion of alert, on-line weapons that would survive a first strike by the other side. *Reliability* is the proportion of surviving, alert, on-line weapons that are estimated to be reliable. Finally, *penetration probability* is the proportion of reliable, surviving, alert, on-line weapons that would penetrate any defenses the first striker may have. In this analysis, these planning factors are held constant for all of the force structures considered. They are applied to the total weapons levels of each side to calculate an estimate of the number of on-line, alert, surviving, and arriving weapons for the United States and Russia in all alert and retaliatory launch scenarios. In equation form,

- On-line weapons = (Fraction on-line) * (Total weapons)
- Alert weapons = (Alert rate) * (Fraction on-line) * (Total weapons)
- Surviving weapons = (Prelaunch survivability) * (Alert rate) * (Fraction on-line) * (Total weapons)

- Arriving weapons = (Reliability * Probability to Penetrate) * (Prelaunch survivability) * (Alert rate) * (Fraction on-line) * (Total weapons).

As an example, consider U.S. bomber weapons in 1991 in the day-to-day alert, ride-out-attack scenario. The total number of U.S. bomber weapons is 4,004, as found in Table 2.2. Other bomber weapon counts are as follows:

- On-line bomber weapons = (0.9) * (4,004) = 3,604
- Day-to-day alert bomber weapons = (0.3) * (0.9) * (4,004) = 1,081
- Surviving bomber weapons = (1.0) * (0.3) * (0.9) * (4,004) = 1,081
- Arriving bomber weapons = (0.9 * 0.9) * (1.0) * (0.3) * (0.9) * (4,004) = 876.

Some of the data in Table 2.5 derive from official sources,[48] but for the most part they are simply one-significant-digit estimates based on plausibility considerations.[49] There is substantial uncertainty in many of these planning factors. The level of uncertainty is a function of whether one's own forces or one's adversary's forces, current or future systems, or targetable or untargetable systems are being characterized. We make no attempt in this analysis to quantify this uncertainty.

Based on the strategic force planning factors in Table 2.5, Table 2.6 displays the quantity of weapons in each of these categories for the United States and the Russian Federation for each of the force structures considered in this study. This table is mainly for reference, as graphical displays of selected data and the measures of effectiveness defined earlier follow.

DETERRENCE STABILITY

Figures 2.2 and 2.3, respectively, provide graphical displays of U.S. strategic nuclear weapons under the prospective START III Treaty (1500) and Russian strategic nuclear weapons under either START II or START III as a function of weapon status. The weapons levels associated with two measures of deterrence stability used in this analysis, maximum retaliation and assured retaliation, are identified. As discussed, these measures of effectiveness are based on arriving retaliatory weapons.

Maximum retaliation is the expected number of arriving retaliatory warheads in the scenario that represents the best case for the retaliator. In this scenario the retaliator is on generated alert and promptly launches his retaliation upon receipt of tactical warning. This scenario plausibly might occur after an extended crisis in which both sides have generated their forces and have the capability to launch on tactical warning. Maximum retaliation is thus best viewed as a metric of deterrence stability in a severe crisis. This

Table 2.5
U.S. and R.F. Strategic Weapon System Planning Factors

	Fraction On-line	Alert Rate (of On-line Forces)		Prelaunch Survivability (of Alert, On-line Forces)					Reliability (of Survivable, Alert, On-line Forces)	Penetration Probability (of Reliable Survivable, Alert, On-line Forces)
				GEN			DAY			
		GEN	DAY	LOTW	ROA	LOTW	ROA			
UNITED STATES										
ICBMs	1.0	1.0	1.0	1.0	0.1	1.0	0.1		0.9	1.0
SLBMs	0.9	1.0	0.67		1.0				0.9	1.0
Bombers	0.9	1.0	0.3, 0.0		1.0				0.9	0.9
RUSSIAN FEDERATION										
ICBMs in silos	1.0	1.0		1.0	0.1	1.0	0.1		0.9	1.0
Mobile ICBMs	1.0	1.0		1.0		1.0	0.1		0.9	1.0
SLBMs	0.9	1.0	0.2		1.0		1.0	0.5	0.9	1.0
Bombers	0.9	1.0	0.0		1.0				0.9	0.9

GEN = generated alert (U.S.) or increased combat readiness (R.F.)
DAY = day-to-day alert
LOTW = launch on tactical warning
ROA = ride-out attack

Table 2.6
U.S. and R.F. Strategic Nuclear Forces in Alternative States

	Total	On-line	Alert			Surviving								Arriving					
			GEN	DAY	LOTW	GEN			DAY			GEN			DAY	
						LOTW	ROA	LOTW	ROA	LOTW	ROA	LOTW	ROA	LOTW	ROA
UNITED STATES
1991	11702	10777	10777	6696	10777	10777	8572	6696	4491	9375	7390	5929	3944
START I	6208	5834	5834	3372	5834	5834	4304	3372	1842	5103	3726	3035	1658
START II	3496	3252	3252	1545	3252	3252	2802	1545	1095	2820	2415	1391	986
START III (2500)	2500	2300	2300	1310	2300	2300	1850	1310	860	2017	1612	1179	774
START III (1500)	1500	1380	1380	773	1380	1380	1110	773	503	1208	965	695	452
RUSSIAN FEDERATION
1991	10808	10388	10388	7117	10388	10388	4994	7117	914	9237	4382	6405	822
START I	2265	2163	2163	1322	2163	2163	1434	1322	164	1900	1244	1189	148
START II, III	1500	1398	1398	557	1398	1398	1249	557	88	1211	1078	501	79

GEN = generated alert (U.S.) or increased combat readiness (R.F.)
DAY = day-to-day alert
LOTW = launch on tactical warning
ROA = ride out attack

Figure 2.2
Measures of Deterrence Stability: U.S. START III (1500) Strategic Forces

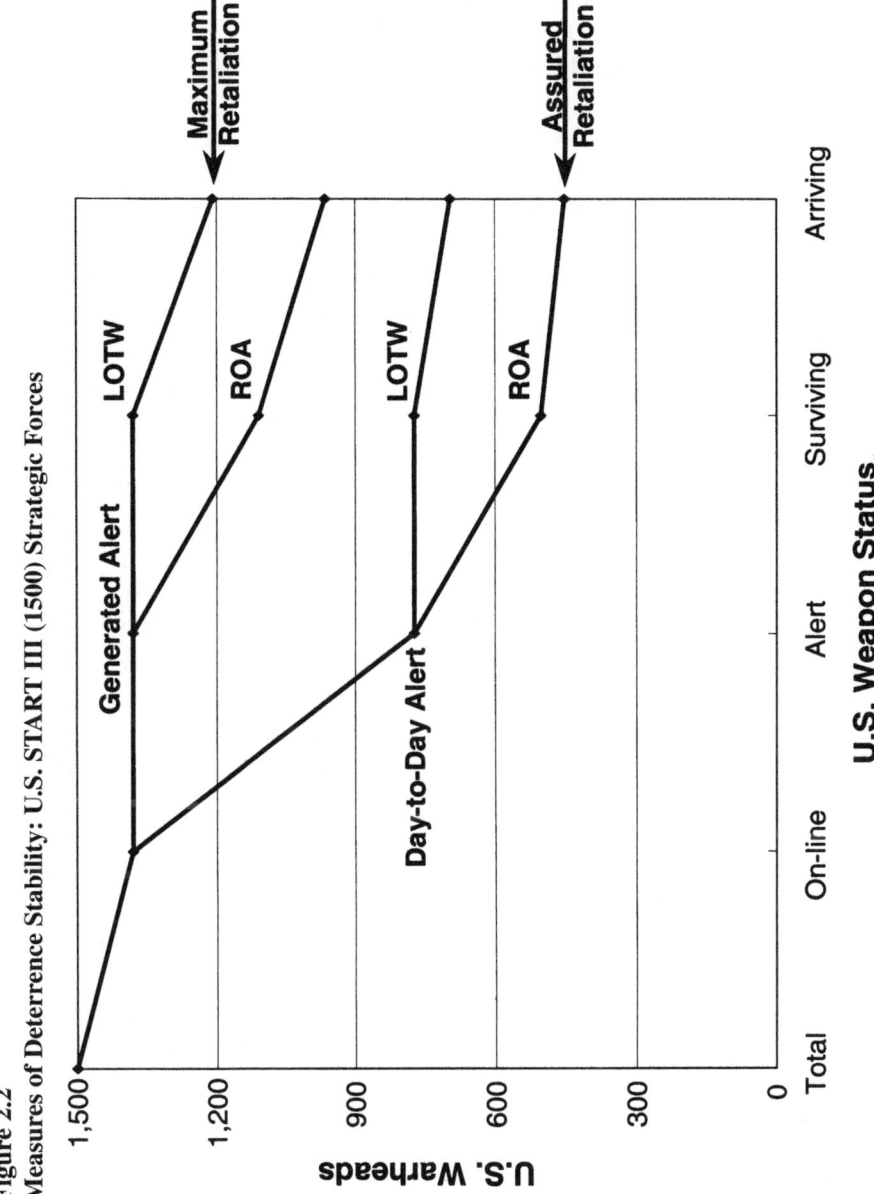

metric, however, is not very useful for planning purposes from the perspective of the retaliator since it is based on the most optimistic assumptions.

Assured retaliation is at the opposite extreme of scenarios from the maximum retaliation scenario. It is the expected number of retaliatory warheads that would arrive on target on the first striker when the retaliator is on day-to-day alert and rides out the first strike before retaliating. This worst case scenario for the retaliator is the lowest plausible level of retaliation that a first striker can anticipate. It assumes the first strike was successful in launching an attack against an unalerted enemy and the retaliator did not attempt to, or failed in trying to, launch his retaliation on tactical warning. The only weapons systems in the assured retaliation are those that are either untargetable on a day-to-day basis (i.e., SSBNs at sea and mobile ICBMs in the field); those that are targetable, but happen to survive because the attack is not perfect (i.e., a portion of ICBMs in silos); and in year 1991 only, bombers on day-to-day alert that are assumed to escape from their bases whether or not vulnerable missiles are launched on tactical warning. To be counted in the calculation of assured retaliation, these surviving weapons must also be reliable and penetrate any defenses of the first striker.

The maximum retaliation of all force structures is compared in Figure 2.4. For the United States, maximum retaliation will drop from over 9,380 weapons in 1991 to some 5,100 weapons under START I and, should START II enter into force, to some 2,820 weapons.[50] Depending on the overall START III weapon limit, maximum retaliation under START III will drop to between 1,210 and 2,020 weapons. Russia's maximum retaliation matched that of the United States in 1991, but, based on the assumptions of this analysis, will drop to some 1,900 weapons under START I and 1,210 weapons under START II and START III. All triad legs are substantially represented in both the U.S. and Russian maximum retaliations.

We are somewhat ambivalent with regard to the adequacy of the START III levels of maximum retaliation. Can we imagine a crisis so severe that these levels of maximum retaliation will not be adequate to dissuade either side from attacking. In a word—no. If deterrence fails, it probably won't be because of the inadequacy of either side's maximum retaliation. But several caveats are in order regarding the U.S. maximum retaliation. First, we're not *certain* of its adequacy and we can't easily characterize just how confident we are. Second, it's easy to fall into the trap of mirror imaging—that is, assuming that what is enough to deter the United States will also serve to deter Russia. We may well be guilty of some of that faulty logic. Third, we are more sure of the deterrence capability of U.S. START I forces today than we were of much more capable forces during the Cold War. So, our assessment of deterrence stability is very much a function of our perceptions of the gen-

Figure 2.3
Measures of Deterrence Stability: R.F. START II and START III Strategic Forces

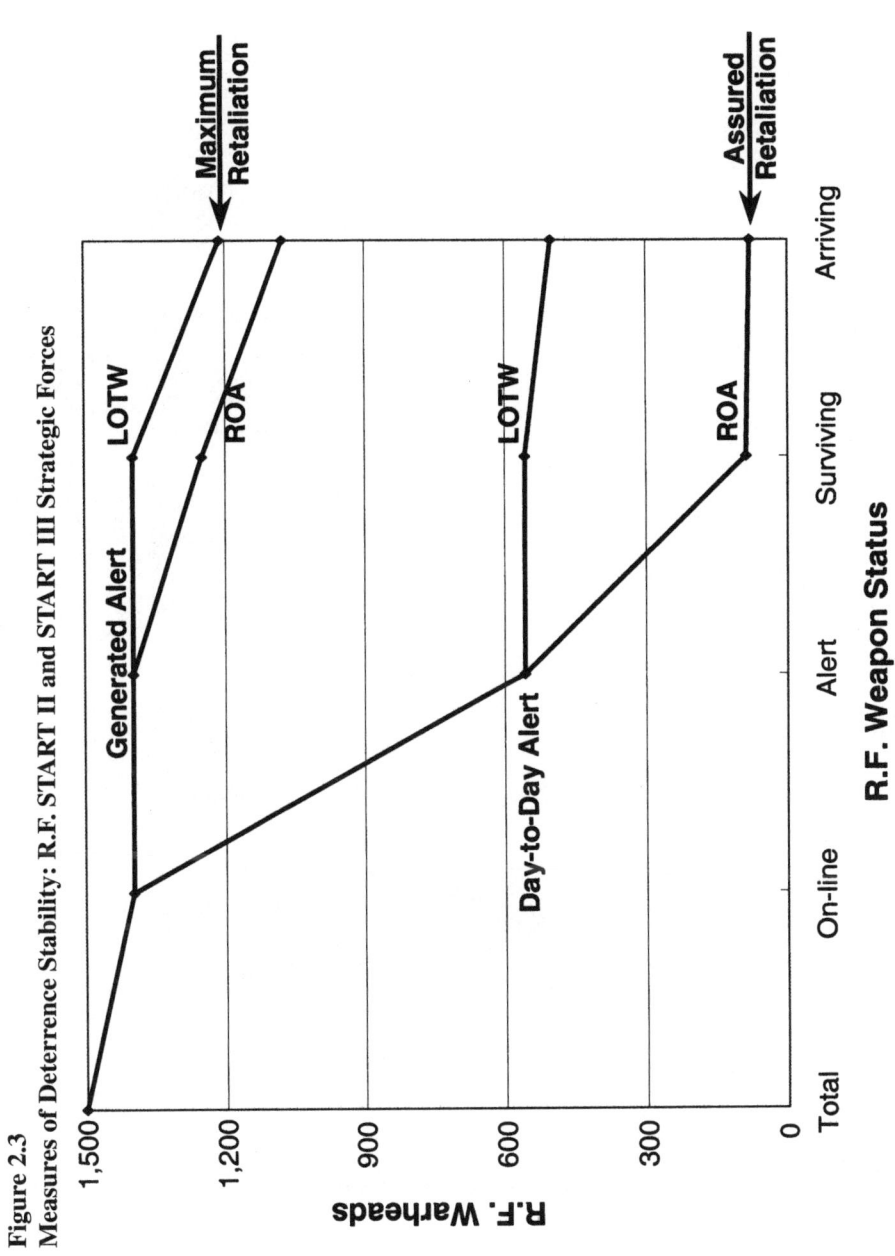

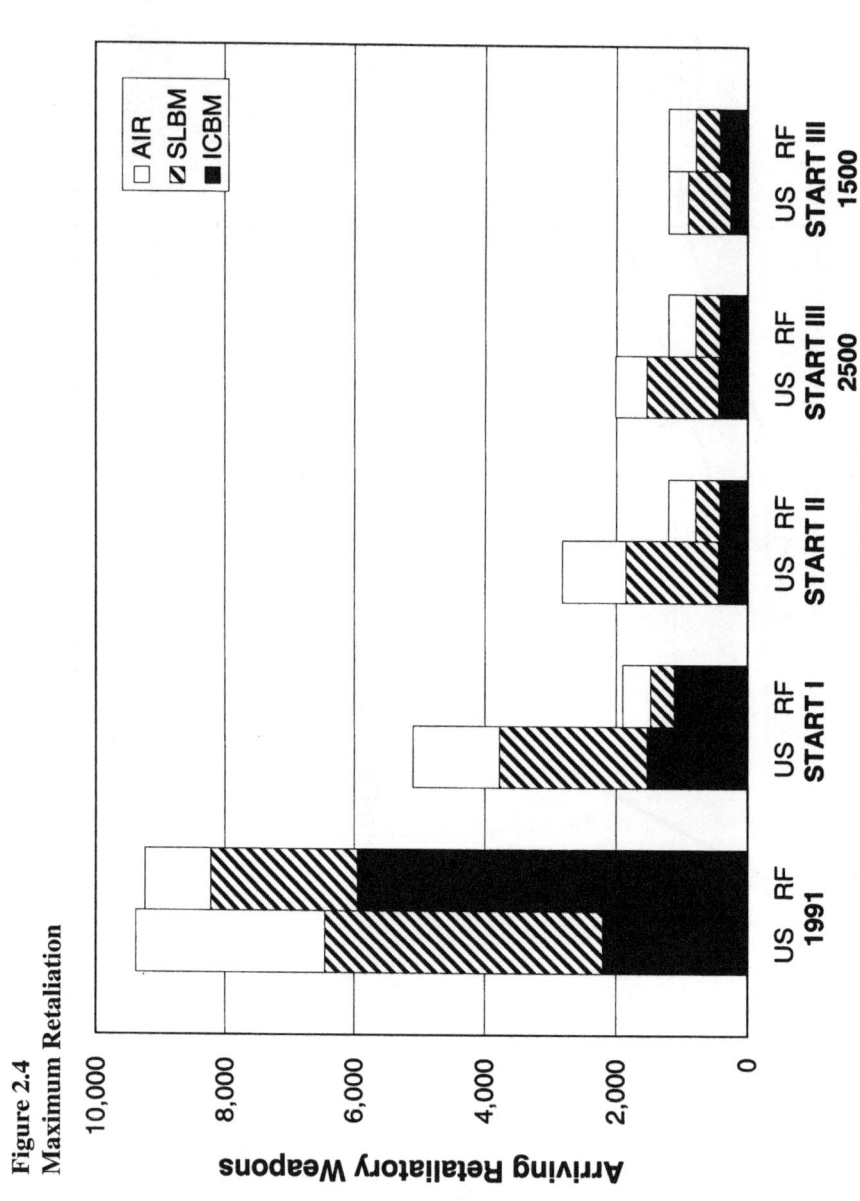

Figure 2.4
Maximum Retaliation

eral state of international relations and our perception of the rationality of Russian leaders. These perceptions could change very quickly. Finally, we are more certain of the adequacy of our maximum retaliation in cases in which there is a large disparity in this metric in favor of the United States. In the START III (1500) case both sides might well be deterred, but they might also perceive the other as equally deterred. These mutual perceptions could lead to an exacerbation of the crisis if they lead to the expectation by both sides that the other side should be more conciliatory.

Another reason for our relatively optimistic assessment of the adequacy of the maximum retaliation levels of both sides is that they are much larger than corresponding assured retaliation levels shown in Figure 2.5. The U.S. assured retaliation in 1991 was over 3,900 weapons. This level declines under each new START treaty to between 450 and 770 under the prospective START III Treaty. Moreover, while in 1991 the U.S. assured retaliation was composed of weapons from all legs of the triad, under START I and subsequent treaties it is now composed of weapons almost entirely from the submarine leg of the triad.

We must ask the same questions of assured retaliation that we did for maximum retaliation—are the U. S. and Russian assured retaliation levels adequate for deterrence? There are conflicting perspectives, but little analysis, of this question. Consider the following assessments of the U.S. assured retaliation, all of which are—or may be—literally true, but do not reflect the depth of analysis necessary to shed light on this important question:

- *Under START II and START III, the United States will have fewer total weapons than it would have had in 1991 after a well-executed Soviet first strike.* This statement is true. After a Soviet first strike in 1991, the United States would have had approximately 3,940 (refer to Figure 2.5 or Table 2.6) surviving retaliatory weapons. Under START II, the United States will have some 3,500 total weapons. The implication of this statement is that the Soviet Union has achieved its counterforce nuclear warfighting goals by arms control agreements, without firing a shot. But this assessment skirts the issue of how much is enough for deterrence. The United States (as well as the Soviet Union) may have had significantly more strategic weapons during the Cold War than were rationally needed for deterrence and either or both sides may need fewer now than then.
- *The U.S. assured retaliation of some 450 weapons under START III (1500) is more than adequate to underwrite deterrence.* This is an assertion with no evident analytical underpinning. It may or may not be true, but it is not a constructive contribution to the debate.
- *Under START III (1500), the U.S. assured retaliatory capability may not reach the McNamara standard of 400 equivalent megatons.*[51] This statement is also true. During the Kennedy administration, Secretary of Defense Robert McNamara suggested that 400 equivalent megatons delivered on target would suffice to deter the Soviet Union. Since the U.S. strategic arsenal contains mostly weapons with yields lower than

one megaton, it needs more than 400 arriving retaliatory weapons to meet this standard. Although the McNamara standard may be achieved under START III (2500), it will not under START III (1500). However, the McNamara standard was based on the ability to destroy one-third of the population and one-half of the industry of the Soviet Union. Given the breakup of the Soviet Union and the tremendous decline in the Russian economy, we must ask what would be the comparable standard today. And given the end of the Cold War, we must also ask whether the comparable standard is even relevant today.

- *The U.S. assured retaliation is greater than Russia's.* This statement is true, but is based on a dubious comparison. A more relevant comparison would be to compare Russia's first-strike capability with U.S. assured retaliation or vice versa. These comparisons result in a far different assessment—the side that strikes first does significantly better than the side that does not.

- *The U.S. assured retaliation is fragile because it is composed almost entirely of forces from the submarine leg of the triad.* Although submarine-based forces do overwhelmingly dominate the U.S. assured retaliation, it does not necessarily follow that this is a problem. On the other hand, one might be generally skeptical of unsubstantiated assertions that U.S. SSBNs are undetectable and thus invulnerable. So, this may or may not be a valid assessment. In any event, should SSBNs at sea become targetable, and if we are aware that they are, we could partially compensate for this by placing some of our strategic bombers on day-to-day alert as we did during the Cold War.

Where does all this leave us? Without more thoughtful and analytically rigorous analyses of the relationship between assured retaliation and deterrence, the adequacy of the U.S. assured retaliation will remain a judgment call and subject to unresolvable debate. Whatever debating points are scored, however, we must always keep in mind that the ultimate decision rests with the Russian civilian and military leadership.

The Russian assured retaliation of some 820 weapons was much lower than that of the United States in 1991. This can be interpreted any number of ways. It could be reflective of a Soviet perception that it didn't take as much to deter the United States as the United States believed it took to deter the Soviet Union. Alternatively or additionally, it could indicate that the Soviet Union believed this scenario of day-to-day alert and ride-out attack was highly improbable. If the Soviet Union was confident that it would receive strategic warning in time to generate its forces and/or if the Soviet union expected to strike first or at least launch its retaliation on tactical warning, assured retaliation would have been a less relevant metric for them.

Of primary importance is the extremely low (by historical standards) Russian assured retaliation under START II and START III. If the United States were to attack Russia while Russia was on constant combat readiness, and if Russia was incapable of or failed to launch on tactical warning, Russia could retaliate with approximately eighty weapons reliably delivered on target. While the United States will likely perceive this as an ade-

Figure 2.5
Assured Retaliation

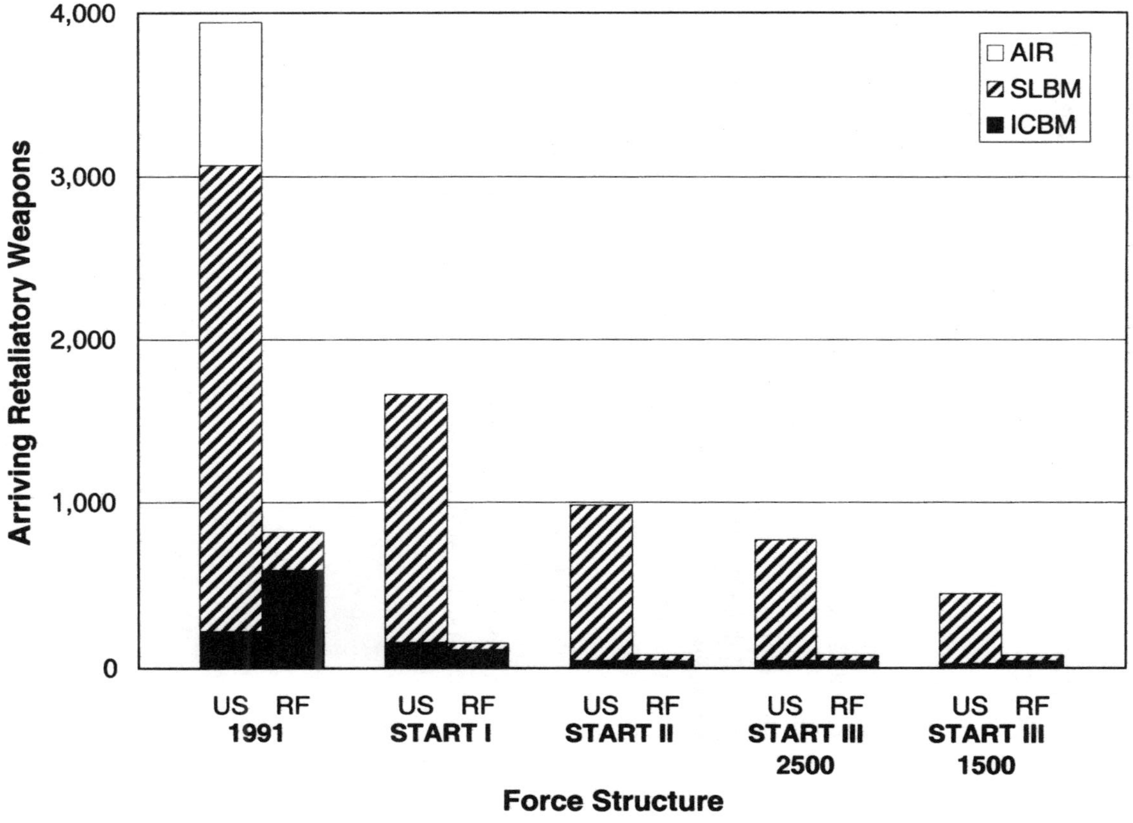

quate deterrent, Russia most certainly does not. Russia's perception of the inadequacy of its assured retaliation explains Russia's objections to U.S. national missile defenses and, we believe, is the greatest structural source of strategic instability in the post–Cold War period.

GENERATION STABILITY AND PROMPT LAUNCH STABILITY

Our measures for generation stability and prompt launch stability are depicted in Figures 2.6 and 2.7 for U.S. START III (1500) forces and Russian START II/ START III forces. To evaluate each of these metrics, a two-step process is involved. For example, for generation stability we first determine the differences in arriving retaliatory weapons between the scenarios in which the retaliator is on day-to-day alert and on generated alert. There are two possible cases, one in which the retaliator launches on tactical warning and the other when the retaliator rides out the attack. These differences are labeled *sensitivity to generation* in Figures 2.6 and 2.7. Similarly, for prompt launch stability we first determine the differences between scenarios in which the retaliator launches on tactical warning and those when he rides out the attack. Again, there are two possible cases, one when the retaliator is on generated alert, and the other when the retaliator is on day-to-day alert. These differences are labeled *sensitivity to prompt launch* in Figures 2.6 and 2.7.

Sensitivity to generation and sensitivity to prompt launch are interesting metrics in their own right, but can be misleading indicators of generation stability and prompt launch stability when comparing force structures with varying total levels. This is because these metrics are strongly correlated with overall force levels. Sensitivity to generation is due to (additional) bombers placed on alert, submarines put to sea, and (for Soviet/Russian forces) mobile ICBMs placed in the field. Sensitivity to prompt launch is due to U.S. and Russian silo-based ICBMs and Russian garrison-based ICBMs and SSBNs alert in port that depend on launch on tactical warning to survive. Without major force structure and/or posture changes, as total force levels decline, these additional contributors to arriving retaliatory weapons also decline. Thus, sensitivity to generation and sensitivity to prompt launch are more appropriate to use in comparisons of alternative forces for which the total number of weapons is unchanging.

The second step in the process of defining generation stability is to determine the ratio of arriving retaliatory weapons in the day-to-day case to the generated alert case. This is illustrated by the charts in the right-hand sides of Figures 2.6 and 2.7. For example, for the U.S. START III (1500) force structure in Figure 2.6, in the day-to-day alert, launch-on-tactical-warning

Figure 2.6
Generation Stability and Prompt Launch Stability: U.S. START III (1500) Strategic Forces

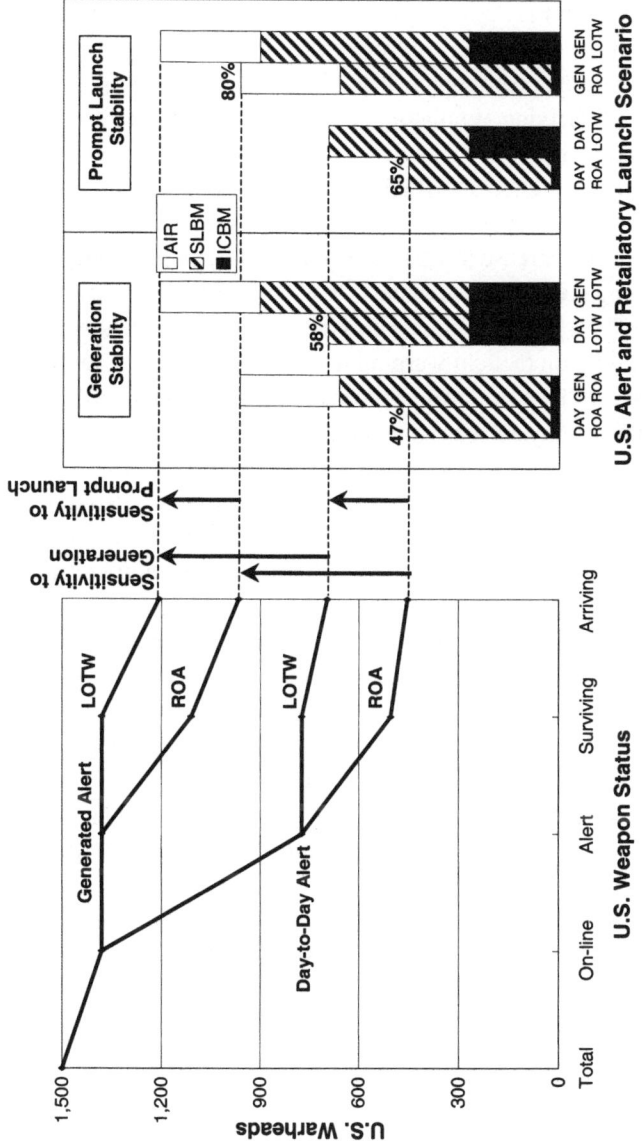

scenario the United States would have a retaliation of 700 weapons; this level of retaliation would increase to 1,210 weapons in the generated alert, launch-on-tactical-warning scenario. Generation stability—the ratio of these two levels—is 0.58, or 58%. The higher this ratio, the less dependent the retaliator is on force generation and thus the more stable the force structure in the day-to-day alert posture.

Similarly, prompt launch stability is depicted in Figures 2.6 and 2.7 as the ratio of arriving retaliatory weapons between the scenarios in which the retaliator rides out the attack and the retaliator launches on tactical warning. Again using U.S. START III (1500) forces in Figure 2.6 as an example, the U.S. retaliation in the generated alert, ride-out-attack scenario is 970 weapons, but would increase to 1,210 weapons in the generated alert, launch-on-tactical warning scenario. Using these data, prompt launch stability is then 970/1,210, or 80%. Again, the higher this ratio, the less dependent is the retaliator on launching on tactical warning and thus the more stable the situation.

We see by comparing Figures 2.6 and 2.7 that Russia's START III forces on day-to-day alert are much less stable than corresponding U.S. START III (1500) forces. In the ride-out-attack scenario, Russia's generation stability is only 7% compared to 47% for the United States. Russia's day-to-day alert prompt launch stability (16%) is also much lower than that of the United States (65%). These low levels of stability are another reflection of Russia's low assured retaliation. That is, Russia's day-to-day alert forces are unstable with respect to generation and prompt launch because without these measures relatively few Russian strategic forces would survive a U.S. first strike.

Both Russia and the United States significantly increase their generation and prompt launch stabilities if they move from the day-to-day alert, ride-out-attack scenario. For example, if Russia or the United States generate their forces, they become much more stable with respect to prompt launch. In the generated alert scenario, Russian and U.S. prompt launch stabilities are 89% and 80%, respectively. Similarly, if they rely on prompt launch, they become much more stable with respect to generation, although generation stability remains lower than prompt launch stability for both sides. In the prompt launch scenario, Russian and U.S. generation stabilities are 41% and 58%, respectively.

To provide some perspective on these levels, we compare generation stability and prompt launch stability for all force structures considered in this analysis in Figures 2.8 and 2.9, respectively. In 1991 U.S. generation stability was 63% in the launch-on-tactical-warning scenario and 53% in the ride-out-attack scenario. For both scenarios, U.S. generation stability drops somewhat under START I and further under START II, then recovers under

Figure 2.7
Generation Stability and Prompt Launch Stability: R.F. START II, and START III Strategic Forces

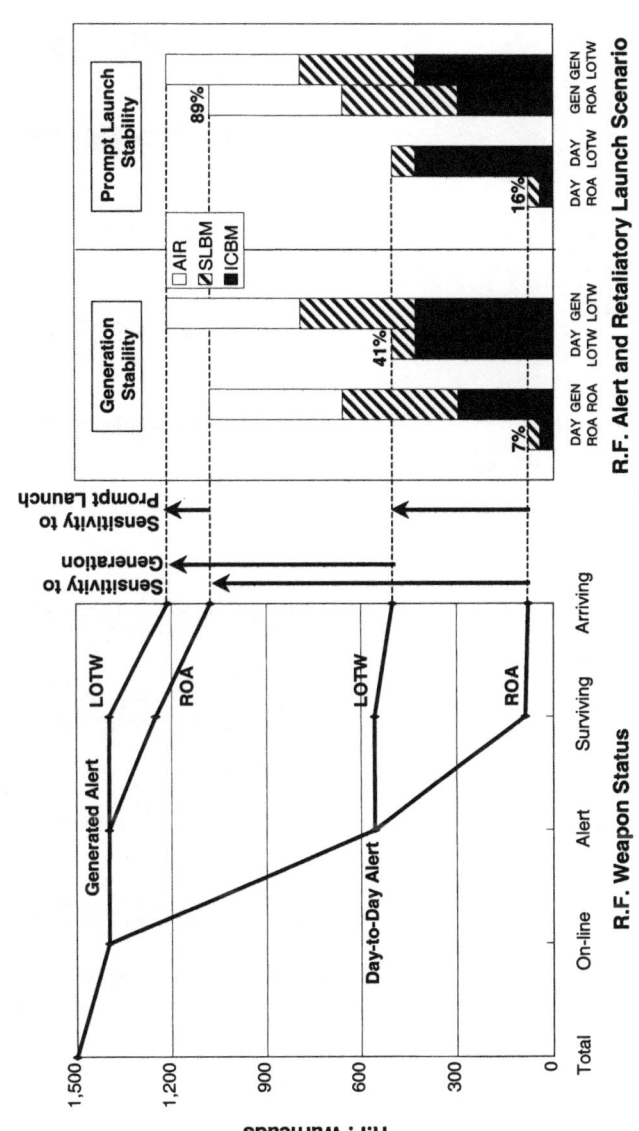

Figure 2.8
Generation Stability

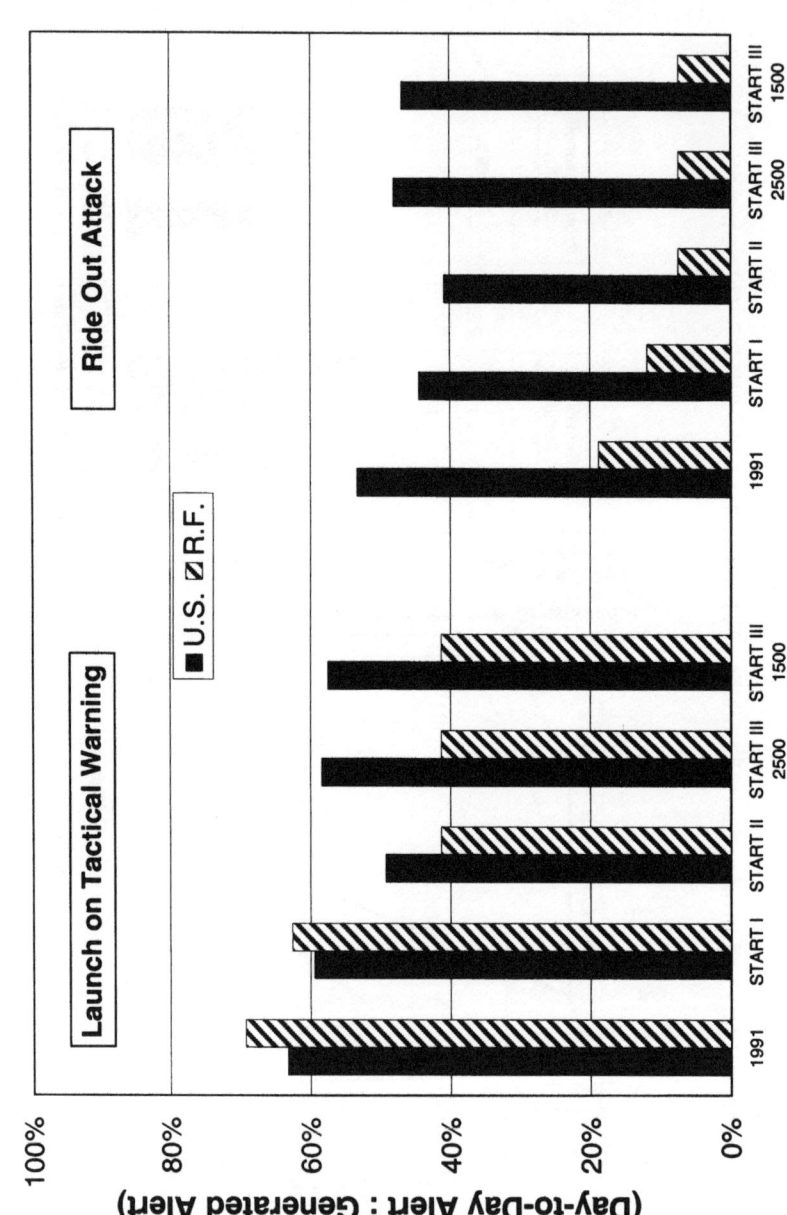

both START III (2500) and START III (1500). The lower U.S. generation stability under START II is due to the decreased proportion of ICBMs, which are not sensitive to generation, in the U.S. force structure.

Russian generation stability follows a similar downward trend from 1991 to START I and START II. Of course, since we assume the same Russian forces under START II, START III (2500), and START III (1500), all Russian stability measures are identical for these three cases. Russia's more pronounced decline in generation stability in the launch-on-tactical-warning scenario is due to a larger decline in the proportion of its ICBM warheads due, in turn, to the impact of the ban on MIRVed ICBMs. In the ride-out-attack scenario, Russia's generation stability was very low in 1991 at 19%, but even lower under START I, and declines further under START II and START III, to less than half its 1991 level. This worrisome decline in Russia's generation stability is due to a greater proportion of Russian forces in SLBMs in port not on alert and mobile ICBMs not in the field.

Turning to prompt launch stability (Figure 2.9), we identify two main points. First, in the day-to-day alert scenario, Russia's prompt launch stability for all cases is very low compared to the United States. It is only slightly improved under START II and START III compared to 1991 and START I. Second, in the generated alert scenario, there are significant increases in Russia's prompt launch stability from 1991 to START I to START II/III. This is explained by the same phenomenon that caused a decline in Russian generation stability—the lower proportion of Russian ICBM warheads under START II.

U.S. prompt launch stability does not vary much across all cases, dipping somewhat under START I and rising slightly under START II, then returning under both START III cases to the 1991 level. These changes are inversely related to changes in the proportion of U.S. ICBM warheads.

CONCLUSIONS

To place our conclusions in perspective, a brief review of this analysis is in order. We began by defending the importance of strategic stability in the post–Cold War period. We then defined strategic stability broadly as a characteristic of the state of international relations in which the probability of strategic warfare was extremely small. We proceeded to define the scope of this analysis to include only the impact on strategic stability of force structure, force posture, and scenarios, thereby excluding other important, but essentially unquantifiable, elements of strategic stability. Thus, we cannot legitimately draw a conclusion on whether or not START III is stabilizing, only whether or not strategic forces under START III are stabilizing.

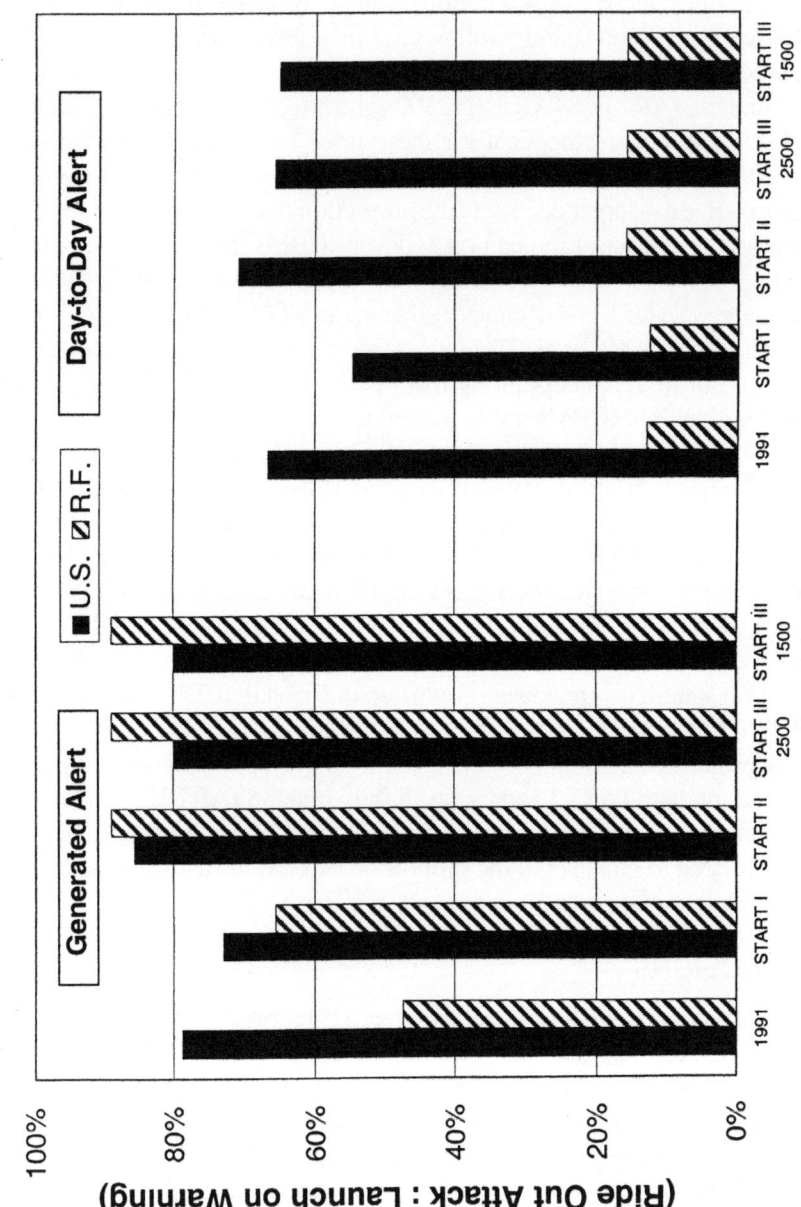

Figure 2.9
Prompt Launch Stability

Rejecting Cold War definitions of strategic stability, we took a crisis decision-making approach to define deterrence stability, generation stability, and prompt launch stability as a more straightforward set of elements of strategic stability that would facilitate understanding of stability issues by minimizing mathematical complexity. Based on our force projections and estimates of strategic force planning factors, all of which have significant uncertainties associated with them, we evaluated these measures and now proceed to draw the following conclusions.

First and foremost, the greatest source of instability related to force structure identified in this analysis is the very low survivability of Russian strategic forces on a day-to-day basis. This instability will exist whether START I, START II, or START III is the controlling arms control treaty in 2010, and it will exist if no arms control treaty is in effect. Fortunately, Russia could diminish this instability by increasing the day-to-day survivability of its strategic forces. A significant improvement would result, for example, from simply maintaining one-third of its submarines at sea and mobile ICBMs in the field. Unfortunately, higher alert rates are costly, both in terms of economic resources and in wear and tear on deployed systems. Thus, Russia is almost certain to reject this option in favor of the less costly alternative of maintaining reliance on one or both of two potentially destabilizing tactics—early generation in a crisis and launch on tactical warning. As a result, the United States needs to be acutely aware of, and responsive to, these Russian dependencies in formulating crisis management and response strategies.

Second, the United States has an opportunity to dramatically affect strategic stability—for better or worse—by maintaining significantly more strategic forces in the foreseeable future than Russia. This largely unexplored option might be the most deterrence-stable one of all, but would come with the risk of increased political and arms race instabilities. The United States could achieve a large asymmetry in strategic forces under START I, START II, and probably START III with a limit of 2,500, but not under START III with a limit of 1,500. If START III negotiations fail to come to fruition, the United States unilaterally could make significant cuts in its strategic forces and still maintain some margin above Russian strategic forces. However, while such cuts might make national missile defenses more politically palatable and ameliorate (not eliminate) Russian concerns with parity, they would not measurably affect Russia's inadequate assured retaliation and associated generation and prompt launch instabilities.

Third, in terms of whether a higher or lower overall weapon limit under START III Treaty is preferable (more stable), the only significant difference found in this analysis between START III with an overall limit of 2,500 weapons and the same treaty with an overall limit of 1,500 weapons is the level of U.S. assured retaliation. The level of U.S. assured retaliation necessary to underwrite deterrence by threatening to inflict unacceptable retaliatory damage is ultimately a political decision informed by military analyses. Unfortunately, military analyses of just how far the United States can safely reduce its deterrent have inadequately examined this critical issue. So long as it remains inadequately examined, erring on the side of caution would appear to be in order.

Fourth, whatever its potential benefits vis-à-vis so-called rogue nations, U.S. deployment of a national missile defense will exacerbate the instabilities identified in this analysis. With Russia's assured retaliation below 100 arriving retaliatory weapons, a national missile defense of only 100 interceptors would seriously undermine that deterrent. Although some weapons would undoubtedly get through, they might not be adequate to assure the level of destruction of the United States required by Russian planners. Thus, Russia will become even more reliant on early generation and/or launch on tactical warning. On the other hand, Russia is *already* dependent on early generation and prompt launch. U.S. national missile defenses may *reinforce* that dependency, but it is unclear whether this increased dependency would result in tangible consequences for deterrence stability.

Fifth, U.S. and Russian strategic forces unconstrained by treaty would have mixed impacts on strategic stability. The United States has the luxury of maintaining strategic forces at any level it chooses up to the START I level. U.S. unilateral reductions below START I would decrease U.S. deterrence stability, but the level of assured retaliation necessary to underwrite its strategy of deterrence is highly uncertain. The other aspects of strategic stability—generation stability and prompt launch stability—need not be greatly affected by U.S. unilateral reductions. For Russia, the primary impact of unconstrained strategic forces would be to allow MIRVing of the SS-27 ICBM and any additional ICBMs Russia may develop. This would improve Russia's deterrence stability and generation stability, but decrease Russia's prompt launch stability. However, these changes would not significantly affect Russia's reliance on the potentially destabilizing tactics of early generation and launch on tactical warning.

Finally, this analysis has highlighted the relatively minor effects on strategic stability of Russian strategic forces in going from START I to START II and the negligible effects in going from START II to START III. There are two reasons for this: (1) the difficulty Russia has in maintaining larger numbers of weapons than START III (1500) would allow and (2) the prior accomplishments of START I and START II in eliminating MIRVed and heavy ICBMs. Thus, the contribution of START III to stability will come from maintaining these achievements, continuing onsite inspections and other cooperative verification activities, assuring greater predictability, supporting our nonproliferation goals, and possibly bringing nonstrategic nuclear weapons under control. There is much analysis to be accomplished to determine whether these possibilities can be realized and thus whether START III is in our interest.

NOTES

1. Parts of this chapter, notably definitions and other introductory material, are based on a contribution by Scouras to the Department of Defense (DoD) START III Stability Study mandated by Congress in the National Defense Authorization Act for Fiscal Year 2000. In addition, the analytical methodology presented here was also used in this DoD study. However, the assumptions, force structures, strategic weapon system planning factors, calculations, and conclusions presented here are *not* based on the DoD study.

2. The INF Treaty also banned ground-launched cruise missiles, but these air-breathing weapons were considered less of a threat to stability because their comparatively long times of flight made them less useful as first-strike weapons.

3. MIRVed and heavy ICBMs (i.e., the SS-18) are generally considered destabilizing because they are simultaneously lucrative targets in a nuclear exchange and, if silo-based or in garrison, vulnerable. Thus, they are much more useful as first-strike weapons than second-strike weapons.

4. *Force structure* includes the type, quantity, and other static characteristics of delivery vehicles and their associated weapons. *Force posture* additionally includes those characteristics that define the state of readiness of these systems.

5. Steven Lee Myers, "Bush Takes First Step to Shrink Arsenal of Nuclear Warheads," *The New York Times*, February 9, 2001. See also Steven Lee Myers, "Bush Repeats Call for Arms Reduction and Missile Shield," *The New York Times*, January 27, 2001.

6. Nations characterized as "rogue" were for a brief period more politically correctly referred to as "nations of concern." However, "rogue" is now back in vogue.

7. See Peter Vincent Pry, *War Scare: Russia and America on the Nuclear Brink* (Westport, Conn.: Praeger, 1999) for detailed accounts of the August 1991 coup attempt against Gorbachev and the January 1995 Norwegian meteorological rocket launch, as well as other Cold War and post–Cold War nuclear incidents.

8. It is telling that the United States didn't foresee the events—including the Japanese attack on Pearl Harbor, the North Korean invasion of South Korea, the Iraqi annexation of Kuwait, and the terror attacks of September 2001—that precipitated its involvement in the most significant wars of the past six decades. The pertinent lessons to be drawn from this history are that the immediate advantages of surprise attack can make it an irresistible tactic and that assurances that similar future unpleasant surprises are unlikely run counter to the historical experience.

9. This term is used to suggest that, notwithstanding the high-level rhetoric devoted to strategic stability, the leadership of neither side takes strategic stability issues as seriously as this analysis suggests is warranted.

10. *Joint Statement Between the United States and the Russian Federation Concerning Strategic Offensive and Defensive Arms and Further Strengthening of Stability*, The White House, June 20, 1999.

11. *Joint Statement by the Presidents of the United States of America and the Russian Federation on Principles of Strategic Stability*, The White House, June 4, 2000.

12. *Joint Statement on Cooperation on Strategic Stability*, The White House, July 21, 2000.

13. *Joint Statement/Strategic Stability Cooperation Initiative*, The White House, September 6, 2000.

14. *Joint Statement on Parameters on Future Reductions in Nuclear Forces*, March 21, 1997.

15. The National Defense Authorization Act for Fiscal Year 2000, Public Law 106–65, Section 1503.

16. The approach described here is based on a methodology first developed in James Scouras, *U.S. Strategic Forces Under the Prospective START Treaty* (Santa Monica, Calif.: The RAND Corporation, 1991).

17. The normal and heightened states of alert of U.S. strategic forces are referred to as day-to-day alert and generated alert, respectively. Confusingly, the U.S. Strategic Command (USSTRATCOM) refers to these states as *alert* and *generated*, respectively. For the Russian Federation, they are referred to as constant combat readiness and increased combat readiness, respectively.

18. Tactical warning is warning, for example by radar detection, that an attack is underway. In contrast, strategic warning is warning that the other side is preparing for an attack. The attack could be minutes to months away, or might never come. Launch on tactical warning and ride-out attack are also referred to as prompt launch and delayed launch and, more recently, prompt response and delayed response, respectively.

19. *Basic Provisions of the Military Doctrine of the Russian Federation*, translated in FBIS-SOV-93–222S (November 19, 1993) and *Draft Russian Military Doctrine*(http://www.fas.org/nuke/guide/russia/doctrine/991009–draft-doctrine.htm, accessed January 9, 2001.)

20. Note that we do not explicitly model a reserve force. That is, all on-line weapons are assumed to be useable in the bilateral nuclear exchange. For the United States, this overestimates the number of weapons usable in the nuclear exchange because some strategic weapons must be reserved to deter or attack nations other than Russia. For Russia, however, this assumption probably is reasonably accurate because Russia can use its tactical, rather than strategic, nuclear weapons against all nations in Eurasia.

21. In our force survivability calculations, we assume all mobile ICBMs that are field-deployed and all SSBNs at sea survive because they are untargetable.

Bombers that are on strip alert are assumed to escape from their bases in both the launch-on-tactical-warning and ride-out-attack scenarios. We further assume that the first striker has enough alert weapons to perform a counterforce attack. This is no problem for the United States from either generated or day-to-day alert postures, but could be a problem for Russia in the future in the day-to-day alert scenario if the U.S. maintains 500 ICBM silos. In that scenario, Russia might have to undertake some degree of force generation for this assumption to be valid.

22. For the mathematically inclined, we note that even if nuclear war were to occur, it would not follow that the probability of nuclear war was high, only that it was above zero. Similarly, even if nuclear war never occurs, we cannot deduce that the probability was low, only that it was not 100%.

23. Peter Vincent Pry, op cit.

24. Although shorter-range weapons may be deemed "strategic" in a local or regional context, here we define "strategic" to include only those weapons of intercontinental range.

25. *Text of Remarks by the President in Address to the Nation*, The White House, Office of the Press Secretary, September 27, 1991, and U.S. Arms Control and Disarmament Agency, "Presidential Initiative on Nuclear Arms," ACDA Fact Sheet, September 27, 1991. The reciprocal Soviet initiative is described in "Gorbachev's Remarks on Nuclear Arms Cuts," *The New York Times*, October 6, 1991.

26. Sources for 1991 data in Tables 2.1 and 2.2 include the *Memorandum of Understanding (MOU) on Data* contained in the START Treaty; Secretary of Defense, *Military Forces in Transition*, September 1991; Secretary of Defense, *Annual Report to the President and the Congress*, January 1991; and United Communications Group, *Periscope United States Naval Institute Data Base*, March 1991.

27. Article VI of the START II Treaty provides that it shall remain in force so long as the START I Treaty remains in force, which is why an extension to START I is required in this case.

28. Article XVII of the START I Treaty provides that it shall remain in force for fifteen years, but can be extended by mutual agreement for an unlimited number of successive five-year periods. Since START I entered into force December 1994, without extension it will expire in December 2009.

29. Under the START I Treaty, bombers that do not carry long-range nuclear ALCMs (LRNA) count as one against the warhead limit of 6,000, regardless of how many bombs they actually carry. Up to 150 U.S. heavy bombers equipped for LRNA count as 10 warheads, but can actually carry up to 20 LRNA. Up to 180 Soviet heavy bombers equipped for LRNA count as 8 warheads, but can actually carry up to 16 LRNA.

30. Secretary of Defense, *Annual Report to the President and the Congress*, 2000. This source states that "to meet the overall START I warhead limits, some of the Minuteman missiles have been downloaded to carry only one reentry vehicle." Interestingly, it does not appear necessary to download *any* Minuteman missiles to remain under either the overall START I accountable warhead limit of

6,000 or the ballistic missile warhead sublimit of 4,900, provided only that the four oldest Ohio-class SSBNs are eliminated or converted to a nonnuclear role before the December 2001 deadline for full implementation. Thus, we apply this statement to only one wing of 150 Minuteman missiles, because this is the smallest reasonable unit for which to make such a change.

31. Ibid. Since this source projects 336 SLBMs (14 Trident SSBNs with 24 missiles each), and the START II Treaty limit for SLBM warheads is 1,750, each missile must be downloaded to 5 warheads for a total of 1,680 SLBM warheads.

32. We do not distinguish between air-launched cruise missiles (ALCMs) and advanced cruise missiles (ACMs) in this analysis.

33. Ibid. For bombers, this source projects keeping all ninety-five strategic bombers (20 B-2s and 75 B-52Hs).

34. *Joint Statement on Parameters on Future Reductions in Nuclear Forces*, op. cit.

35. *Joint Statement on Parameters on Future Reductions in Nuclear Forces*, op. cit.

36. Secretary of Defense, *Annual Report to the President and the Congress*, 2001, p. 91.

37. Bill Gertz, "Joint Chiefs Oppose Russian Plan to Cut 1,000 U.S. Warheads," *Washington Times*, May 11, 2000; "Arbatov on U.S.-Russian Arms Reductions," *Carnegie Non-Proliferation Project*, May 18, 2000 (http://www.ceip.org, accessed February 5, 2001).

38. Department of State, *Fact Sheet: START I Aggregate Numbers of Strategic Offensive Arms*, October 1, 2000.

39. Dean A. Wilkening, *The Evolution of Russia's Strategic Nuclear Force*, Center for International Security and Cooperation, Stanford University, July 1988, pp. 29–31.

40. *Russia's Arms and Technologies, The XXI Century Encyclopedia, Strategic Nuclear Forces,* Volume I, 2000 (Moscow: Publishing House "Arms and Technologies"). Although Russia has developed a variant of the Bear that can carry sixteen ALCMs, this source appears to indicate that current Bear bombers carry six ALCMs.

41. Jon Brook Wolfsthal, Cristina-Astrid Chuen, and Emily Ewell Daughtry, eds. *Nuclear Status Report* (Carnegie Endowment for International Peace and Monterey Institute of International Studies, 2001), p. 18.

42. Ibid., p. 18.

43. Jon Brook Wolfsthal, op. cit., p. 18.

44. Exploiting these upload potentials in a "breakout" would require downloaded weapons to be maintained in reserve or the ability to rapidly produce new nuclear weapons, as well as a significant logistics infrastructure to accomplish the uploading process in a relatively short period of time.

45. We say "apparent" advantages mindful of the admonition, "Beware what you wish for."

46. Although there is an unresolvable argument whether the U.S. strategic nuclear advantage or its local conventional military advantage was more important during the Cuban missile crisis of October 1963, no serious scholar has argued that we would have been better off with nuclear parity with the Soviet Union during that crisis.

47. Article VI of the Nonproliferation Treaty, signed July 1, 1968, states, "Each of the Parties to the Treaty undertakes to pursue negotiations in good faith on effective measures relating to cessation of the nuclear arms race at an early date and to nuclear disarmament, and on a treaty on general and complete disarmament under strict and effective international control."

48. Secretary of Defense, *Annual Report to the President and the Congress*, 2001. This source provides that one or two SSBNs are undergoing long-term overhauls (off-line); two-thirds of operational SSBNs are routinely at sea; almost all ICBMs are on day-to-day alert; and no bombers are on day-to-day alert. We do not distinguish SSBNs that are at sea from those that are on station (i.e., in position to fire).

49. For example, assignment of 90% reliability to all systems is based loosely on the notion that no system is perfect. The figure of 90% probability of penetration for Russian bombers reflects minimal U.S. air defenses; the same probability of penetration for U.S. bombers reflects a combination of considerations—gaps in Russian early warning coverage and deterioration in their air defenses, an assumed capability of U.S. ICBMs and/or SLBMs to destroy key air defense installations before the arrival of bomber weapons, and credit for stealth technology. The 10% survivability of ICBMs in silos reflects the assumed imperfect reliability of ICBMs and SLBMs. See James Scouras, *U.S. Strategic Forces Under the Prospective START Treaty*, The RAND Corporation, 1991, for a similar estimate of strategic weapon system planning factors.

50. All quantities are rounded to the nearest ten. This represents a compromise between providing enough detail to replicate our results and implying more precision in these calculations than is warranted. We err on the side of precision.

51. The equivalent megatonnage of a nuclear weapon is its yield (in megatons) taken to the two-thirds power. Equivalent megatonnage provides a more accurate comparison of blast effects on the ground due to weapons with different yields.

3

FRICTION AND NUCLEAR DETERRENCE

Nuclear weapons were thought by many to contradict much that had been taught previously about military strategy. Nuclear weapons would keep the peace by means of deterrence. The threat of using means of destruction so absolute in their consequences would suffice to replace war, and friction along with it. Generations of nuclear strategic thinkers in the United States and some policymakers treated the end of the Cold War as confirmation of this logic. Both the peaceful withdrawal of Soviet military power from East Central Europe and the demise of the Soviet Union itself without war provided for some observers the proof that nuclear deterrence worked by freezing the frame of war until communism collapsed in Europe.

This reading of the Cold War and of the reasons for Soviet peaceful disengagement or demise is wrong: We and others have elaborated on that topic elsewhere.[1] The expectation that nuclear deterrence has invalidated great power wars and thereby circumvented friction—and Clausewitz—is even more mistaken than the assumption that nuclear weapons gave the West victory in the Cold War. Nuclear and other deterrence as practiced during the Cold War was marked by a dangerous and unavoidable component of friction, and so too will it be in the future. Friction is not determined by the size of arsenals or by the devastation that weapons can inflict if fired, but by the human relationships that must be engaged in order to deter or, if need be, to fight with weapons of mass destruction, including nuclear ones.[2]

A great deal was assumed about human behavior by deterrence theory, and that theory has been subjected to numerous critiques that will not be repeated here. Instead, this chapter asks about the impact on deterrence of friction as Clausewitz understood the term and as further elaborated in this study: Friction is the difference between expected outcomes and actual results. In the first part of the chapter, we review the different kinds of deterrence and their implications. The second section considers how friction might be related to past and future nuclear weapons issues, including war plans, crisis management, and offensive and defensive force operations. Friction has special pertinence to post–Cold War nuclear proliferation and efforts to contain it with missile defenses.

TYPES OF DETERRENCE

This book is more about nuclear deterrence than conventional. Nevertheless, some points of comparison and contrast between the two types of deterrence must be brought forward. Conventional deterrence is thought to depend mainly on the credible threat to deny the enemy his military and political objectives. Nuclear deterrence, on the other hand, is judged by most experts to depend mainly on the credible threat of retaliatory punishment.[3] These assumptions are captured in Table 3.1.

It is not the case that nuclear deterrence rests exclusively on punishment, or conventional deterrence on denial. Nuclear weapons can destroy armies, navies, air forces, and supporting military assets of opponents, thus denying them significant combat capabilities. Conventional forces can, and have in historical cases, punished the societies and economies of their opponents: economic blockades and strategic air bombardment by conventional munitions in World War II are illustrative.[4] The economic blockades and conventional air wars carried out by the United States and its allies in that war were not done only for the purposes of deterrence, of course; they were also ex-

Table 3.1
Deterrence by Denial and by Punishment

	Denial Capability	**Punishment Capability**
Conventional Deterrence	X	
Nuclear Deterrence		X

pected to wear down by attrition enemy war-supporting infrastructure and destroy military assets in Germany and Japan. Nevertheless, it is fair to say that deterrence, based on the threat of more air war or increased economic strangulation to come, was part of the equation.

Deterrence can have active or passive forms. The strategic air bombardment of Germany and Japan was an active form, or compellence.[5] Compellence aims to induce the state or other actor to cease conduct already in progress, and/or to undo an action already taken. President Kennedy's demand that the Soviet Union remove its nuclear capable missiles from Cuba in 1962 is an example of compellence. British air power theorists hoped that bombing of German cities during World War II would coerce (i.e., compel) dehoused and discontented Germans to demand of their government a strategic surrender. Unfortunately for air power optimists, the devastation was less than expected and the power of public opinion to coerce Hitler was negligible.

Nuclear deterrence rests mainly on the threat of punishment and that threat has two parts: capability and credibility.[6] Capability implies the means to retaliate once having been attacked or in the expectation of an attack (more on that later). Credibility implies that the deterrer understands the threat being made and believes that if the specified behavior is engaged in, the deterrer will actually carry out the threat. Capability is easier to show than credibility, on the evidence. It seemed relatively simple for the Cold War superpowers to demonstrate that they could not only blow themselves up simultaneously or sequentially, but much of the exterior world besides. But this capability endured for most of the Cold War as a constant. It did not necessarily follow that, in the variable circumstances of a specific crisis or attack, deterrence would work as expected to.

During the Cold War there was another complication. Because of alliance commitments by the United States to the defense of NATO Europe, conventional and nuclear deterrence were commingled. So too were conventional and nuclear defense problems. NATO relied after 1967 on a "flexible response" strategy of graduated deterrence that promised to meet any conventional attack with an initial conventional response. Soviet escalation to the first use of theater nuclear forces would presumably bring a response in kind from NATO TNF. Finally, if the Soviets were to employ strategic nuclear weapons against the United States or its allies, Washington would respond by invoking the SIOP (Nuclear War Plan). Whether the Soviets believed NATO declaratory policy on these points was arguable, Soviet military planners were obliged to pay attention to NATO's nuclear capabilities based in Europe and in North America.

There is some controversy whether deterrence is truly a strategy or an experiment in applied psychology. Successful deterrence means that a war does not have to be fought, but success is defined in a very short-term manner. In the Agadir crisis several years before the start of World War I, the outbreak of war among the major powers was avoided, so Germany was presumably deterred by the denouement of that crisis. However, Germany (at least the Kaiser) was also frustrated and enraged, and resolved not to yield the next time around. So being deterred in the short term can light the fuse for failed deterrence later. Deterrence in history also suffers from a lack of evidence of its effects. One cannot prove that deterrence "worked" when one state failed to attack another; there are many reasons why a state contemplating an attack might stay its hand. Deterrence is also latent as well as manifest. A latent deterrence system exists among all states dependent on self-help for military security. The possibility of war in general is ever present, although the specific causes for war and the lineup of enemies may vary. Manifest deterrence takes place when a state or other actor has issued a specific threat against another, has stated conditions for compliance, and has explained what will happen if compliance is not forthcoming. It follows that states that cannot or will not communicate cannot play at deterrence; they can engage in other mischief though, including aggression.

Deterrence can also be misread to assume that arsenals deter one another independently of the purposes for which they are intended, or independently of the nuances of war plans, alerts, and other operational matters pertinent to military threats and campaigns. Nuclear weapons were supposedly of this sort: contributory to more or less automatic deterrence once deployed in large numbers and in survivable basing modes. This "apes on a treadmill" mystique about nuclear armed states in the Cold War led to a related assumption that the nuclear arms race was fallout from misunderstanding between Americans and Soviets rather than serious policy disagreements.

Weapons-driven explanations ignore the fact that policy disagreements create the need for deterrence to be exercised instead of the reverse. Nevertheless, it is also reasonable to assume certain feedback effects onto policy from the kinds of nuclear arsenals that are deployed. Survivable and flexible nuclear forces will permit leaders to develop war plans with more potential for adaptation to unforeseen circumstances particular to time and place. Nuclear combatants even more than conventional war fighters would be prudent to assume that prewar plans will not survive the first encounter with the enemy, a la Field Marshal von Moltke's warning to that effect. The U.S. nuclear war plans of the Cold War years were the product of very generalized policy guidance issued by persons who involved themselves little, if at all, in the details of nuclear option planning and targeting. As a result, hubristic objectives not attainable with the existing technology (e.g., controlled and protracted nuclear wars) found their way into U.S. declaratory policy.

If we imagine a line separating those theorists and policymakers who approached nuclear weapons and deterrence issues from an arms control perspective, compared to those who adopted a military–strategic orientation, the summary of the differences in their attitudes toward strategy and deterrence in Table 3.2 might be apropos:

During the Cold War it was assumed by most Western policymakers and military analysts that technology favored the offense over the defense in the case of nuclear weapons. The defender's task was judged as especially problematic if it aspired to defend cities instead of retaliatory forces. The ABM Treaty of 1972 was regarded by U.S. arms control advocates, but apparently not by Soviet military or political leaders, as an acknowledgment that this state of affairs could never be changed. Soviet leaders continued to work on the development of antinuclear strategic defenses and deployed an ABM sys-

Table 3.2
Arms Control and Strategic Orientations to Strategy and Policy

	Arms Control Orientation	**Strategic Orientation**
Military requirements for deterrence	Forces adequate to guarantee survivability and assured retaliation (with or without flexible targeting)	Forces require survivability and flexibility to ensure ability to dominate any process of competitive escalation
View of Soviet strategy and policy objectives	Geopolitically assertive, but opportunistic and realistic; capable of reaching accommodations on issues of mutual interest	Motivated by ideology as well as geopolitics, Soviets will create pressure against any perceived weak point in U.S./NATO or allied defense perimeter
Attitude toward missile defenses, robust counterforce capabilities, and other aspects of nuclear force employment	Doubtful of effectiveness *for deterrence* of missile defenses and counterforce, considering them either superfluous or dangerous to stability based on assured vulnerability	Acceptant of highly competent counterforce in support of deterrence, although suspicious of any notion of U.S. - Soviet "nuclear war fighting" or victory in a nuclear war; acceptant of defenses for the retaliatory force, less friendly (with exceptions) to population defense for the homeland

tem around Moscow subject to treaty constraints. In 1983 President Ronald Reagan called on the U.S. defense technology community to produce a multitiered missile defense system that could protect the American homeland even against large-scale Soviet attacks. After the Cold War, the U.S. research and development program was scaled back to one favoring a smaller defense system for limited strikes by rogue states or accidental launches.

This rejection of defense and embrace of offensive retaliation as a necessary evil or a desirable condition simplified arms control negotiations, but also nullified much of traditional military strategy. Traditional strategy for conventional deterrence or for prevailing in war regarded offenses and defenses as competitive and interactive war forms. Historically, a temporarily superior form of attack had eventually produced its antithesis: a countervailing form of defense. Nuclear weapons seemed to exist apart from this action–reaction dynamic, although it was possible that the years between 1945 and 1990 offered too short a time interval to tell. Some argued in the 1980s that eventually space and terrestrially based nonnuclear weapons, which were founded on new physical principles, would unlock the deadlock of deterrence based on assured retaliation. This futuristic technology remained out of reach at century's end, and congressional advocates of limited national missile defense (NMD) for the U.S. homeland plumped for ground-based, kinetic kill interceptor, and other technologies closer to hand.

The potential for first-strike stability and central deterrence is partly related to the prevailing technology environment: offense dominant, defense dominant, or mixed. Central deterrence exists if, in a two-sided relationship, neither side can calculate "in cold blood" that a first strike would pay. First-strike stability requires, in addition to the standards for central deterrence, that neither side be tempted to launch its forces preemptively on the assumption that it is under attack or about to be attacked. Table 3.3 summarizes possible relationships between technology environments and optimism or pessimism about central deterrence and first-strike stability.

Some prominent military thinkers now hold that nuclear weapons may give pride of place to a "revolution in military affairs" led by improved electronics, information, and communications technologies.[7] Nuclear weapons would not be defeated so much as circumvented. The United States and other high technology societies that were first to exploit advanced information technologies for military purposes would, in this view, have a rich deterrent in the form of "dominant battlespace awareness." This meant being able to see and interpret the entire battlefield and to deny the opponent a clear vision of it, perhaps by confusing or distorting the opponent's own information systems themselves. Some visionaries foresaw techniques for cyberwar that could bypass the actual destruction of armies and missile silos by holding hostage or

Table 3.3
First-Strike Stability and Central Deterrence in Three Environments

	Offense Dominant	Defense Dominant	Offense-Defense Competitive
Central Deterrence	STRONG Assured retaliation by offenses	STRONG Replaced by denial of attack objectives	UNCERTAIN Retaliatory threats may not be credible
First Strike Stability	STRONG No advantage to going first—both destroyed	STRONG No advantage to going first—both survive	UNCERTAIN Survival may be dependent upon first strike

Source: Adapted from Glenn A. Kent and David E. Thaler, *First Strike Stability and Strategic Defenses* (Santa Monica, Calif.: RAND, 1990), p. 4. We have reworded some cell entries in keeping with our purposes, but not changed the thrust of the Kent/Thaler model.

incapacitating enemy communications, computers, electric power grids, banking records, or other social and economic necessities for modern life. Cyberwar might make possible both "counterforce" and "countervalue" attacks against nuclear command and control systems and against civilian infrastructure without firing a single shot in anger.

In summary thus far, both conventional and nuclear deterrence can rely on punishment or denial, on offensive or defensive technology, and on offensively or defensively oriented military doctrines. We will ignore for purposes of this discussion the fact that politicians and others use the terms "offensive" and "defensive" for pejorative and approbative references to the strategies of their enemies and allies. The terms have familiar meaning to readers of this book. The preceding considerations are necessary prologue to the more specific arguments that follow. They establish that friction in war or deterrence depends on the specifics of strategy and force structure as well as on the generalities to which theorists are naturally attracted. What kind of friction relative to nuclear deterrence might be of interest to theorists and military operators in the new century, based on experience?

FRICTION IN POLICY AND OPERATIONS

Friction pertinent to nuclear deterrence might apply to various aspects of the decision-making process. Let us take as examples war plans, crisis management, offensive force operations, and defenses against nuclear attack. Of course, the extent to which friction applied at these various stages would depend on the preferred strategy for deterrence. Broadly speaking, one can identify three types of nuclear strategies that were advocated by policymakers or theorists during the Cold War and that have continued to command interest thereafter. We will refer to these as assured retaliation, defense emphasis, and minimum deterrence. We might suppose that each of these strategies implies its own estimate of the kinds of friction that matter more, and of those kinds that matter less. Proponents of an assured retaliation strategy, for example, are willing to accept higher levels of destruction if deterrence fails compared to advocates of defense emphasis. Those in favor of defense emphasis, on the other hand, are more willing to run the risk of a continuing competition between offensive and defensive technologies.

We have not included in this list of families of strategy "nuclear war fighting" because the phrase is oxymoronic and because we take Colin Gray's point as valid: All military strategies, at the sharp end of the spear, are about the fighting of war. What else would they be about?[8] Gray is no more willing than we are to minimize the danger of nuclear war and its effects. But he believes on the evidence that, nuclear weapons having been invented and made available to potential enemies of the United States and its allies, it required thinking through how nuclear weapons might actually be used. Moreover, scholars and other military strategists might refuse to consider nuclear war fighting as a serious subject for study, but policymakers and commanders would be tasked to produce policy guidance, plans and forces for the conduct of nuclear warfare in case deterrence failed. The point of deterrence, as Bernard Brodie said in 1946, was to avoid war.[9] Avoiding war by means of deterrence meant being able to fight if war was forced upon you. On this, if little else, U.S. and Soviet militaries agreed.

Some scientists argued that assured retaliation was not really a strategy, but a condition. This argument assumed that offensive technology would forever prevail over the defense, and for the duration of the Cold War this was so. However, the end of the Cold War makes the argument for a "condition" of assured retaliation weaker, even if technology does not change rapidly to favor defenses relative to offenses. More important than technology, the politics of strategy have changed. The demise of the Soviet Union has uncoupled much of American and other military thought from its Soviet and bipolar focus.[10] This cautionary note includes nuclear strategic thinking. Since politics drives strategy, it follows that a friendly or at least not hostile Russia diffuses the "enemy" in the equation for U.S. nuclear war planners. In fact, it is not clear at this writing whether it makes sense for the United States to continue with preplanned nuclear strike options targeted on a particular country or countries.

Having acknowledged the diversity of possible strategies for force development and employment, we nonetheless intend to proceed with a broad brush, using illustrations of friction in decision-making related to deterrence that could apply to any, or all, of these strategies. This approach avoids getting bogged down in the acute hermeneutics of nuclear theology that is beside our purpose here. A large literature already covers that ground. But it was necessary to note that a decision for or against a particular strategy such as assured retaliation or finite deterrence does help to shape the kinds of friction that can bedevil policymakers and planners and limit their choices in a crisis.

The kinds of friction and the two illustrations for each kind could be classified as it appears in Table 3.4.

Of necessity, policymaking overlaps with military operations, but the distinction between types of general friction is useful. Friction in policymaking related to nuclear deterrence shows up in the matrix of political expectations built into war plans. It also appears in the crisis management behaviors of public officials, both civilian and military. Examples from U.S. and Soviet behavior in the Cold War years are instructive.

War Plans

The most interesting feature of Cold War nuclear planning might be called the "Pushkin paradox." U.S. nuclear war plans were in some ways very Russian, and Soviet war plans were in some ways very American. The U.S. Single Integrated Operational Plan (SIOP) for strategic nuclear war was driven by required Damage Expectancies (DE) against a preselected target list grouped in the following categories: nuclear forces; OMT (conventional forces and their supporting infrastructure); command and control; and economic and social assets of the opponent.[11] Elaborate National

Table 3.4
Types of Friction

	Policy-related Friction	**Friction in Military Operations**
War Plans and Crisis Management	X	
Offensive Force Operations and Defenses		X

Strategic Target Lists (NSTL) based on loose policy guidance were used by Strategic Air Command targeters at Omaha. Air Force and Navy targeters actually operated in a void much of the time; target lists expanded to meet growing inventories of weapons. Policymakers rarely interested themselves in the details of nuclear war planning and, when they did, they were sometimes astonished or dazed. Declaratory policy not infrequently veered far from operational capabilities of the force and from actual target plans. The SIOP was fairly rigid, offering few major attack options and posing formidable problems to any president or secretary of defense who decided to improvise options not previously programmed into the system.

Americans, who pride themselves as a culture on creative improvisation and innovation, wedded themselves to a Schlieffen plan for nuclear retaliation. Meanwhile, in Moscow, the Soviet General Staff was tasked by the Politburo to guarantee retaliation (if not preemption) under any conditions of military surprise attack. The Soviet approach to nuclear war planning, in contrast to the American, was more contingent and open-ended. Prepared strike packages certainly existed and, in the event, would have been employed. But the Soviets faced three problems: war in Europe; war against China; and possible escalation to world war involving the Americans. Nuclear strikes might be called for against NATO in Europe or against China in Asia while a firebreak was kept between theater and strategic nuclear war. Of course, in their declaratory policy the Soviet Union said no such thing was acceptable; so did NATO. These were necessary political declamations, like Lloyd George's assertions of religious nonconformism.

According to lectures given at the Voroshilov Military Academy in the 1970s, the Soviet military was to be prepared for an outbreak of regional or larger war growing out of a deliberate enemy nuclear surprise attack, by escalation to nuclear war from conventional war, or by accidental or inadvertent initiation of nuclear strikes. The prepared strike plans might or might not fit the exigent circumstances. This lesson, of the possible irrelevancy of prewar plans, the Soviets had learned on June 22, 1941, as Hitler's Operation Barbarossa crushed their forward defenses. Accordingly, it was acknowledged by the General Staff that improvised options after the outbreak of war might be necessary. A command system had to provide for the conduct of a war after its initial phase.

U.S. planners also confronted the problem of possible variants of a nuclear war, but American efforts to devise war plans suitable for unexpected contingencies were confounded by the broad policy debates within which matters of strategy and force structure were hammered out. Beginning with the "Schlesinger doctrine" of 1974 with regard to limited nuclear options, U.S. officials became more explicit in declaratory policy about the need for flexible targeting and adaptive planning for more than one kind of nuclear war. The Carter administration was even more explicit, calling for "countervailing" capabilities that could offset Soviet ones at every level of escalation from limited strikes to protracted nuclear war.

The Reagan administration continued to endorse the countervailing strategy (as a "prevailing" strategy) and, in 1983, added a call for a defensive antimissile shield. Countervailing strategy is not really consistent with defense dominance, but this contradiction is not the point here. These U.S. efforts to provide for flexible nuclear options produced a firestorm in the body politic among arms controllers, academics, and media pundits whenever they trickled into declaratory policy. And, although U.S. nuclear planning was much more flexible by the 1980s than it had been in the 1950s or 1960s, there was an outer limit imposed on U.S. nuclear flexibility by the attentive antinuclear "public" suspicion that providing leaders with more options would make them more willing to wage war. Meanwhile, the SIOP soldiered on.

Apart from this contrast in the political psychology of war plans, one might also note that friction was implicit in U.S. extended deterrence commitments to NATO. These commitments were based on a complementary, but not identical, understanding of military strategy, especially about the problem of escalation. For most of the Cold War, U.S. leaders wanted conventional forces in Europe sufficient to require an extended pause of days or weeks before NATO was forced into nuclear first use. Although NATO adopted "flexible response" as its official policy in 1967, its European members did so in order to couple America's strategic nuclear deterrence to Western Europe's conventional defense and theater nuclear forces. NATO Europe's worst case was a war confined to Europe that spared American and Soviet homelands; if the Soviets expected to limit any war in this fashion, deterrence would be weaker. The French predicated their entire nuclear strategy on this assumption, which was not, in the event, a weak assumption. The coupling of U.S. to European deterrence was never road tested above the level of crisis management.

The U.S. leaders, on the other hand, sought nuclear flexibility in addition to a firebreak between conventional defense and nuclear first use. When McNamara first briefed the idea of nuclear flexibility to Europeans in 1962, they were aghast. It was not that they objected to the technical aspects of the secretary's brief, but to the politics. The idea of flexible nuclear options placed NATO's European pillar at a singular disadvantage and invited the Soviet Union to think of a political demarche that, in a crisis, might divide NATO down the middle of the Atlantic. Of course, the Soviets needed no incentive: Dividing Europe from North America was their strategic and political obsession. Nevertheless, it was felt by NATO Europeans that

McNamara was inviting Soviet misperception of American resolve to defend Europe by means of nuclear threat and, if necessary, nuclear first use.

U.S. and NATO war plans simply bypassed this policy and strategy debate about nuclear flexibility. NATO deployed so-called tactical and theater nuclear weapons in Europe in such a way that they would inevitably be involved in any large-scale war. NATO's doctrine of first use therefore invited a Soviet readiness for first strike, against U.S. strategic nuclear forces and against NATO theater nuclear weapons, once Soviet leaders were convinced that policy had failed to avert war. And so Soviet leaders did plan. Supposed revelations from the post–Cold War Russian archives have disclosed that the Soviets planned some of their military operations on the assumption of nuclear first use by them. But some archivists have overread this discovery into a conclusion that the Soviets would inevitably have begun a war in Europe with limited nuclear strikes against a variety of target sets. This is reading the Soviet planning process in too deterministic a way; it is a fair reading of what U.S. leaders playing the part of Soviets in a war game would have done.

The Soviets, believing in adaptive war planning that takes into account the actions of the enemy, would have been prepared for nuclear first use, but not necessarily dependent on it. In fact, they grew their conventional forces in the 1970s and early 1980s to give themselves the option of beginning a war without nuclear first use and putting that onus on NATO. In some conditions such a posture would have been politically advantageous for them; the Soviets always remembered that public opinion in Western Europe and in North America mattered in the equation of war. And Soviet planners were as aware as NATO's were of the results of their own war games, with regard to the effects of nuclear weapons on friendly *and* enemy troops on the field of battle. A one variant war plan dependent on nuclear first use was not in the Soviet tradition unless the General Staff had subcontracted nuclear strategic planning to French officers.

Considerable friction could have been expected if either NATO or the Soviet Union had been called upon to implement its nuclear strike plans. The deployment of theater nuclear forces by either side assumed that, in war, a lower than armageddon threshold could be maintained in the field without escalation to total war. This possibility was denied in official Soviet pronouncements and discounted by some European members of NATO. The difficulty for the United States was that flexible response offered a porous umbrella for extended deterrence, but inflexible response based deterrence on the willingness to bring prompt attacks on North America. There was no getting around the problems created by political sovereignty and geography.

The deployment of NATO tactical nuclear weapons near probable Soviet invasion corridors was presumably intended to create a nuclear trip wire that the Soviets would not dare to cross. However, if a war started under unpredictable conditions growing out of a political crisis (Checkpoint Charlie, Cuban Missile Crisis, Arab–Israeli war), U.S. leaders might wish that those nuclear weapons had not been deployed so far forward or so immediate to the tactical maneuvers of Soviet and NATO forces. The early contacts between forces would probably have been "meeting engagements" in which forces collided into one another in a mushy pattern similar to the first day at Gettysburg. It might be the priority of their political leaders to get them disengaged from maneuvers and separated from their opposite numbers while negotiations ensued to stop the fighting. Although NATO's nuclear release might take some time for political approval and for wending its way through the military bureaucracy to field forces, Soviet forces moving into contact would almost certainly have been granted contingent authority for nuclear first use or nuclear response in kind to NATO strikes (much as General Pli'yev, commander of the Group of Soviet Forces in Cuba, was temporarily granted in 1962 for retaliation with tactical nuclear weapons in case of a U.S. invasion of Cuba that interrupted communications between Moscow and Havana).

The largest degree of friction in war plans of both Americans and Soviets was probably the "people" factor. Both sides repeatedly offered reassurances that, once the balloon went up, persons in the chain of command from chief of staff to latrine orderly would carry out their instructions faithfully and without question. There is a great deal of difference between exercises and the actuality of war, however. There is also a great deal of difference between prewar expectations based on hubris of national assertiveness and the sentiments of military combatants after battle has been joined. That field forces would have continued to fight under the strain of even "limited" nuclear war in Europe is an assumption that defies historical precedent. It also defies the evidence of the best studies of human behavior in combat. It is entirely possible, of course, that S.L.A. Marshall, John Keegan, and Clausewitz are all wrong on these points, and that troops would continue to persevere in battle as their comrades and surroundings were atomized. This possibility does not merit serious consideration, and even less consideration is merited by the idea of postattack America and Russia carrying on a protracted global war after their home continents have been turned into Chernobyls.

It is more probable that, at the moment that orders were given by politicians for nuclear first use or first strike, some resistance in the chain of command would assert itself. A little resistance or doubt goes a long way, especially in the case of forces dependent on prompt launch. "Resistance" does not have to be active, visible, or assertive. Orders are misunderstood, lost, or misdirected. Standard operating procedures allow each level of command certain room for interpolation of the procedures as they apply to its tasking; in short, there is always "room to wiggle." It was often argued by Cold War military analysts that even if doubting Thomases slowed down the U.S. war machine, the Soviet forces would carry out any and all orders without question. This assumption of stick-figure Russians was based on peasant infantry forces of the Tsarist years and offered little insight into the probable behavior of officers actually in possession of nuclear launchers, weapons, and launch codes. Could Soviet leaders opt for preemption against North America and, absent any preceding attacks on Mother Russia, count on commanders in charge of nuclear forces, their operators, and their political supervisors all falling in line toward doomsday?

Crisis Management

The preceding discussion has spilled us over from war plans into nuclear crisis management. There is a large literature on crisis management during the Cold War as a result of the intensive study of the Cuban missile crisis, several Berlin crises and the U.S.–Soviet confrontation over the October war of 1973. Any reader of this literature who comes away reassured by these studies of decision-making behavior is a candidate for the Pangloss Pantheon. Crisis management in the nuclear age has fulfilled all the conditions that Clausewitz ascribed to the environment of military operations, including heavy doses of friction, uncertainty, and chance. Optimists say that there was no nuclear war for the forty-five years of Cold War and no conventional war in Europe during the same period, so why worry?

Studies of security decision-making often reach pessimistic judgments about the quality of the decision-making process by taking an incorrect route. If one turns up the level of magnification on the microscope high enough, one is bound to see many examples of dysfunctional attitudes, behavior, and personality in any crisis. The devil is indeed in the details. Not all of these details matter. Whether, for example, the personality of Richard Bissell or Allen Dulles contributed much to the outcome of the Bay of Pigs invasion is not clear. It is much clearer that CIA hubris, an inexperienced president and national security team, and compartmentalization of information did play important parts in the denouement of the failed invasion. Analysts can get lost in personality to the detriment of understanding why a *process* did, or did not, work.

For example, take the Soviet side of the Cuban missile crisis of 1962. Although a bookshelf of studies had captured the drama of the tense days in

October after U.S. intelligence discovered the Soviet missiles in Cuba, we know less about the decision-making process in the Kremlin pertinent to the actual deployment decision.[12] This process took place in the spring and early summer of 1962. We have Khrushchev's memoirs (in two editions), recollections from other crisis participants, and various studies by journalists, historians and political scientists. Khrushchev gives two reasons for the MRBM and IRBM deployment decision: to equalize the nuclear balance of power and to deter invasion of Cuba. These are not implausible motives. However, when one asks who was consulted by Khrushchev about this decision, the answers are vague and not at all reassuring. He apparently discussed it with Deputy Premier Anastas Mikoyan and Foreign Minister Andrei Gromyko; Mikoyan advised against it, and Gromyko was, as always, noncommittal on policy matters.

Only after having made up his own mind did Khrushchev bring in military experts and ask whether the deployments could be done *secretly*, that is, without U.S. discovery of the missile launchers and their contiguous air defenses before the MRBM and IRBM deployments had been completed. Military experts were then tasked to draw up appropriate plans. There is no record that Khrushchev considered the implications of his decision for mobilization of the Soviet armed forces in general or for the readiness of the Strategic Rocket Forces in particular. It appears that he entirely disregarded the possibility that his scheme would fail, did not task the military to prepare a fallback position, and was unprepared to offer counterproposals when Kennedy demanded withdrawal of the missiles and warheads from Cuba. Nor does it appear that his military advisors, including the defense minister and armed forces chief of staff, offered any remonstrances to this effect. In addition, Khrushchev placed his crony General Pli'yev, a World War II cavalry officer, in charge of the entire contingent of Soviet forces deployed in Cuba.

The matter of how much authority over nuclear weapons to delegate to Pli'yev was up for grabs in the summer and fall of 1962. Khrushchev, worried that the Americans might attack Cuba before the MRBM and IRBM missile deployments were completed, initially considered turning Soviet tactical nuclear weapons (not the MRBMs or IRBMs but Frog surface-to-surface, nuclear capable tactical missiles) over to the Cubans. He later thought better of this. The Soviet Presidium, or highest policy making body, at first told Defense Minister Rodion Malinovskiy to order Pil'yev to use all available Soviet and Cuban forces *except* the nuclear weapons to meet any U.S. attack. After some second thoughts of its own, the Presidium weighed a possible message authorizing the Group of Soviet Forces commander to use tactical nuclear weapons, but not the MRBMs or IRBMs. Malinovskiy was not content with this instruction and it was changed before it could be sent to the field; the earlier version withholding approval for any use of nuclear weapons except by explicit permission from Moscow was sent to Pli'yev.[13]

The performance of U.S. policymakers and their military advisors during, and prior to, the Cuban missile crisis also raises serious concerns about the demands made on any policymaking process by the requirements of nuclear crisis management. After discovering the missiles, the United States entered into the crisis with a strong hand. The United States had a second-strike capability while the Soviet Union had only a first-strike capability in its strategic nuclear forces. An altercation in the Caribbean would favor the superiority of U.S. naval and other conventional forces in a theater of operations close to home. The Soviets had been caught in a clandestine deployment that put the diplomatic initiative in Washington and created much public embarrassment for the Kremlin. Despite these favorable background conditions, the Kennedy ExComm deliberations involved extreme stress, great disputation among participants, uncertainty in intelligence estimates, and a great deal of guesswork about why the Soviets had deployed the missiles and what they would do in response to various U.S. moves to get the missiles removed. One cannot escape the verdict that the crisis was resolved favorably for the United States not on account of superior crisis management or a favorable balance of forces, but due to improvised crisis communications, dead reckoning, and good luck.

Worse is yet to come. On the evidence, U.S. performance during the Cuban missile crisis reached a relatively high standard for Cold War crisis management. If we compare American crisis decision-making in October 1962 to that of October 1973, the earlier crisis shows an administration performing with far greater effectiveness and in the face of graver danger. In October 1973 U.S. intelligence was caught by surprise when several Arab states attacked Israel. Egyptian and Syrian offensives made serious gains in the early days of fighting before Israel rallied its forces, stabilized its defensive lines, and went over to the offensive. The success of Israeli counteroffensives led to a Soviet threat of unilateral military intervention to enforce a cease-fire unless the United States joined in a Soviet effort to do so or caused Israel to cease its threat to an encircled Egyptian Third Army Corps.

The senior crisis management group was called to an evening meeting to decide how to respond to Soviet President Leonid Brezhnev's ultimatum of October 23 to this effect. The group included President Nixon's National Security Advisor (Henry A. Kissinger) and other principals of the administration with defense, foreign policy, and national security portfolios. Kissinger chaired the meeting in Nixon's absence, since the president was "unavailable," although on the premises. In the absence of the president, Kissinger and his crisis management group decided to order into effect a global military alert, including the alerting of nuclear forces. This was intended as a deliberate signal to the Soviet leadership that they could not miss. The United States was signaling its vital interest in preventing any Soviet military intervention in this conflict while Kissinger's shuttle diplomacy and other political demarches were at work to resolve it.

The crisis managers ordered the alert into effect on the assumption that it would serve to intimidate the Soviet Union but not alarm the U.S. domestic public. The intended effects were the reverse of the actual results. The Soviets were not intimidated, since the conditional threat of unilateral Soviet intervention was actually a bit of "coercive diplomacy" in American terms, not a guaranty of military action under certain conditions. And awareness of the alert spread almost immediately to the media, Congress, and the public, producing a backdraft of accusations that the Nixon administration was deliberately overplaying the crisis in order to distract public attention from Watergate.

In addition, the raising of diplomatic temperatures and popular anxieties was not the only side effect of the alert and reactions to it. Soviet naval forces and their American counterparts in the Mediterranean were already playing tag and keeping close company in the event that crisis turned to war. Some of these maritime maneuverings were quite assertive on both sides, and the possibility of miscalculation growing out of an incident at sea could have coincided with a stalled diplomatic process and more menacing Soviet troop movements. As it was, some Soviet airborne forces were moved from their peacetime deployment locations to jumping off points, possibly but not necessarily points of departure for the Middle East. The U.S. intelligence observed these and other troop movements by the Soviets that could have been construed by American watchers as prudent preparatory steps for an actual invasion or other military intervention.

In some ways the 1973 confrontation was less dangerous compared to the Cuban missile crisis, and in other ways more so, from the perspective of friction in policymaking or in military operations related to crisis management. For example, Kennedy's team *knew* that they were in a serious crisis from the moment that photographic evidence of the missiles in Cuba was available. The president also established a clear objective for crisis managers: find some way to remove the missiles, if possible without war. In 1973, neither the awareness of a U.S.–Soviet crisis nor the specification of U.S. policy objectives was as clear. Irrefutable evidence of Soviet missiles in Cuba pushed Kennedy into an immediate, direct confrontation with Khrushchev. The October war of 1973 did not create an immediate showdown between Washington and Moscow; it evolved into one as the two superpowers lost control over the diplomatic and military endgame. Client states became potential causes of escalation and inadvertent war between U.S. and Soviet forces in the local theater of operations or globally.

Although the quality of U.S. crisis management appears superior to that of its Soviet counterpart in 1962, the reverse is the case in 1973. The Brezhnev threat of unilateral military intervention was never fully explicit or unconditional. It was stated as an "if, then" clause, conditional on our willingness to "cooperate" and agree to the possible insertion of a joint peace imposition force. United States officials were rightly suspicious of the motives behind this proposal, but they played the response badly. It was neither necessary nor prudent to declare in effect a global military alert, including nuclear capable forces. It was intended to send a loud signal to the Russians, but in the midst of Watergate it also sent a signal of panic.[14]

It was inexcusable for a military alert of this magnitude to be ordered into effect without presidential knowledge and approval (until after the fact). It may well have been the case that President Nixon was incapable of rendering a timely judgment on the evening that Brezhnev's message, about the possibility of unilateral Soviet military intervention, arrived. But, if so, the alerting decision could easily have been taken pending presidential approval the next day. The excuse for an immediate U.S. decision despite presidential noninvolvement was that the Soviets were alerting and repositioning airborne and other forces that might be spearheads for intervention. If so, the Soviet maneuvers were intended as a signal of their serious interest in a diplomatic settlement of the crisis without destruction of the Egyptian Third Army Corps.[15] Any actual Soviet deployment of combat forces into the Middle East could involve a shooting war between Soviet and Israeli forces; the risk was not worth any possible gain to Moscow. Among other risks, Israel had nuclear weapons that could be air delivered against Soviet targets, and Soviet intelligence knew this. Brezhnev's "invitation" to settle the conflict by joint military action if necessary, and his threat of possible Soviet military action without U.S. support in extremis, were examples of coercive diplomacy.

Throughout the Cold War, policymakers in Washington and in Moscow were too optimistic about the clarity with which nuclear alerts could be used to send messages and too poorly informed about the complexity of alerting operations.[16] Even peacetime operations in the United States led to occasional failures of equipment or of man–machine interfaces, leading to congressional investigations and public embarrassment. For example, simple-component failures and/or operator errors at NORAD in 1979 and in 1980 caused streams of messages to be fed through the warning and information systems of other major military commands, suggesting an imminent attack. Dangerous incidents complicated the efforts of U.S. leaders to manage the Cuban missile crisis, including a misguided U-2 spy plane that strayed into Soviet air space during one of the most tense periods of the crisis. The U-2 was supposedly on a routine training flight; the incident is, quite literally, Strangelovian, and no one has satisfactorily explained it to this day. The Soviets had their own fiascoes. Khrushchev initially approved a contingent delegation of authority to his field commander in Cuba for the first use of nuclear weapons in case of an American invasion, then rescinded it after the crisis started. It is not clear, however, whether the Soviets at that time had electronic locks to prevent arming of warheads for their tactical, surface-to-surface Frog missiles or if field commanders had decided to "misunderstand" their orders under the duress of a later, and actual, U.S. invasion of Cuba.

Offensive Force Operations

Accounts of U.S. or Soviet strategy for nuclear war published during the Cold War years had an antiseptic, unreal quality, something like Clausewitz's reference to "war by algebra." Statistical estimates of the outcomes of nuclear wars were necessary substitutes for the real thing. The danger was that models of nuclear war might distort probable outcomes by ignoring friction and assuming best case performances for missiles, bombers, and command systems never tested in combat conditions. Contributors to the academic literature on nuclear strategy and arms control during the Cold War tended to assume away the significance of operational issues. The large and redundant force structures of the nuclear superpowers, it was presumed, would make irrelevant any comparisons among postattack states of affairs.

The assumption of nuclear operations irrelevancy was not necessarily correct, even for the years of Cold War. It becomes even more important to consider offensive and defensive operational issues, including those related to friction, when American and Russian forces are greatly reduced from their Cold War levels. Both governments have agreed to reduce total strategic nuclear weapons drastically below current levels.

These promising hopes for reducing the sizes of deployed forces are dependent on the confidence that both Washington and Moscow can have in the capabilities of their remaining forces. Even if their respective launchers and warheads are no longer aimed at one another's territory (nowadays a matter of no more than several minutes to adjust), neither the United States nor Russia wants to doubt its retaliatory capability even after absorbing a surprise attack. Planners will continue to use their survivability against one another's arsenals as the "worst case" test case. How would friction in offensive force operations reduce the numbers of surviving and retaliating

U.S. or Russian forces under various START III conditions, compared to START I- and START II-compliant forces?

One way to measure the impact of friction on second-strike retaliation is to vary the operational conditions under which retaliatory forces are assumed to perform. As discussed in Chapter 2, forces can be raised to high levels of alert during a crisis or they can remain at normal peacetime "day-to-day" alert levels. Launch doctrines for retaliatory forces may also vary: from comparatively hair trigger "launch on warning" to the more laid-back posture of launch after riding out an attack. Levels of preattack alertness and launch doctrines will have an obvious influence on the numbers of warheads that retaliate successfully against their assigned targets. Let us compare the numbers of arriving retaliatory warheads for U.S. and Russian START I, START II, and START III (2500 warhead limit) forces under four conditions:

- Generated alert, launch on warning: *maximum retaliation*.
- Generated alert, ride-out attack: *intermediate retaliation*.
- Day-to-day alert, launch on warning: *intermediate retaliation*.
- Day-to-day alert, ride-out attack: *assured* or *minimum retaliation*.

Table 3.5 summarizes these comparisons. The force structures used to develop this table are those developed in Chapter 2 and summarized in Tables 2.2 and 2.4, and the weapon system planning factors used are those found in Table 2.5.

The results of this analysis are a two-sided coin: good news and bad news for proponents of nuclear force reductions. Lowering the force size creates a need to downsize target sets or to accept lesser criteria for unacceptable damage in retaliation.[17] If, for example, the United States assumes that it will be striking back from a posture of day-to-day alert and after riding out the attack, then fewer of its available second strike forces will survive a first strike than would be the case at higher alert levels and/or with a prompt launch doctrine. The charts show that at START I, START II, and START III (2500) force levels there are significant differences in the numbers of arriving retaliatory warheads under the four alertness/launch conditions specified earlier. Reducing the size of retaliatory forces will require policymakers to either: (1) routinely operate with higher alert levels and/or become more dependent on early generation and prompt launch doctrines; or (2) reduce the damage expectancy criteria for retaliatory forces, perhaps redefining the "assured destruction" mission at much lower levels than hitherto.

We might want to ask an additional question about friction, relative to our interrogation of the dependency of either side's forces on prompt launch or

Table 3.5
U.S. and Russian Arriving Retaliating Weapons

		U.S. START I	U.S. START II	U.S. START III (2500)	R.F. START I	R.F. START II	R.F. START III (2500)
MAXIMUM RETALIATION (Generated Alert, Launch on Warning)	ICBM	1530	450	450	1117	428	428
	SLBM	2246	1404	1089	363	363	363
	Air	1327	966	478	420	420	420
	Triad	5103	2820	2017	1900	1211	1211
INTERMEDIATE RETALIATION (Generated Alert, Ride Out Attack)	ICBM	153	45	45	461	295	295
	SLBM	2246	1404	1089	363	363	363
	Air	1327	966	478	420	420	420
	Triad	3726	2415	1612	1244	1078	1078
INTERMEDIATE RETALIATION (Day-to-Day Alert, Launch on Warning)	ICBM	1530	450	450	1117	428	428
	SLBM	1505	941	729	73	73	73
	Air	0	0	0	0	0	0
	Triad	3035	1391	1179	1189	501	501
ASSURED RETALIATION (Day-to-Day Alert, Ride Out Attack)	ICBM	153	45	45	112	43	43
	SLBM	1505	941	729	36	36	36
	Air	0	0	0	0	0	0
	Triad	1658	986	774	148	79	79

generated alert for survivability. How do U.S. and Russian forces compare in their relative dependency on generated alert and/or prompt launch? Our model permits us to interrogate this issue in the following manner. We can compare *generation stability* and *prompt launch stability* for the two states' forces. Generation stability is defined as the percentage of arriving retaliatory warheads in day-to-day alert compared to generated alert, for a given launch condition. Similarly, prompt launch stability is defined as the percentage of arriving retaliatory warheads when riding out the attack compared to launching on warning, for a given alert condition. These stability ratios can be calculated by our model, and those results are displayed in Figures 3.1 and 3.2. Figure 3.1 shows generation and prompt launch stabilities for U.S. START III (2500) forces; Figure 3.2 provides similar information for Russia.

Figures 3.1 and 3.2 show that Russian START III forces on day-to-day alert are much more sensitive than U.S. forces are to the difference between riding out an attack and prompt launch. And Russian forces either launched on warning or under attack are more sensitive or dependent on force generation than are the U.S. forces of comparable size.

Does this exercise matter? All nuclear war calculations, until a nuclear war actually takes place, are equivalent to Clausewitz's "war by algebra."

Figure 3.1
Generation and Prompt Launch Stability: U.S. START III (2,500) Forces

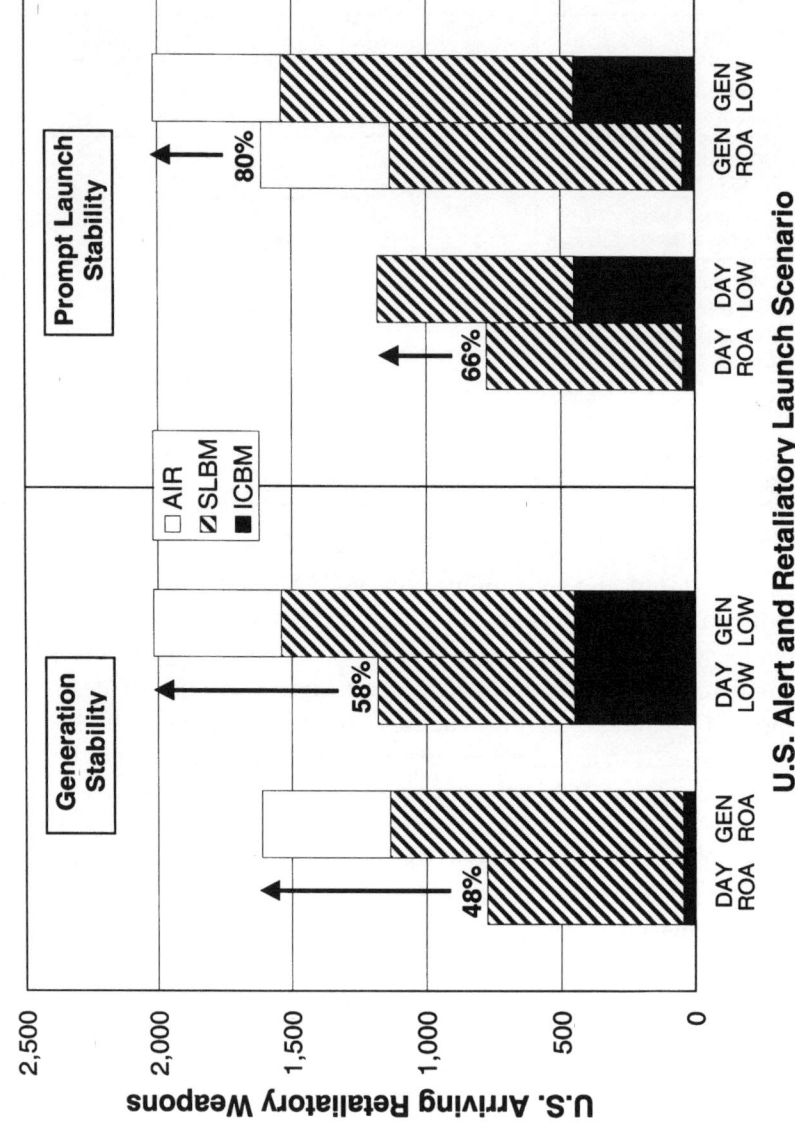

Figure 3.2
Generation and Prompt Launch Stability: R.F. START III (2500) Forces

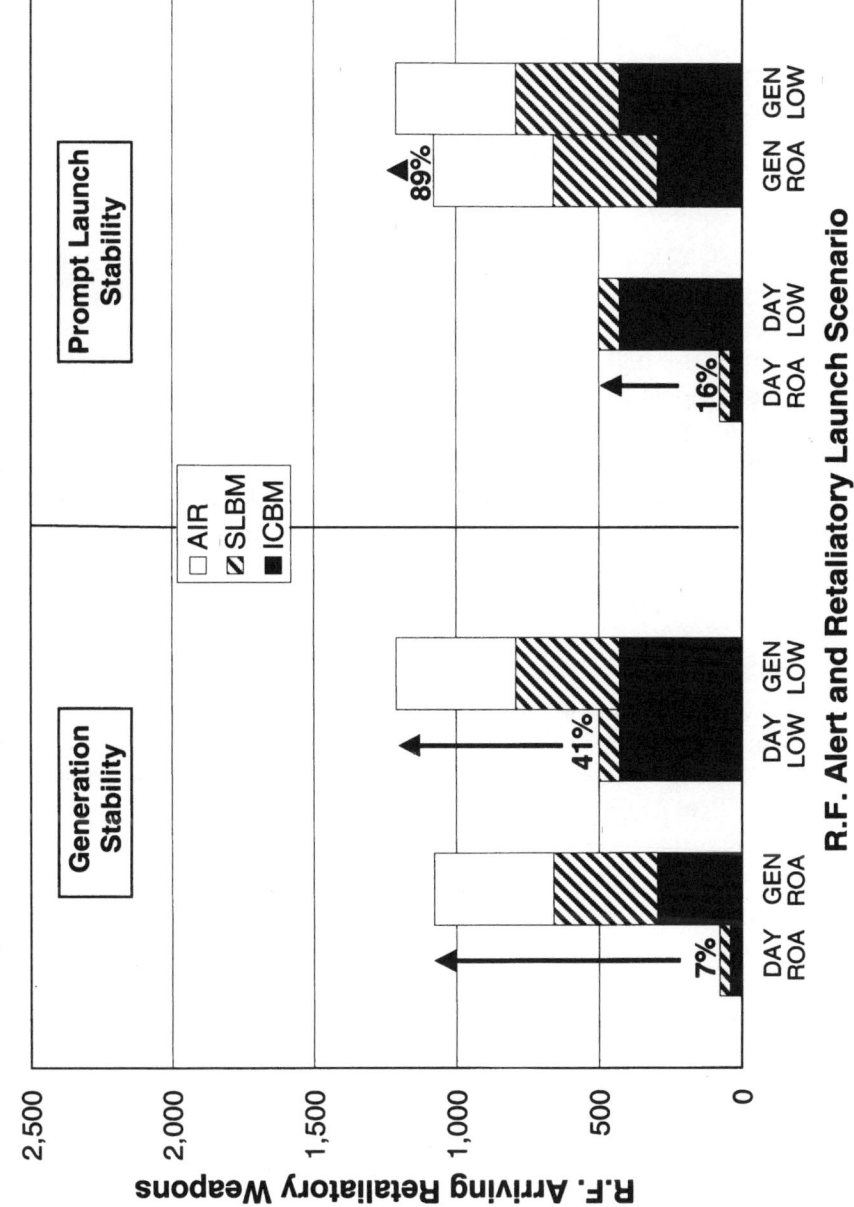

We simply do not know what will happen. But we know enough about the effects of nuclear weapons to hazard this guess: even one hundred or so arriving and penetrating warheads is enough to ruin a modern society and dethrone the politicians who caused it. Winners and losers will be hard to distinguish. The mission of nuclear weapons remains as it was: the avoidance of war by means of deterrence through credible threat of unacceptable retaliatory punishment.

Defenses

Post–Cold War U.S. and Russian officials still have reason to worry about another kind of friction: the possibility of accidental/inadvertent war or small attacks from third parties that might draw in the Americans and Russians. Some of these scenarios are rather far-fetched, including a Russia that implodes and allows its government to fall into the hands of a "Red–Brown" military dictatorship brandishing the nuclear sword. However, both Russian and U.S. political and military leaders have expressed serious concern about the possibility of rogue state attacks or accidental launches, and Boris Yeltsin on at least one occasion suggested that the United States and Russia might collaborate on joint defense deployments.[18] In 1999 the Clinton administration indicated it would proceed unilaterally to make a decision by fall of 2000 on a possible deployment of a limited National Missile Defense system (NMD) to protect U.S. territory against limited strikes. Eventually Clinton decided to defer the decision to President George W. Bush, and the Bush administration stated its clear intent in January 2001 to proceed with deployment of a national missile defense system against accidental or deliberate light attacks.

Offensive technologies are mature compared to antinuclear missile defenses (hereafter, BMD for ballistic missile defenses). It was easier to identify possible points of friction in offensive force operations than it would be for defenses since the latter are still in the stage of exploratory technologies. During the Cold War the Soviets deployed a limited, early generation ABM (antiballistic missile, early nomenclature for BMD) system around Moscow, causing some U.S. partisans of BMD to demand an arms race in defenses as well as in offenses. The United States deployed a one-site BMD system (Safeguard) to defend ICBM fields at Grand Forks, North Dakota, until 1974. Neither the Soviet nor the U.S. technologies of the Cold War years could have coped with a large-scale attack. The Soviets feared in the 1980s that President Ronald Reagan's "Strategic Defense Initiative" would produce a technological leap ahead in missile defense for the United States that would undermine the Soviet deterrent. But the technology to make the president's dream a Cold War reality was not at hand. Under the first President Bush and Clinton, the United States has reduced its research and development objectives for NMD to defense against limited strikes. The Clinton administration, goaded by the Rumsfeld Report issued in 1998 on ballistic missile threats, moved hesitantly toward a decision to begin to deploy a limited NMD system scheduled for completion in 2005. The second President Buch committed his administration to NMD deployment and increased research and development spending for missile defense.

A notional BMD system based on nonnuclear exoatmospheric intercept might involve different kinds of friction. First, space and terrestrially based radars would have to track incoming reentry vehicles and the warheads they dispensed. Second, interceptors would have to accelerate very rapidly in order to attain the velocities necessary for nonnuclear kill by impact with incoming warheads. Third, command, control, and communications (C3) would have to synchronize threat detection with the appropriate pattern of response. C3 would be even more important if the defenses involved a preferential firing doctrine instead of one that was random subtractive. Also related to C3 is the necessity for political leadership to take a timely decision to fire. Fourth, offensive countermeasures to defeat the defense might include chaff or other devices to blind or confuse radar tracking. Fifth, the "footprint" or area covered by the missile might not be as extensive as planners hoped; targets outside the footprint would be vulnerable. Friction in any or all of these components of the defense might add to "leakage" or the overall rate at which attackers succeed in penetrating the defense.

Table 3.6 does not cover the entire range of possible sources of friction in defenses any more successfully than the earlier short resume of problems in offenses. And we have the additional disadvantage of dealing in hypothetical technologies instead of actual forces deployed and (occasionally) alerted. Despite these handicaps in discussing defenses, some discussion of friction even in defenses based on very simple concepts, and tasked against very limited attacks only, might be useful now.

The present-day concern of Russia, in response to the possibility of a U.S. national missile defense, is that a U.S. defense might be expanded into something that could nullify Russia's second or retaliatory strike. The current political relationship between the United States and Russia is such that some might argue the irrelevancy of any such concern about second-strike stability. But this perception of irrelevancy is mainly a U.S. and not a Russian one. Russia sees any failure to maintain essential nuclear strategic parity with the United States as tantamount to being dropped from the league of major powers into the minors. This possibility concerns the Russian leader-

Table 3.6
Possible Sources of Friction in Missile Defenses

Detection	Detection might not take place in time for response or mischaracterize innocent event as attack
	Large-scale or sneaky attack might overwhelm or confuse defenses
Interception	Extreme accuracies and velocities required for exoatmospheric nonnuclear kill
	Firing doctrine must be appropriate to the attack
Command and control	Policymakers must react quickly and decisively to indications of attack, which might be ambiguous
	C3 system must provide for feedback on intercept failures to correct follow-on forces
Enemy countermeasures	Chaff, decoys, and other devices might confuse detection and tracking
	Enemy might use nonstandard methods of attack (e.g., low trajectory ballistic or cruise missiles)
Footprint	Not all areas within the footprint of the defender are equally important in terms of military assets, population, or other values
	Enemy method of attack may outsmart defensive firing doctrine, making some areas within the footprint vulnerable

ship, not only because of its weak conventional forces compared to those of NATO, but also because Russia fears an empowered post–Cold War NATO that might interfere in its military–strategic backyard. In addition, Russia's military leadership, intent on modernizing its debilitated conventional forces, does not want to enter into a missile defense arms race with the United States that plays to U.S. technology advantage. Therefore, any U.S. missile defense system can raise the negatives in Russian threat assessments and U.S. officials who dismiss this as Russian paranoia or propaganda have missed the point.[19]

CONCLUSION

Friction is related to deterrence in both its policymaking and military operational aspects. The likelihood of friction in war plans, crisis management, offensive force operations, and in antimissile defenses is considerable. On the historical evidence, considerable friction has been attendant to war plans, crisis management, and offensive and defensive battle even with conventional forces. With nuclear weapons, the probability of friction of an intensity and character sufficient to cripple deterrence, thereby resulting in accidental or inadvertent nuclear war, is more than trivial. The spread of nuclear weapons and the possibly contingent spread of missile defenses will introduce additional friction into states' estimates pertinent to war. Growing interest on the part of regional powers and some dissatisfied states in nuclear weapons and in long-range delivery systems argues for conservative planning on the subject of friction as related to deterrence.

NOTES

1. William E. Odom, *The Collapse of the Soviet Military* (New Haven, Conn.: Yale University Press, 1998), esp. pp. 388–404; Edward A. Kolodziej, "The Pursuit of Order, Welfare and Legitimacy: Explaining the End of the Soviet Union and the Cold War," Ch. 2 in Stephen J. Cimbala, ed., *Mysteries of the Cold War* (Aldershot: Ashgate Publishing Ltd., 1999), pp. 19–48, and, in the same volume, Peter Rainow, "The Strange End of the Cold War: Views from the Former Superpower," pp. 49–69.

2. Carl von Clausewitz, *On War*, edited and translated by Michael Howard and Peter Paret (Princeton, N.J.: Princeton University Press, 1976), pp. 119–121.

3. Lawrence Freedman, *The Evolution of Nuclear Strategy* (New York: St. Martin's Press, 1981) is exemplary.

4. George H. Quester, *Deterrence before Hiroshima: The Airpower Background of Modern Strategy* (New Brunswick, N.J.: Transaction Books, 1986), pp. x–xi and passim.

5. Thomas C. Schelling, *Arms and Influence* (New Haven, Conn.: Yale University Press, 1966), passim. explains the concept of compellence.

6. Colin S. Gray, *Modern Strategy* (Oxford: Oxford University Press, 1999), Ch. 11, esp. p. 309, offers some interesting retrospective, and contemporary, appraisals of U.S. nuclear strategy and strategy debates.

7. For views on the RMA and information based warfare, see John Arquilla and David Ronfeldt, "A New Epoch—and Spectrum—of Conflict," Ch. 1 in Arquilla and Ronfeldt, eds., *In Athena's Camp: Preparing for Conflict in the Information Age* (Santa Monica, Calif.: RAND, 1997), pp. 1–22. See also, on definitions and concepts of information warfare, Martin Libicki, *What Is Information Warfare?* (Washington, D.C.: National Defense University, ACIS Paper 3, Au-

gust 1995); Libicki, *Defending Cyberspace and other Metaphors* (Washington, D.C.: National Defense University, Directorate of Advanced Concepts, Technologies and Information Strategies, February 1997); Alvin Toffler and Heidi Toffler, *War and Anti-War: Survival at the Dawn of the 21st Century* (Boston: Little Brown, 1993), *passim*. John Arquilla and David Ronfeldt, *Cyberwar Is Coming!* (Santa Monica, Calif.: RAND, 1992); and David S. Alberts, *The Unintended Consequences of Information Age Technologies: Avoiding the Pitfalls, Seizing the Initiative* (Washington, D.C.: National Defense University, Institute for National Strategic Studies, Center for Advanced Concepts and Technology, April 1996).

8. A truly strategic, as opposed to an arms control, appraisal of nuclear weapons must confront the possibility of their actual use in war, in addition to their coercive nonuse. See Colin S. Gray, *The Second Nuclear Age* (Boulder, Colo.: Lynne Rienner, 1999), esp. pp. 93–96.

9. Bernard M. Brodie, ed., *The Absolute Weapon: Atomic Power and World Order* (New York: Harcourt, Brace, 1946).

10. Keith B. Payne, *Deterrence in the Second Nuclear Age* (Lexington: University Press of Kentucky, 1996).

11. Bruce G. Blair, *The Logic of Accidental Nuclear War* (Washington, D.C.: Brookings Institution, 1993), passim. See also Desmond Ball, "The Development of the SIOP, 1960–1983," in Desmond Ball and Jeffrey Richelson, eds., *Strategic Nuclear Targeting* (Ithaca, N.Y.: Cornell University Press, 1986), pp. 57–83.

12. For some of the more recent revelations, see Ernest R. May and Philip D. Zelikow, eds., *The Kennedy Tapes: Inside the White House During the Missile Crisis* (Cambridge, Mass.: Harvard University Press, 1997), pp. 666–90 on the Soviet decision-making process. See also Aleksandr Fursenko and Timothy Naftali, *"One Hell of a Gamble": Khrushchev, Castro, and Kennedy, 1958–1964* (New York: W.W. Norton, 1997).

13. May and Zelikow, eds., *The Kennedy Tapes*, p. 682.

14. See Raymond L. Garthoff, *Detente and Confrontation: American-Soviet Relations from Nixon to Reagan* (Washington, D.C.: Brookings Institution, 1985), pp. 377–380. Kissinger interpreted Brezhnev's communication as an "ultimatum." The meeting (absent Nixon) that decided on a Defense Condition 3 alert (higher than normal, but short of full readiness) included the Secretary of Defense, Chairman of the Joint Chiefs of Staff, Director of Central Intelligence, White House Chief of Staff, Deputy National Security Advisor, and Kissinger's NSC military assistant.

15. Some of these indicators are noted in Garthoff, *Detente and Confrontation*, pp. 377–378. Garthoff's note 68, p. 377, is especially pertinent.

16. Richard Ned Lebow, *Nuclear Crisis Management: A Dangerous Illusion* (Ithaca, N.Y.: Cornell University Press, 1987).

17. For elaboration of these points, see National Academy of Sciences, Committee on International Security and Arms Control, *The Future of the U.S.–Soviet*

Nuclear Relationship (Washington, D.C.: National Academy Press, 1991), pp. 26–29.

18. Jennifer G. Mathers, *The Russian Nuclear Shield from Stalin to Yeltsin* (London: Macmillan Press Ltd., 2000), p. 166.

19. Possible points of convergence between Russia and the United States on theater and/or strategic defenses are explored in Konstantin Cherevkov, "Security on a New Principle: Russia Would Do Well to Factor ABM into the Balance of Nuclear Deterrence," *Nezavisimaya voennoe obozrenie*, February 2, 2001. We are grateful to Peter Rainow for calling this source to our attention.

4

TRIAD AND TRIBULATION: U.S. AND RUSSIAN START OPTIONS

The ratification of the START (Strategic Arms Reduction Talks) II agreement by the Russian Parliament in 2000, albeit with conditions that made its ultimate entry into force uncertain, opened the door to additional nuclear arms reductions by Washington and Moscow. U.S. President George W. Bush and Russian President Vladimir Putin agreed in November 2001 on a general goal of two-thirds reductions in their strategic nuclear forces. Both states' approaches to further arms reductions under a de facto or de jure START III regime would depend in part on their respective modernization plans, their budgetary assumptions about how much was affordable, and their perceptions of one another's commitment, or lack thereof, to mutual deterrence based on offensive retaliation.

One question facing U.S. and Russian defense planners and arms controllers was whether either state needs to maintain its three-cornered "triad" of strategic nuclear delivery systems: land-based missiles, sea-launched missiles, and bomber-delivered weapons. This chapter considers various U.S. and Russian options for strategic nuclear forces consistent with the lower overall limit of 1,500 weapons for START III proposed by Russia. It is at this lower level that the challenge to the traditional triad is greatest. First, we discuss issues of force structure and modernization pertinent to the two states' strategic nuclear forces. Second, we compare the performances of various U.S. and Russian START III compliant forces under several operational conditions. Third, we discuss some of the political and strategic reasons why, despite the findings of analysts, both states may prefer to adhere to a strategic nuclear "triad" even at greatly reduced force levels.

FORCE STRUCTURES AND MODERNIZATION

It was an accepted truism during most of the Cold War that U.S. strategic nuclear forces had to be distributed among three kinds of delivery systems: land-based ballistic missiles, submarine-launched ballistic missiles, and a variety of weapons delivered by bombers of intercontinental range, including gravity bombs, short-range attack missiles, and air-launched cruise missiles (ALCMs). (SRAMs are no longer in the U.S. inventory; today's bomber force carries gravity bombs and ALCMs.) In addition to ALCMs, nuclear armed cruise missiles could also be launched from surface ships or submarines (SLCMs, for sea-launched cruise missiles). Air and sea-launched cruise missiles also can be tasked for conventional missions as they were during the Gulf War in 1991 and against Yugoslavia in 1999.

The strategic rationales for this triad of forces were of three kinds.[1] First, by distributing retaliatory forces across three kinds of launchers, the United States could complicate the plans of any attacker. A first striker would have to attack the various United States land-based, sea-based, and air-delivered delivery systems in different ways. On account of this first factor, the attacker's plans would be confounded by necessary and undesirable trade-offs. For example, an attacker might have to choose between simultaneous or sequential launches of its ICBMs and SLBMs. If land- and sea-based missiles were launched simultaneously against U.S. targets, the early arriving SLBMs (targeted against bomber bases and SLBM ports) would provide additional warning time for U.S. ICBMs to escape destruction via prompt launch. On the other hand, if attacking ICBMs and SLBMs were launched sequentially in order to destroy more of the U.S. land-based missile force, then additional time would be available to scramble U.S. bombers out from under the attack.

A second argument for the triad was that each leg created a different problem for any missile or air defenses deployed by the other side. Having bombers and two types of missiles meant that even highly competent ballistic missile defenses could not obviate destruction from air-delivered weapons. For the same reason, air defenses were of no value against attacking missiles. A third aspect of the triad touted by its defenders was the avoidance of vulnerability due to any single technology breakthrough. If, for example, the United States were to reduce its offensive retaliatory forces to a monad based on submarines as some have advocated, then a singular breakthrough in antisubmarine warfare technology would negate the U.S. deterrent. (Current or foreseeable technology offers no such possibility, it should be noted.)

These strategic rationales were supported by strong forces in domestic politics. Each military service wanted a piece of the action of strategic nuclear warfare. The navy's sea-based ballistic missile force was a complement to the air force's Strategic Air Command. The air force and the army contested for at least a decade the issue of who would control land-based missiles. After many battles, a truce of sorts allotted the mission of offensive retaliation by means of land-based ballistic missiles to the air force. The army acquired ballistic missile defense as its turf. These decisions about roles and missions, reached during the latter 1950s and early 1960s, have largely carried forward to the present day. Modernization of nuclear forces and research and development on potential antinuclear defenses (from Project Defender through the present Clinton version of limited defenses against accidental launches or rogue attacks) has continued to distribute the domestic economic spillovers of weapons procurement and deployment across the various services and across many Congressional districts as well.

The end of the Cold War and the demise of the Soviet Union led to an acknowledgment by virtually all observers that American and Russian nuclear weapons could be greatly reduced in number. The United States and Russia signed START II in 1993; it requires that each state reduce the number of its accountable warheads on long range delivery systems to 3,000–3,500. Both the Clinton and Yeltsin governments discussed further reductions under a START III regime that would reduce both sides' accountable forces to some 2,000–2,500 warheads. Russian ratification of START II was expected to open the door to speedy agreement between the two governments on the lower START III levels. Some arms control analysts and government officials in Washington and Moscow (including President Putin) have proposed even further reductions, for example, a START III limit of 1,500 accountable warheads for each state.

Economics is only one determinant of possible arms control outcomes, however, and not necessarily the most important. Russia's threat perception is equally important, if not more so. The end of the Cold War means that political relations between the United States and Russia are not ideologically hostile as they were between the United States and the former Soviet Union. But many Russian military and political leaders remain wedded to Cold War thinking about missile defenses. And the United States' announced plans to make a decision about possible NMD (national missile defense of the U.S. territory against accidental launches or light attacks) by June 2000, with a possible beginning of NMD deployment in 2005, had temporarily increased opposition in Russia to ratification of START II. (President Clinton later kicked this can down the road and left the decision on deployment of

NMD to his successor.) By itself, Russian concern about U.S. NMD and American abrogation of the ABM Treaty in 2001 might not be an arms control "war stopper." But Russian threat perceptions during the Clinton administration were also raised by the enlargement of NATO to include Poland, the Czech Republic, and Hungary in 1999. Russians noted that the formal accession of these states to the North Atlantic Treaty took place during NATO's air war against Yugoslavia (Operation Allied Force).

Russia's options for modernizing its forces after 2000 will be constrained by the state of its economy. Russian intercontinental ballistic missiles (ICBMs) remain as the backbone of its strategic retaliatory forces. At the end of 1998, nineteen ICBM bases held 756 missiles of five types: SS-18s, SS-19s, SS-24s, and SS-27s in underground silos; rail mobile SS-24s; and road mobile SS-25s. START II entry into force would eliminate all SS-18s and SS-24s and all except 105 SS-19s; remaining SS-19s would be downloaded to a single warhead. Some ICBM silos may be converted to accept the SS-27 Topol-M.[2] General Vladimir Yakovlev, CINC of the Strategic Rocket Forces, called in 1999 for a production schedule of 20–30 Topol M (SS-27) becoming operational for each of the next three years, and for 30–40 per year for the following three years, although such production rates have not yet been achieved.

With regard to ballistic missile submarines, Russia's START exchange data of 1998 included forty-two submarines of six classes, but the actual number of submarines available and fully operational is fewer than that. The Russian navy considers only twenty-five SSBNs as operational, sixteen in the Northern Fleet and nine in the Pacific Fleet.[3] Operational tempos of the Russian SSBN fleet have been drastically reduced since the end of the Cold War, and Russia might have as few as ten to fifteen operational SSBNs by the end of 2003 (consisting of Delta IVs, newer Delta IIIs, and Typhoons). Although the keel for the first Borey-class SSBN was laid in November 1996, construction was suspended in 1998 at least temporarily amid official statements that the ship was being redesigned.[4] In the autumn of 1998 Russia was already below the START II established ceiling for warheads carried on SLBMs (1,750).

The modernization plans for the Russian strategic bomber force are as vague as those for the navy. Russia claimed some seventy strategic bombers at the end of 1998, but fewer were actually operational due to lack of funds. The current generation of air-launched cruise missiles (ALCMs) is approaching the end of their service lives, adding an additional modernization requirement for airborne resources already stretched. The commander in chief of the Russian Air Force has announced plans to replace the Tu-95MS Bear H with a new aircraft after 2010, a rather distant date. Only two of the six Tu-160 Blackjack bombers listed as operational at the end of 1998 were actually able to take off, and plans to purchase additional Blackjacks from Ukraine fell through in 1997. The number of operational strategic bombers deployed in the next decade will surely fall below current deployments, and the possibility of Russia's going out of the bomber business entirely cannot be discounted as impossible.[5]

The uncertain status of Russia's economy dictates prudence in making projections about Russia's nuclear or other force modernization. Russia has to balance its desire to appear essentially equivalent in strategic nuclear retaliatory power to the United States, and thus to retain its asserted claim to major power status, against the constraints imposed by its limited resources and post-Soviet decade of fiscal mismanagement. Options available on the "back of an envelope," however attractive in principle, may be simply unaffordable. Absent a dramatic improvement in Russia's economy within the next decade, there is a fiscal straitjacket imposed on Russia's force modernization that U.S. arms negotiators must take into account. Constrained Russian force modernization is a mixed blessing: "Less" is not necessarily "better" unless reduced forces compared to those now deployed can be operated without excessive dependency upon generated alert or prompt launch doctrines.

The U.S. and Russian START I accountable strategic nuclear forces are summarized in Tables 4.1 and 4.2, as given in the joint Memorandum of Understanding of July 2000.

U.S. AND RUSSIAN OPTIONS: DATA ANALYSIS

Given reasonable assumptions about projected U.S. defense spending in the first decade of the twenty-first century, the United States will have more options than Russia with regard to the modernization of its strategic nuclear forces. Throughout the Cold War and since it ended, various proposals have been made for reducing force sizes by downsizing the existing "triad" of strategic nuclear delivery systems or reducing the triad to a dyad or monad. Four options are considered next. They offer a range of candidate forces and a mix of alternative basing modes and delivery systems. Some are more politically plausible than others, but we are more interested in their attributes related to arms race and crisis stability. Shifting either U.S. or Russian forces from the familiar "triad" to something else has implications for strategy as well as arms control, a matter that will be addressed later in the chapter.

A nuclear exchange model of force attrition was used to compare the performances of four hypothetical U.S START III compliant forces with the performances of four notional Russian counterparts, all within a lower START III limit of 1,500 warheads. The various U.S. and Russian forces in the analysis are listed in Tables 4.3 and 4.4, respectively.

Table 4.1
U.S. Strategic Nuclear Forces: Memorandum of Understanding, July 2000

Weapon System	Launchers	Warheads Per Launcher	Total Warheads
MM II	1	1	1
MM III	608	3	1824
MX/Peacekeeper	50	10	500
Total ICBM	**659**		**2325**
Poseidon	16	10	160
Trident I	192	8	1536
Trident II	240	8	1920
Total SLBM	**448**		**3616**
B-52H/ALCM	142	10	1420
B-2	20	1	20
B-1	91	1	91
B-52	47	1	47
Total Bomber	**300**		**1578**
Total Triad	**1407**		**7519**

Source: Fact Sheet, U.S. Department of State, Washington, D.C., October 1, 2000. Bombers are counted according to START I counting rules. Some missing information supplied by interpolation.

The 1,500 warhead ceiling is well below current U.S. planning guidance and below limits preferred by the Pentagon. But the Putin adminstration has indicated an interest in discussing limits well below 2,500 warheads for each side, and some expert analysts suspect that Russia will not be able to afford a larger force than 700 warheads.[6]

Our model will interrogate the relative performances of these forces under various operational conditions, as defined as follows:

1. *Maximum retaliation*—forces are on generated alert, and are launched on warning of attack.

2. *Intermediate retaliation*—forces are either:

   a. on generated alert, and launched after riding out the attack, or

   b. on day-to-day alert, and launched on warning of attack.

3. *Miminum Retaliation*—forces are on day-to-day alert, and are launched after riding out the attack.

Figure 4.1
Arriving Retaliatory Weapons

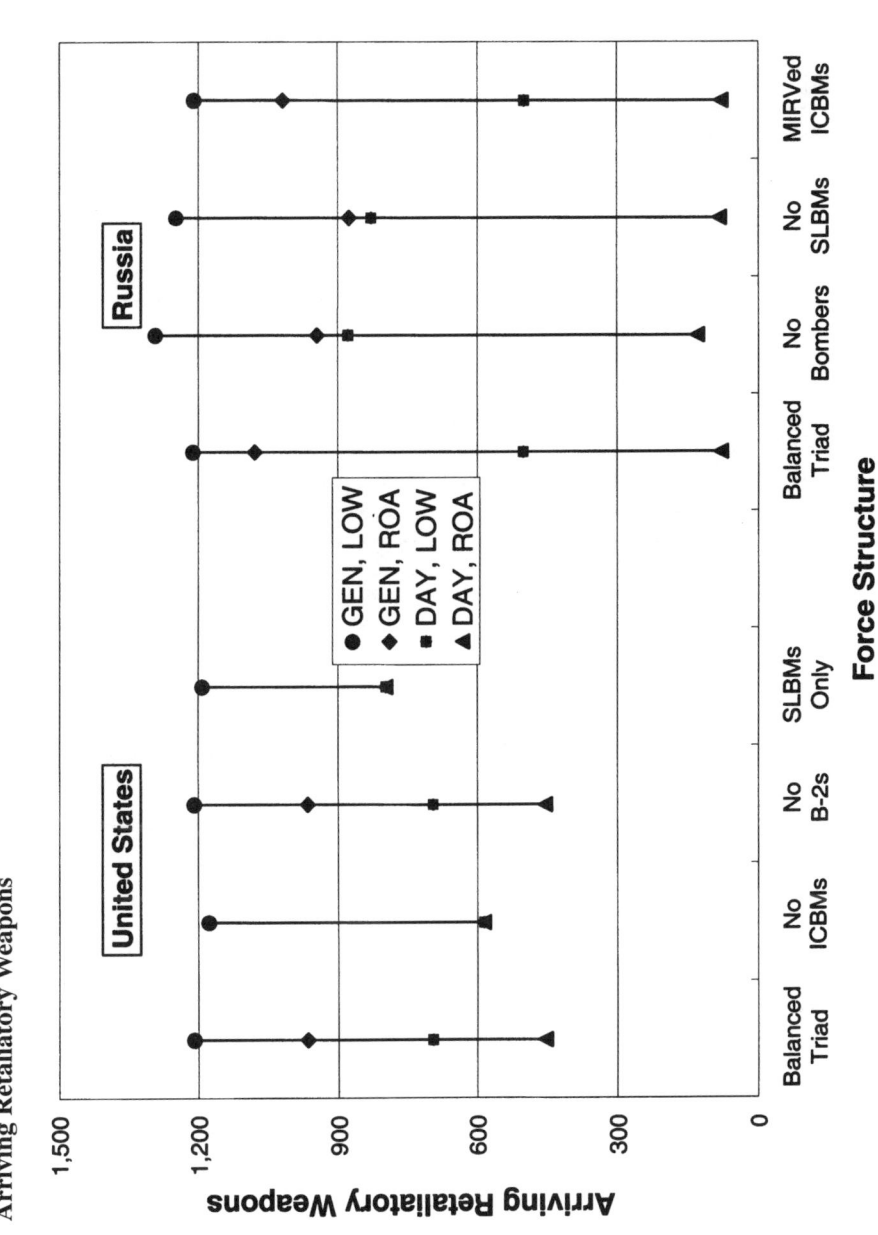

Table 4.2
Russian Federation Strategic Nuclear Forces Memorandum of Understanding, July 2000

Weapon System	Launchers	Warheads Per Launcher	Total Warheads
SS-25	360	1	360
SS-27 silo	20	1	20
SS-19	150	6	900
SS-18	180	10	1800
SS-24 silo	10	10	100
SS-24 mobile	36	10	360
Total ICBM	**756**		**3540**
SS-N-8	48	1	48
SS-N-18	192	3	576
SS-N-20	120	10	1200
SS-N-23	112	4	448
Total SLBM	**472**		**2272**
Blackjack/ALCM	15	8	120
Bear/ALCM	66	8	528
Bear/Bomb	4	1	4
Total Bomber	**85**		**652**
Total Triad	**1313**		**6464**

Source: Fact Sheet, U.S. Department of State, Washington, D.C., October 1, 2000. Bombers are counted according to START I counting rules. Some missing information supplied by interpolation.

In Figure 4.1, the estimated numbers of arriving retaliatory warheads for each of the four U.S. and Russian START III-compliant forces are summarized. The data analysis summarized in Figure 4.1 indicates that, within a START III ceiling of 1,500 warheads, there is considerable variation among force postures and operational modes, in terms of the numbers of arriving retaliatory warheads. To examine this variation in more detail, we require several more refined and disaggregated sets of calculations.

In Figure 4.2, the numbers of surviving and retaliating warheads for each of the four U.S. and Russian forces under the operational condition of generated alert and launch on warning, or maximum retaliation, are summarized. Figure 4.2 shows that, under assumed conditions of maximum retaliation, each side retains approximately 1,200 surviving and retaliating

Table 4.3
U.S. Forces in the Analysis

System	Loading	Delivery Vehicles / Weapons			
		Balanced Triad	No ICBMs	No B-2s	SLBMs Only
Minuteman III	1	300 / 300		300 / 300	
Total ICBM		**300 / 300**	**0 / 0**	**300 / 300**	**0 / 0**
Trident D5	14x4	196 / 784		196 / 784	
Trident D5 Pacific	14x5		98 / 588		
Trident D5 Atlantic	14x6		98 / 490		
Trident D5 Pacific	14x7				98 / 686
Trident D5 Atlantic	14x8				98 / 784
Total SLBM		**196 / 784**	**196 / 1078**	**196 / 784**	**196 / 1470**
B52H	4 ALCMs	64 / 256	64 / 256		
B52H	8 ALCMs			52 / 416	
B52H					
B2	8 bombs	20 / 160	20 / 160		
B2	8 bombs				
Total Bomber		**84 / 416**	**84 / 416**	**52 / 416**	**0 / 0**
Total Triad		**580 / 1500**	**280 / 1494**	**548 / 1500**	**196 / 1470**

Table 4.4
Russian Forces in the Analysis

System	Loading	Delivery Vehicles / Weapons			
		Balanced Triad	No Bombers	No SLBMs	MIRVed ICBMs
SS-19	1	105 / 105			
SS-25	1	251 / 251			
SS-27 mobile	1	60 / 60	430 / 430	460 / 460	
SS-27 silo	1	60 / 60	430 / 430	460 / 460	
SS-27 mobile	3				79 / 237
SS-27 silo	3				79 / 237
Total ICBM		**476 / 476**	**860 / 860**	**920 / 920**	**158 / 474**
Delta IV equivalent	16x4	112 / 448	160 / 640		112 / 448
Total SLBM		**112 / 448**	**160 / 640**	**0 / 0**	**112 / 448**
Bear H	6 ALCMs	66 / 396		66 / 396	66 / 396
Blackjack	12 ALCMs	15 / 180		15 / 180	15 / 180
Total Bomber		**81 / 576**		**81 / 576**	**81 / 576**
Total Triad		**669 / 1500**	**1020 / 1500**	**1001 / 1496**	**351 / 1498**

**Figure 4.2
Maximum Retaliation
Generated Alert, Launch on Warning**

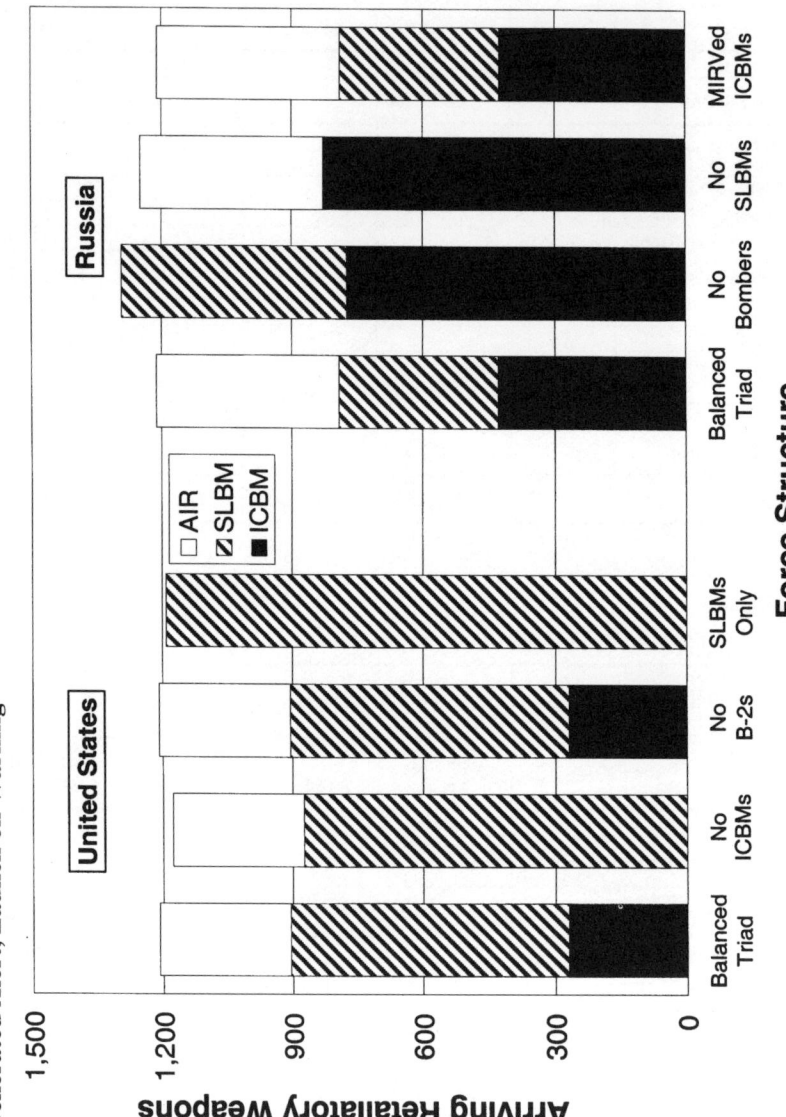

warheads regardless of its force posture. Not surprisingly, there are wide variations in the contribution to maximum retaliation from each triad leg.

In Figure 4.3, we compare the U.S. and Russian forces under the first condition of intermediate retaliation: generated alert and riding out the attack. Under this assumed condition of intermediate retaliation, Russia's "Balanced Triad" and "MIRVed ICBMs" forces outperform its "No Bombers" and "No SLBMs" forces. The U.S. "SLBMs Only" and "No ICBMs" forces provide for more retaliating weapons than do its "Balanced Triad" or "No B-2" forces.

In Figure 4.4, we compare the performances of the various forces under the second condition of intermediate retaliation: day-to-day alert and launch on warning. Under the assumed second condition of intermediate retaliation, Russia's "No Bomber" and "No SLBM" forces outperform its other force structures, "Balanced Triad" and "MIRVed ICBM" forces. The U.S. "All SLBM" forces provide for more surviving and retaliating warheads than do its other forces, with "No ICBMs" forces providing the lowest level of U.S. retaliation under these conditions.

In Figure 4.5, we compare the numbers of surviving and retaliating warheads for the eight START III compliant forces under the assumed operational conditions of minimum retaliation: day-to-day alert and launch after riding out the attack. The analysis summarized in Figure 4.5 does show some differences in the projected performances of various Russian forces, compared to one another, and among U.S. forces, compared to one another. But more important than the intrastate variations are the interstate differences. Regardless of force posture, U.S. forces provide for significantly more survivable and retaliating warheads than their Russian "counterparts" (admittedly an inexact comparison, since the force structures cannot be made identical for the two sides). The *lowest* assured retaliation for the U.S. is some 450 arriving retaliatory warheads, while the *highest* assured retaliation for Russia is only some 130 arriving retaliatory warheads.

Some clues exist in the preceding figures to suggest that Russian forces, compared to U.S. START III forces, are more dependent on prompt launch and force generation for survivability. If so, this presents a concern for U.S. planners and arms negotiators about preserving crisis stability as force sizes are reduced. In order to measure the relative dependency of the two sides' forces on prompt launch or on force generation, we calculated the ratios of U.S. and Russian "Balanced Triad" forces operating on day-to-day alert compared to generated alert, and under delayed launch orders compared to prompt launch. The higher these ratios, the less sensitive to generation and prompt launch, thus the more crisis-stable the force posture. Figure 4.6 summarizes the results of the comparison between different alert statuses

Figure 4.3
Intermediate Retaliation: Generated Alert, Ride Out Attack

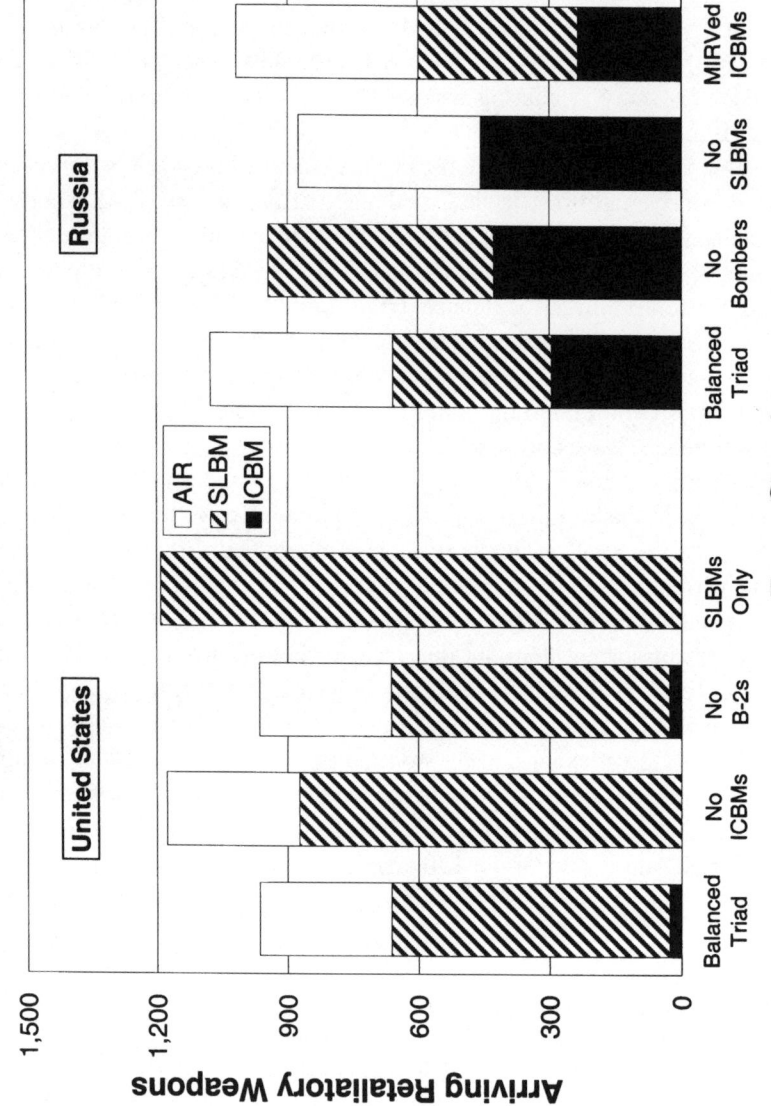

Figure 4.4
Intermediate Retaliation: Day-to-Day Alert, Launch on Warning

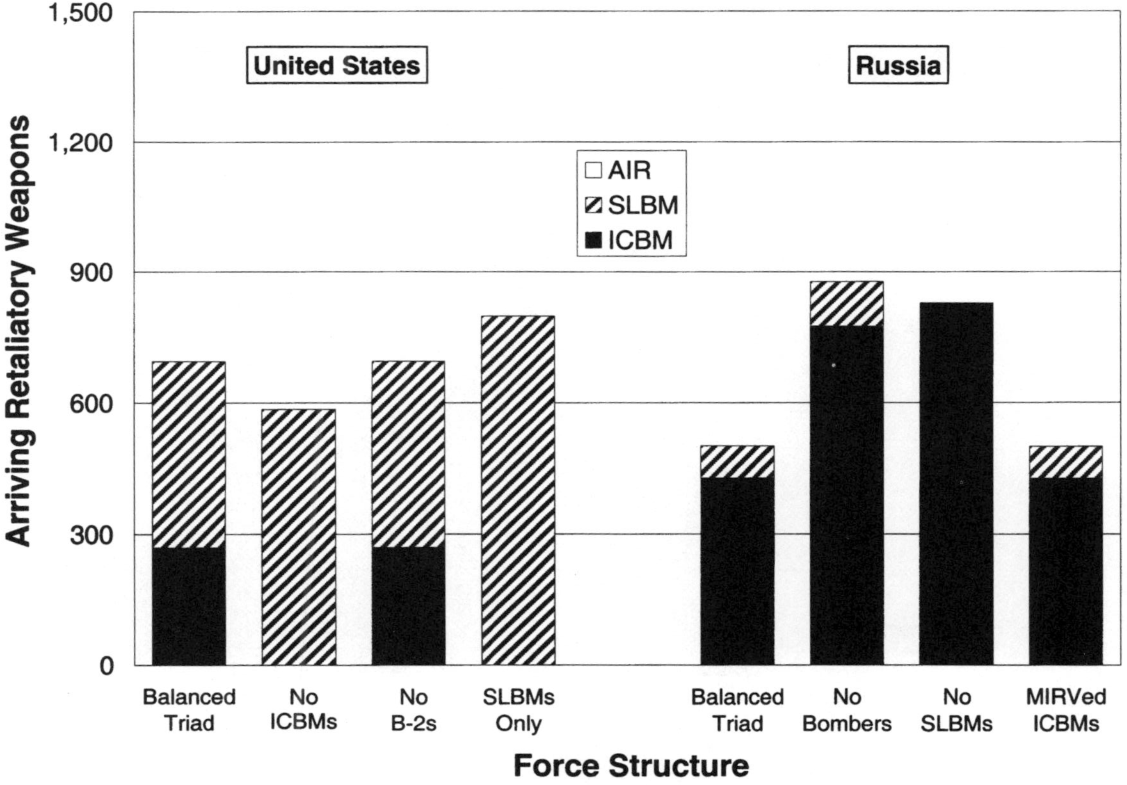

Figure 4.5
Assured Retaliation: Day-to-Day Alert, Ride Out Attack

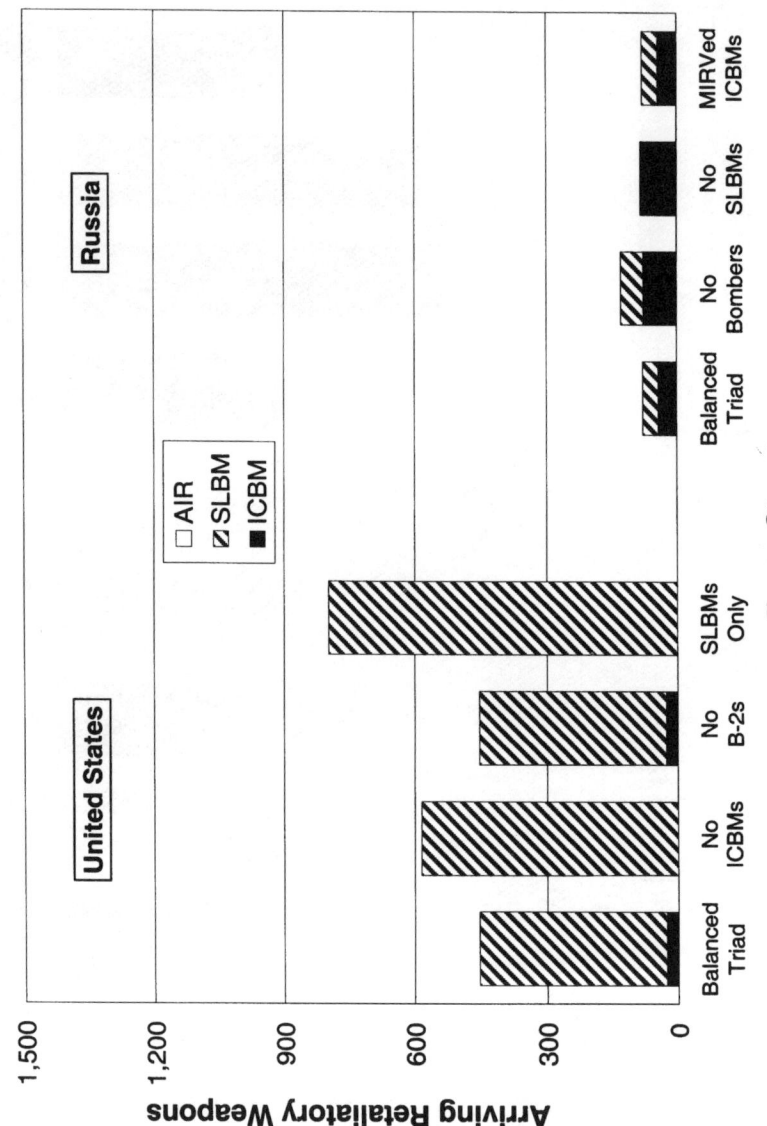

Figure 4.6
Generation and Prompt Launch Stability: U.S. Balanced Triad Strategic Forces

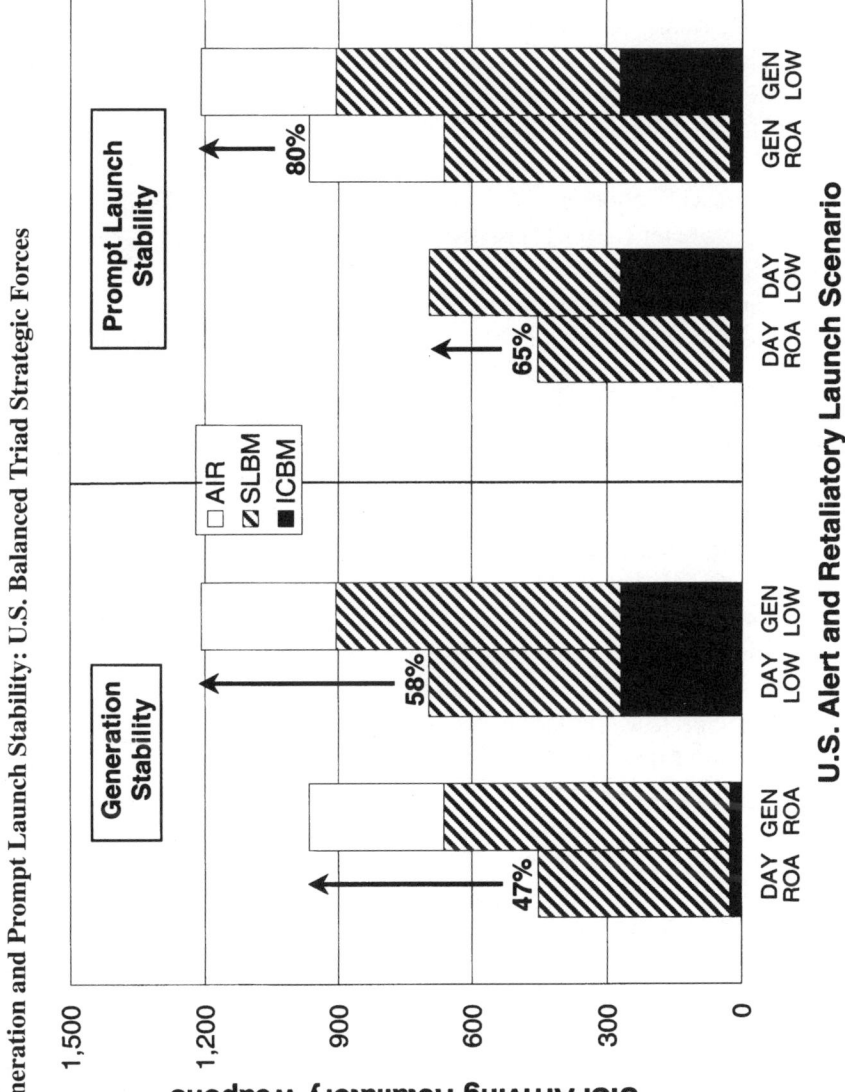

and launch conditions for U.S. "Balanced Triad" forces. Those forces are relatively more sensitive to generation than they are to prompt launch.

Similar data are interrogated for Russia's "Balanced Triad" in Figure 4.7. Russian "Balanced Triad" forces are more sensitive to alert levels than to prompt launch. How do Russian sensitivities compare to U.S. figures? Russian "Balanced Triad" forces are about as sensitive to prompt launch as their U.S counterparts, when on generated alert. But Russian forces on day-to-day alert are much more sensitive to prompt launch than U.S. forces. With regard to force generation, Russian "Balanced Triad" forces launched on warning are slightly more sensitive to generated alert than their U.S. counterparts. On the other hand, Russian forces riding out an attack are much more sensitive to the difference between generated and day-to-day alert, compared to U.S. forces.

Traditions and strategy are likely to persuade U.S. and Russian planners to continue modernization of all three legs of their strategic nuclear triads, although Russia will be hard put to afford much in the way of new bomber or SLBM forces. The traditional argument for a nuclear triad is that it complicates the strategy of an attacker by dispersing launch platforms among three different basing modes. On the other hand, if one of those basing modes invites attack on itself, such as the silo-based ICBM, then it might be more crisis stable for the United States to trade off ICBMs for SLBMs and bomber-delivered weapons, and for Russia to deploy more mobile as opposed to fixed base ICBMs. Russia's land-based missile modernization plans (Topol-M) are apparently moving in this direction of greater emphasis on mobiles. Mobiles are more survivable than silo-based ICBMs, but their command and control are more complicated: Moving mobiles out of garrison as a precautionary measure during a crisis can also lend itself to misunderstanding by the other side as a provocative measure.

With regard to U.S. force options and regardless of what Russia does, the pressures of domestic politics almost guarantee that the ICBM and bomber components of the American triad will continue well into the next century. Nevertheless, it is also clear that the SLBM force will remain as the cornerstone of American strategic nuclear retaliatory forces well into the twenty-first century. And, barring any unforeseen breakthrough in antisubmarine warfare technology for surveillance and detection of submarines on patrol, the U.S. choice of an SLBM-heavy triad does seem to provide both a reliable deterrent and one that is not dangerously dependent on early crisis generation or prompt launch for survivability. Moreover, based on our analysis, there is not a great deal of variation among the various triads, dyads, and monads at the START III

Figure 4.7
Generation and Prompt Launch Stability: R.F. Balanced Triad Strategic Forces

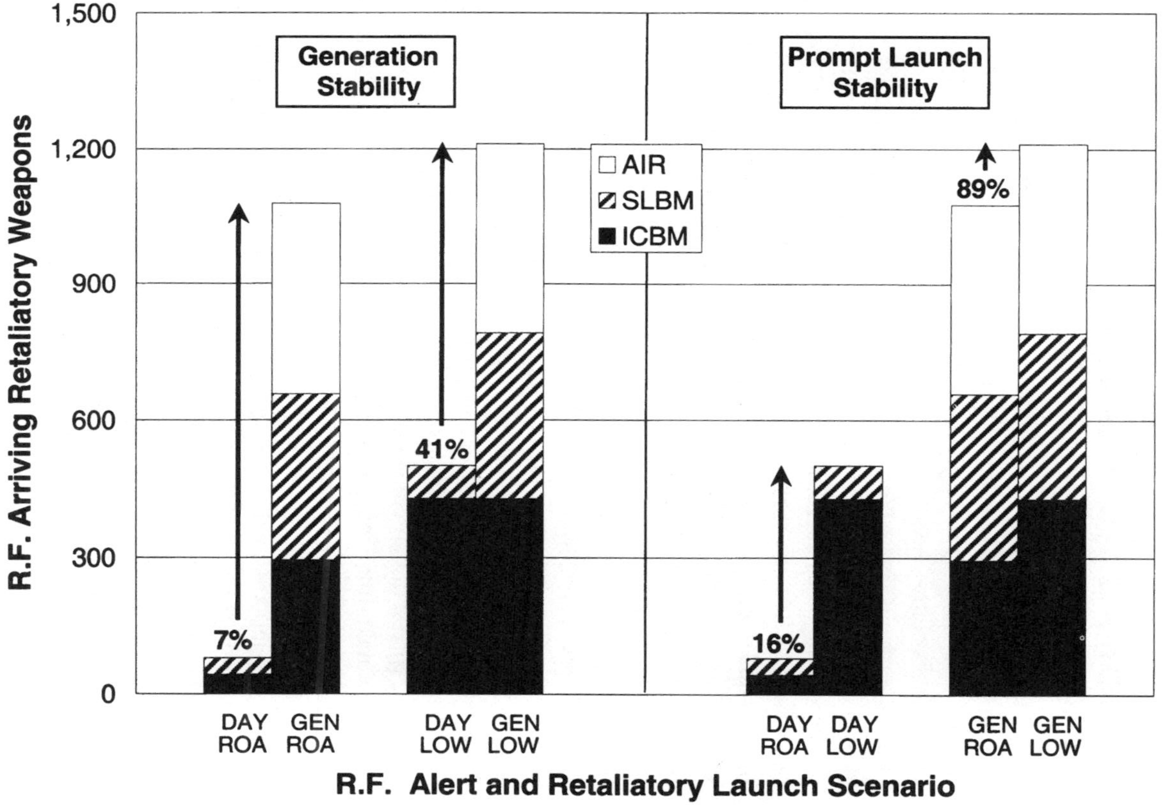

level, in terms of their ability to guarantee an acceptable number of survivable warheads or in their relative crisis stability as measured by lack of sensitivity to force generation or prompt launch.

BEYOND NUMBER CRUNCHING: ISSUES OF STRATEGY AND POLICY

What significance do these findings have for a post–Cold War deterrent system characterized by nonhostile political relations between the U.S. and Russia? One might reasonably argue that nuclear "deterrence" between the two states is neither necessary nor desirable in the next century. This is certainly the case if favorable to United States trends continue in Russia and Russia moves further toward democracy and a free market economy. Even if Russia's pathway to democracy and capitalism is full of potholes, any non-imperial Russian regime content to live within its current Federation borders and to practice nonoffensive defense poses no military threat to the United States or NATO. Deterrence, nuclear style, may have become passe between the two nuclear superpowers of the Cold War.

Perhaps so, given these optimistic expectations. But more pessimistic futures can be imagined between the U.S. and Russian governments. And even optimistic projections must acknowledge that the two states have a shared interest in maintaining essentially equivalent strategic nuclear arsenals and weapons that are superior in quality and in quantity to those of any third party. The new world order will not allow to the Americans or the Russians the nuclear suasion that their forces held over diplomacy in the Cold War. The spread of nuclear and other weapons of mass destruction together with advanced, long-range delivery systems is one of the major threats to world peace in the next century. United States and Russian nuclear forces can help to retard the spread of nuclear weapons and long-range ballistic missiles by supporting diplomacy intended to dissuade or discourage rogue states or nonstate actors from acquiring these weapons. Superior (to everyone else) U.S. and Russian nuclear arsenals also provide a disincentive to would-be regional hegemons or aspiring peer competitors. If, for example, American and Russian nuclear forces were reduced in size and diminished in capability to an extent that permitted, say, China to leap forward into nuclear parity within two decades or so, stability in Asia would be diminished and the positions of Taiwan, Indonesia, and Japan less secure.

The idea that peace is supported by continuing American and Russian nuclear strength is one that professional arms controllers and disarmament advocates find hard to take. Equally repugnant to many in the same communities is the possibility that the United States would commit itself to deploy ballistic missile defenses regardless of Russian sentiments or of the need to amend or abrogate the ABM Treaty. The authors will not revisit the entire Cold War debate about ballistic missile defenses here. The Cold War debates about BMD were swamped by two exogenous factors: excessive technicism, and ideological fanaticism by proponents and opponents. Plainly stated, there was a great deal of lying and sloppy analysis on both sides of the issue.

Answering the question of national missile defense now is vitally important, and it plays into the problem of deciding whether the United States needs a two-sided or three-cornered strategic retaliatory force in the early years of the twenty-first century. If the United States deploys a light system to defend against rogue attacks or accidental launches, it will do so either with or without the concurrence of the Russians. Russia is not in a position to prevent the United States from deploying defenses. But Russia can make U.S. and NATO political life more complicated, as in its support or lack thereof for START III, the comprehensive test ban treaty (CTBT), and other measures contributory to the reduction of vertical or horizontal nuclear proliferation. The United States also needed, and still needs, Russian cooperation in other matters, including the war in Afghanistan beginning in October 2001 and the extended campaign against global terrorism. The long-term stabilization of Europe and central Asia cannot be accomplished without the cooperation of Russia. And the cooperation of Russia will only be obtained if Russia feels secure.

The United States and NATO cannot jeopardize their own security to pay homage to Russian insecurity. But they can and must contribute to a realistic conception of Russian security. Russian concerns about the enlargement of NATO to its very borders (Kaliningrad) and those of Ukraine (historically commingled with Russia) are not mere propaganda. NATO includes a nuclear guaranty. And Russian military planners recognize that their underpaid, poorly equipped and ill-trained conventional forces are ill suited to the defense of eleven time zones worth of borders. Contiguous to Russia are former Soviet states caught up in political turbulence that has, or may soon, spill over into Russia itself. Also bordering Russia is China, a major nuclear power with regionally hegemonial ambitions (at least) in the Pacific basin. Parts of Russia caught up in Islamic revolution against Russian rule (Chechnya, Dagestan) are in the volatile Caucasus region located between Russia and Iran. Iran openly seeks to acquire nuclear weapons and ballistic missiles. An Iranian regime armed with nuclear weapons and ballistic missiles of appropriate range would be in a position to counter deter Russia's incursion against Chechnya as in 1994–1996 and again in the autumn of 1999. An Iranian bomb shared with Afghanistan and Pakistan could create an arc of Islamic extended nuclear deterrence used against Russia or against former Soviet states bordering Iran, Afghanistan, and Pakistan (including oil-rich Turkmenistan on the Caspian Sea). Iranian efforts to develop a nuclear weapons capability have been supported by China.

Russia can be its own worst enemy, however. Intentions do matter, and the United States is not Iran or China. NATO is not planning any incursion into Russia. And the debate over ballistic missile defenses has gone beyond the "Star Wars" era with its hubris of near-perfect shields and space armadas. Current U.S. proposals for NMD deployments, possibly to begin as early as the year 2005, leave open the decision about specific NMD technology. The U.S. congressional and other domestic policy debate on NMD has already shifted its center of gravity away from the Cold War–era exclusive emphasis on offensive retaliation for deterrence. The United States does not threaten Russia by intention, and will not inadvertently do so if Russia is kept informed of U.S. technology developments and offered an opportunity to share in development and deployment.

Should Russia worry that a U.S. NMD system originally intended for use against rogues could grow into a light NMD system that might be inadequate against Russia's first strike, but sufficient to negate a Russian second strike, following a U.S. first strike? This would be the functional equivalent of "deterring Russia's deterrent." Some Russians may worry about this possibility, but the Uniited States has little interest in deterring Russia's deterrent unless the character of U.S.–Russian political relations changes drastically from its contemporary condition. Apart from politics, would the very existence of a U.S. NMD technology create the sum of its own fears? The United States might have reason to be fearful of Russian fears, but for reasons having less to do with quantities of warheads than with qualitative issues related to crisis stability. A prematurely deployed U.S. missile defense system might cause the Russian military to decide to rely on prompt launch for force survivability to an even greater extent than hitherto.

CONCLUSIONS

Strategy is more complicated than arms control. From a strictly arms control and cost-efficiency perspective, one might argue for either U.S. or Russian (or both) START III strategic nuclear forces based on a dyad instead of a triad. However, reducing the quantities of nuclear weapons also requires careful attention to the qualitative aspects of the U.S.–Russian nuclear relationship. These qualitative attributes include the propensity of some kinds of forces to be more reliant on higher alert levels and hair triggers compared to others. Crisis stability involves more than force balances, of course. But a component of crisis stability is the likelihood that some kinds of force structures lend themselves more than others to operationally problematical behaviors, with respect to nuclear crisis management and arms control.

We did not find great differences among the four types of Russian forces, or among the four types of U.S. forces, with respect to their propensity for leading to operationally problematical behavior. Despite this finding of minimal intrastate variations, the differences *between* U.S. and Russian forces were significant (using the balanced triad forces for each state as a benchmark). Especially when riding out the attack, Russian forces were much more dependent on generation than American forces were. And Russian forces on day-to-day alert were more dependent on prompt launch than their American counterparts. Added to Russia's declared doctrine permissive of nuclear first use and a history of 1990s uncertainties about the *peacetime* command and control of Russia's nuclear forces, Russia's larger START III dependency on high alert levels and prompt launch, under certain conditions, should induce caution in U.S. crisis management behavior. This finding might be modified slightly if either or both states were to shift from a strategic nuclear triad to a dyad, but such a decision by Washington or by Moscow is unlikely, given inertial forces in both camps and some valid strategic concerns about the flexibility and survivability of a U.S. or Russian dyad.

NOTES

1. See Center for Counterproliferation Research, National Defense University, and Center for Global Security Research, Lawrence Livermore National Laboratory, *U.S. Nuclear Policy in the 21st Century: A Fresh Look at National Strategy and Requirements* (Washington, D.C.: U.S. Government Printing Office, 1998), pp. 3.12–3.15 for a summary of arguments for the U.S. strategic nuclear triad.
2. NRDC (Natural Resources Defense Council) *Nuclear Notebook*, Vol. 55, No. 2, March/April 1999, pagination uncertain due to electronic transmission.
3. Ibid.
4. Ibid.
5. Ibid.
6. Suggested by Alexander Golts at a conference on Russian security policy in December 2000, U.S. Army War College, Carlisle, Pennsylvannia.

5

PROLIFERATION IN AN UNSTABLE WORLD

India and Pakistan's nuclear detonations in May 1998 underscored the post-Cold War risk of regional arms races in weapons of mass destruction. The danger of nuclear weapons spread is aggravated by the spread of delivery systems, including ballistic missiles, capable of delivering nuclear and other WMD over thousands of kilometers. The U.S. supremacy in high-technology, conventional military power tempts aspiring regional hegemons to acquire nuclear weapons as deterrents against possible deployment of U.S. and allied forces into hostile theaters of war.[1] The potential for nuclear leakage from already weaponized states into the hands of frustrated state and nonstate actors is considerable and, in some cases, already documented.

Despite these trends, some highly regarded scholars have minimized the risk of nuclear proliferation or even argued that, under certain controlled or fortuitous conditions, the spread of nuclear weapons would improve stability. The same perspective on proliferation also raises important issues about how theory in international relations can predict or explain policy. The optimists about proliferation follow the logic of models that explain and predict well for conventional war and deterrence, but not for a more nuclearized world.

In the following discussion, we first consider the assumptions of political realism on which many arguments dismissive of the risks of nuclear weapons spread are based. Second, we argue that the assumptions and logic of political realism lead to some important wrong inferences about the relationship between nuclear weapons and peace during the Cold War and, therefore, to mistaken projections about the future. Third, we consider the significance of the potential combination of weapons of mass destruction and proliferating missile delivery systems, noting several important and troubling cases. Last, we explore the question of conflict termination between two nuclear armed states at war, both prior to and after nuclear first use.

PROLIFERATION AND REALISM

The argument that the post–Cold War world may be compatible with a hitherto unknown, and unacceptable, degree of nuclear weapons spread rests on some basic theoretical postulates about international relations. These basic theorems, most frequently associated with the "realist" or neorealist school of international political theory, are as follows.[2] First, states seek to balance power through international rivalry in order to prevent any single state or coalition from attaining a hegemonial position. Some states may be more powerful than other states, but no state or group of states should be permitted to become so dominant that the others' basic security and autonomy are at risk. Realists are divided on whether a true balance, or equilibrium, of power or the domination of international relations by one imperial superstate, such as ancient Rome, is actually more stable. But they assume that the likelihood of any global empire has been slight to nonexistent since the emergence of the nation-state as the preferred form of political unification in Europe during the sixteenth and seventeenth centuries. Since no international Leviathan is actually possible, the realistic choice comes down to power balances within large regions of the globe, as in Eurasia.

The second theorem of international power politics associated with realists is the assumption that power is measurable or, at least, comparable in units of consensual understanding. Thus, if one state holds more economic and military power than another, both will understand that this conveys on the former state the advantage in situations of conflict or of potential conflict. For realists, this is a strong argument for the connection between nuclear weapons and peace. Nuclear weapons make power immediately commensurable: few doubt that even a small number of nuclear explosions can cause unacceptable damage. Conventional forces, even those deployed by potential antagonists in very large numbers, leave open to military planners and strategists ample room for prewar arguments about which state's forces are actually capable of prevailing in battle. Only a small number of nuclear weapons on each side, provided each is confident that its weapons can survive against a first strike, suffice to make calculations about expected cost very simple.

The notion of shared interstate agreement on what constitutes power, both power resources and the means of influence, is very important. If, for example, one group of states thinks that only landpower is important in creating credible means of defense, and another state feels that only maritime forces matter, then each of these two states has neglected at least one important dimension of potential power. States have frequently miscalculated their relative degrees of military effectiveness, sometimes because they overrated their own capabilities and at other times because they underrated the capabilities of their opponents. For example, from the time of the Napoleonic wars until the end of World War II, the size of a country's population was assumed to be positively related to its power ranking: the larger the population, the more powerful the country. Now this is no longer the case; power today is acknowledged by most leaders to rest more on the qualities of the population, such as its educational attainments and cultural composition, than it does on its size or scale. The "soft" power of a country's political and social institutions and their international appeal may count for as much as the "hard" power of military formations and manufacturing capacity.[3]

The important issue for realist theories is not that there is any single measuring rod of power, but that leading states agree on what those key indicators of power are. If they do, then they can rapidly arrive at an assessment of the balance of power without having to fight a war to settle the issue. If not, an uncertain status ranking and an outbreak of violence are more likely. From the Peace of Westphalia to the conclusion of World War II, it was generally accepted by leaders of states that military and economic power together constituted the basis of international influence.[4] The period since the end of World War II has not seen total abandonment by leaders of this persuasion, but the assumption that a state's power is based on its military and economic strength has been diluted at the margin under the pressure of new technology, nationalism, and cultural revivalism.[5]

The third necessary assumption for a realist or power-oriented perspective is that states seek to advance their interests, but at a risk and cost that are manageable.[6] Balance-of-power-oriented states are not willing to bet their entire fortune on an unpredictable roll of the iron dice. The major powers of Europe, during the July crisis of 1914, violated this canon of the realist persuasion to their everlasting detriment. They sought absolute instead of limited aims once the war had broken out. The empires of Austria-Hungary, Russia, Germany, and Turkey were destroyed, reaping instability that led directly to a second world war twenty years later. According to the assumptions made by realist theory, the alliances or states engaged in fighting World War I should have cut their losses and settled for lesser objectives instead of prolonging the fighting to their infinite ruin. As a result, even the "winners" of World War I not only lost an entire generation of fighting men, but their societies were so traumatized that they were unable to respond to Hitler's aggression in the 1930s.

Because realist theories talk so much about the requisites and uses of power, critics mistakenly assume that realists are more optimistic about the actual use of military power than are the adherents of other schools of thought. In fact, realists are skeptical that power can be used repeatedly and effectively by states, and especially by democracies. Therefore, realist theory does not depend on the willingness of states to abolish war or to avoid unnecessary involvement in crises that might lead to war. Realists are fundamentally pessimists about human nature, including the nature of world leaders. Instead, realists assume that war will occur, but that most wars will take place on the periphery of the international system, meaning outside of Europe or central Eurasia, and not among the major actors in the international system.

Realist theory makes other assumptions that are important for scholarly debates, but the ones noted here are most significant for purposes of this discussion about realist assumptions and nuclear proliferation. The assumptions that power requires balancing by power, that states should measure and evaluate power in roughly similar ways, and that states should moderate their objectives in crisis or time of war to preserve the major actors and international order are pertinent to the issue of whether realist analysis can be joined to nuclear weapons spread. Some realists assert that it can, despite considerable skepticism from those who distrust the very notion that proliferation and stability can be made compatible.

Realists do not flinch from making the assumptions that power must be used to balance against power, that power can be commensurable, or that actor objectives within the international system must be moderated. For example, Kenneth N. Waltz argues for these assumptions assertively in his widely cited *Theory of International Politics*.[7] He argues that system stability is a derivative of polarity: bipolar systems are more stable than multipolar systems. The ability of the United States and the Soviet Union to dominate the international order during the Cold War years, according to this reasoning, accounted for much of the stability in the international system as a whole. The U.S.–Soviet rivalry established the essential political dividing lines between East and West that muted other axes of potential conflict, in this view. Competition between bipolar antagonists also has a built in metric toward accommodation: The two powers share an interest in maintaining their predominant positions relative to others.

The argument that bipolar international or regional state systems are more stable than multipolar systems, or vice versa, has stimulated many academic debates that are not necessarily pertinent to the relationship between nuclear weapons spread and stability. The point is that the case for the greater stability of bipolar interstate relations is as yet unproved, for several reasons. First, there are very few legitimate instances of bipolarity; the number of cases is small relative to the scope of the theory that they are asked to support. Ancient Greece (Athens and Sparta) was an interesting regional bipolar system, but not a global one. Its outcomes, however, provide little comfort for the prediction that bipolarity is more stable than multipolarity. Nor do the incessant wars between ancient Rome and Carthage, a better example of a bipolar system, support the assumption that bipolarity is more stable. The Cold War bipolar system is definitely stable, but would a multipolar Cold War system have been unstable?

Waltz, John J. Mearsheimer, and other realists acknowledge that the relationship between system polarity and international stability between 1945 and 1990 is complicated by the existence of nuclear weapons.[8] The complication is both theoretical and historical. Theories of nuclear deterrence and of system polarity may lead to the same propositions in some cases, but to divergence in others. For example, although bipolarity preceded the development of a U.S.–Soviet arms race and nuclear deterrence relationship, a double helix of interdependency between bipolarity and nuclear weapons obtained during most of the Cold War. Therefore, when analysts argue for the greater stability of bipolar compared to multipolar systems using the Cold War as an illustration, the illustration leaves open the question of historical causation: Which was the chicken, and which the egg?

Realists do not depend only on system polarity or other variables highly correlated with system polarity, including alliance formation and the "bandwagoning" or "balancing" tendencies of states, in order to predict international outcomes. They also assume that rational decision-making is, over the long run, more typical than not for states and their leaders, especially for great powers. Rationality in this sense is not necessarily the taking of a correct or logical decision as seen after the fact by impartial observers. Rationality is a relationship between the ends that states seek and the means that they use to obtain those preferred objectives. Rational decision-makers, according to this model, are those who follow some consistent logic in their relationship between means and ends as seen from the decision-makers' own perspective.

Nuclear realism is of value to the extent that it acknowledges the importance of the nuclear revolution. The nuclear revolution separated the accomplishment of military denial from the infliction of military punishment. The meaning of this for strategists was that military victory, defined prior to the nuclear age as the ability to prevail over opposed forces in battle, now was permissible only well below the level of total war. And less than total wars were risky as never before. Nuclear realists admit that these profound changes have taken place in the relationship between force and policy. They argue, however, that the new relationship between force and policy strengthens rather than weakens some perennial principles of international relations theory. Power is still king, but the king is now latent power in the form of risk manipulation and threat of war, instead of power actually displayed on the battlefield. Peace is now guaranteed by threat of war unacceptable in its social by-products, instead of being dependent upon the defender's credible threat to defeat the attacker's armed forces in battle.

THE LIMITS OF NUCLEAR REALISM

Other schools can concur with the realists on some of these major points, but implicit in the realist model of deterrence stability are some theoretical limitations. Each of these limitations or sets of problems with realist explanatory theory limits the inferences that can be drawn from a realist perspective. Four problem areas are: whether the realist view is based on exceptional cases; whether the economic theories on which some realist arguments about deterrence stability are based can be transferred from economics to international politics; whether realism can account for both general and immediate deterrence situations; and whether rational decision-making as conceived by realists is dependable for explanation and prediction of arms race and war-provoking behavior.[9]

Exceptional Cases

First, realist arguments for the possibility of a stable nuclear multipolar world are based on the Cold War experiences of the United States and the Soviet Union. The supposition is that, just as the U.S. and the Soviet political and military leaderships worked out over time rules of the road for crisis management and the avoidance of inadvertent war or escalation, so too would aspiring nuclear powers among the current nonnuclear states. However, there are reasons to doubt whether the U.S. and Soviet experiences can be repeated after the Cold War. First, the U.S.–Soviet nuclear relationship between 1945 and 1990 was also supported by bipolarity and an approximate equality, although an asymmetrical one, in overall U.S. and Soviet military power. Neither bipolarity nor, obviously, U.S.–Russian global military equity is available to support stable relations in the post–Cold War world; in fact, both are irrelevant so long as Russia evolves in a democratic, capitalist direction and prefers cooperative U.S.–Russian foreign relations.

A second reason why the U.S. and Soviet Cold War experiences are unlikely to be repeated by future proliferators is that the relationship between political legitimacy and military control was solid in Moscow and in Washington, but uncertain for many nuclear powers outside of Europe. The issue here is not whether democracies are less warlike than dictatorships. The question is whether the regime can impose either assertive or delegative military control over its armed forces, and, if it does, the consequences for its crisis management and normal nuclear operations. Assertive control implies a great deal of civilian intervention in military operations and management, delegative control, more willingness to let the military have their own way on operational and organizational issues. Strict rules about nuclear custody are an example of assertive control; for example, in the early years of the nuclear age, atomic weapons were withheld from the military under normal conditions. An example of delegative control is the understanding among U.S. Cold War policymakers that, in the event of a nuclear attack disabling the president and/or the civilian chain of command, the U.S. deterrent would not be paralyzed. Military commanders could, under carefully defined and admittedly drastic conditions, launch in response to unambiguous indications of attack.[10]

Organizational process factors and other decision-making attributes of states with small, new nuclear arsenals may push their militaries toward doctrines that favor nuclear preemption. First-strike vulnerable forces may invite attack on themselves. Newly acquired nuclear arsenals may not be "fail safe" against accidental launch or military usurpation of civil command prerogative. Among nuclear aspirants in 1998, several states, including North Korea, Iran, Iraq (temporarily thwarted by UN inspections), and Libya, the distinction between "civil" and "military" was as opaque to many outside observers as it was to some of their own poorly informed citizens. In Pakistan, a declared nuclear power since May 1998, the military has run the nuclear weapons development program from the time of its inception to the present. Neither Indian nor Pakistani nuclear release protocols are clear to outside observers, and uncertainty marks U.S. understanding of "first use" or "no first use" doctrines in New Delhi and Islamabad. The possibility cannot be excluded that nuclear command authority rests de facto in the hands of brass hats, unaccountable to civil control, in any one or more of the new nuclear powers or nuclear aspiring states. For example, according to one U.S. study prepared for Lawrence Livermore National Laboratory in 1991,

The nuclear chain of command is likely to reflect the military's dominance in Pakistani decision making. Thus, although formal authority to launch a Pakistani nuclear strike could be expected to reside with the President (as does control over the nuclear program today), the Pakistani military is all but certain to obtain *de facto* control over nuclear weapons and the decision to use them. A future civilian government could ignore the military's advice on nuclear use only at its own peril.[11]

Another reason why the U.S.–Soviet experience may not be normative for newer nuclear powers is that there were no pieces of territory or other vital interests for which one of the sides was committed to go to war rather than to suffer defeat or stalemate. The two sides were generally satisfied by *bloc consolidation* and *internal power balancing* instead of external adventurism and zero sum competition for territory or resources. The preceding observation does not imply that Cold War crises, such as those that occurred over Berlin and Cuba, were not dangerous. They were dangerous, but the danger was mitigated by the awareness that neither state had to sacrifice a vital piece of its own territory or its own national values (allies were another matter) in order to avoid war. What was at stake in the most dangerous U.S.–Soviet Cold War confrontations was "extended" deterrence, or the credibility of nuclear protection extended to allies, and not defense of the homeland per se.

Economics and International Politics

The second major set of theoretical problems with nuclear realism lies in the adaptation of arguments from microeconomic theory to theories of interstate relations. Kenneth Waltz explicitly compares the behaviors of states in an international system to the behavior of firms in a market. As the market forces firms into a common mode of rational decision-making in order to survive, so too does the international system, according to Waltz, dictate similar constraints on the behavior of states. The analogy, however, is wrong. The international system does not dominate its leading state actors; leading states define the parameters of the system. The international system, unlike the theoretical free market, is *subsystem dominant*. The "system" or composite of interactions among units is the cross product of the separate behaviors of the units.[12]

International politics is a game of oligopoly, in which the few rule the many. Because this is so, there cannot be any "system" to which the leading oligopolists, unlike the remainder of the states, are subject against their wishes. The system is determined by the preferred ends and means of its leading members. Structural realists assume that some "system" of interactions exists independently of the states that make it up. This is a *useful heuristic* for theorists, but a very mistaken view of the way in which *policy is actually made in international affairs*. Because realists insist on reification of the system independently of the principal actors within the system, they miss the subsystemic dominance built into the international order. Napoleon Bonaparte and Adolf Hitler, for example, saw the international order not as a system that would constrain their objectives and ambitions, but as a series of swinging doors, each awaiting a fateful, aggressive push.

An important test of whether meaningful theory can proceed on the basis of the realist, or realpolitik, premise of "system" separateness, or whether domestic political forces must also be taken into account by theorists, is to test realist and domestic/constrained hypotheses against historical evidence. According to Bruce Bueno de Mesquita and David Lalman, the realist perspective as formalized in their models is not supported by the past two centuries' experience of interstate behavior.[13] The authors deduce an "acquiescence impossibility" theorem that shows that, in a logically developed game structure based on realist assumptions, it is impossible for one state to acquiesce to the demands of another "regardless of the beliefs held by the rivals, regardless of the initial demand made by one of the states, and regardless of initial endowments of capabilities, coalitional support, propensities to take risks, or anything else."[14] None of the deductions derived from the realist or neorealist versions of their international interactions game, according to Bueno de Mesquita and Lalman, were supported in the empirical data set that included 707 dyadic interactions.[15]

One might argue, in defense of realists on this point, that the assumption of system determinism is a useful falsehood. It allows for parsimony in expression and in focus on the essential attributes of the international system. But, again, the assumption of "apartness" of the system and its essential state or nonstate actors is only useful, and methodologically defensible, if it leads to insights that are both accurate and not otherwise attainable. Neither exceptional accuracy nor exceptional attainability of insight has been demonstrated by realists for the assumption of system and actor "apartness." This is probably one reason why traditional realist thinkers did not exclude what Waltz, in another study, refers to as first and second image variables.[16] Realism fails to explain the high degree of international cooperation that takes place despite a legally anarchic international order because of the biased manner in which realism deals with imperfect information. According to Bueno de Mesquita and Lalman,

In the realist world, imperfect information can only encourage violence. Incorrect beliefs about the intentions of rivals can only steer disputes away from negotiation (or the status quo) and toward the blackmail inherent in a capitulation or the tragedy inherent in a war. Incorrect beliefs, secrecy, misperception, misjudgment, and miscalculation are routine features of human intercourse. In that sense, a realist world could be a dangerous world indeed.[17]

General and Immediate Deterrence

The preceding discussion also points to the third general set of problems with realist theories and nuclear weapons spread. The structure of the international system is not related to *general* deterrence in the same way as it is to *immediate* deterrence. According to Patrick M. Morgan, the need for general deterrence is inherent in the normal day-to-day relations of states, based on the distribution of power and states' assumptions about one another's intentions. General deterrence is the latent possibility that any state may opt for war within an anarchic or nonhierarchical international order.[18] Immediate deterrence is a situation in which one side has actually made specific threats against another, the second side perceives itself threatened, and a significant likelihood of war exists in the minds of leaders in at least one of the two states.[19] For example, the onset of a crisis often signifies a failure of general deterrence, but as yet immediate deterrence has not failed because states have not yet abandoned diplomacy and crisis management for battle.

It makes sense to assume that there might be a strong correlation between success or failure in general deterrence and system attributes such as distributions of actor capabilities and objectives. However, the relationship between international systems and failures of immediate deterrence is much more indirect. State and substate variables, including the attributes of individuals, groups, and bureaucratic organizations, are among the filters through which any "system" forces must pass before those forces are manifest in state decisions and policies. The distinction between general and immediate deterrence helps to explain why perfectly logical deductions from deterrence theory based on rationality postulates often fly in the face of states' actual behavior.[20]

The significance of the distinction between general and immediate deterrence is illustrated by the Cuban missile crisis. The decision by Khrushchev to put Soviet medium and intermediate range ballistic missiles into Cuba was intended, among other objectives, to diminish the publicly acknowledged (by U.S. government officials) gap between U.S. and Soviet strategic nuclear capabilities. Khrushchev's decision, made in the spring of 1962 after consulting very few key advisors, represented a failure of general deterrence. The Soviet leadership had decided to risk the emplacement of its nuclear weapons outside of Soviet territory and in the Western Hemisphere for the first time. However, it was not yet a failure of immediate deterrence. Immediate deterrence was not involved in Khrushchev's clandestine deployment program because the deployments were deliberately kept secret. Had Khrushchev carried through his original plans, he would have completed the missile deployments and then announced their existence.

In that eventuality, the mere existence of Khrushchev's missiles on Cuban soil, however threatening it seemed to U.S. policymakers, would not have created a situation of immediate deterrence. Only the completion of deployments followed by a coercive threat would move the situation from a failure of general deterrence (Soviets make a dangerous move in the arms race) to one of immediate deterrence (e.g., Soviets now demand that the United States and allies leave West Berlin immediately). The preceding supposition is of the "what if" or counterfactual kind: We may never know the full story of Khrushchev's motives for the missile deployments.[21] The actual shift from a general to an immediate deterrence situation took place on October 22 when President Kennedy ordered the Soviet missiles removed from Cuba, announced that the United States was imposing a quarantine on Soviet shipments to Cuba, and stated that a nuclear missile launched from Cuba against any target in the Western Hemisphere would call forth a full U.S. retaliatory response against the Soviet Union.

Realist perspectives help to explain the background to general deterrence failure in this instance, but they do little to clarify why the U.S. and Soviet political leaderships chose as they did. If the international power positions of states yield unambiguous inferences about their crisis management strategies, Khrushchev should never have dared to put missiles into Cuba. And the United States, once the missiles had been discovered, need not have hesitated to invade Cuba or to launch an air strike to destroy the missile sites, collocated air defense sites, and other nuclear capable weapons platforms deployed in Cuba by Moscow.[22] Realists would argue, against the preceding statement, that nuclear weapons made the Soviets and the Americans cautious during the Cuban missile crisis. The danger created by nuclear weapons helped to end the crisis without war, following the logic and against my earlier argument.

However, realist arguments will not work in this context. Nuclear weapons did not make the crisis easier to manage, but harder. They added to the risk of escalation, to be sure, and leaders were well aware of these risks. The United States deliberately and, some would say, successfully manipulated the risk of escalation and war to force Khrushchev's withdrawal of the missiles. But the argument, for nuclear coercion as the path to Cuban crisis settlement, will not work because nuclear weapons, and the Soviet sense of inferiority in the nuclear arms race, were major causes for the crisis.[23] If it is argued that nuclear weapons helped to resolve the crisis, that is true only as a historical tautology: Having caused it or helped to cause it and by making it more dangerous, they played a part in ending it.

Realism aided by an appreciation for historical serendipity and indeterminacy fares better in explaining the Cold War relationship between nuclear weapons and peace. For example, John Lewis Gaddis contends that nuclear weapons influenced post–World War II international relations in at least four ways. First, nuclear weapons helped to support an already existing reluctance of the great powers to wage war against one another. Second, states that possessed nuclear weapons became more risk averse. Third, nuclear weapons did not create bipolarity after World War II, but they did prolong its life, and so too helped to prolong stability. Fourth, nuclear weapons helped to perpetuate the Cold War by saving the United States, the Soviet Union, and their allies military expenditures on conventional forces, expenditures that, if necessary, might have forced rethinking of Cold War assumptions sooner.[24]

This summary shows that nuclear stability attributed by realists was purchased with significant trade-offs. For example, Gaddis's fourth form of nuclear influence acknowledges that *political* relations between the United States and the Soviet Union remained adversarial longer than necessary, in part due to ingrained habits of *military* hangover. To the realists' contention that nuclear weapons made war less likely because fighting became more dangerous, Gaddis's fourth argument for nuclear relevancy points to the downside of that contention. The very weapons of mass destruction that some would contend were instruments of deterrence or peace were also causes of U.S. and Soviet leaders' fears of devastating surprise attack. The capabilities of these weapons were so unprecedented that the very fact of their being targeted at another state made a relationship hostile in military-operational terms even when it had passed into a stage of nonhostility in policy.

Rational Decision-Making

As anticipated in our previous comments, a fourth problematical aspect of realism as the basis for optimism about nuclear weapons spread is the question of rational decision-making. The assumption of rational decision-making is a necessary condition for making testable hypotheses and verifiable generalizations about social behavior. In and of itself, the rationality postulate does no harm. It becomes dangerous, however, when it is assumed that particular notions of rational decision-making can be transferred from one culture or society to another. United States policymakers have on more than one occasion substituted assumptions for evidence or intelligence about the behavioral propensities or mind-sets of foreign leaders. For example, throughout the summer and early autumn of 1962, U.S. leaders simply assumed that Khrushchev would not dare to put Soviet missiles into Cuba because it was illogical and too risk acceptant. As another example, American policymakers between 1965 and 1968 assumed that selective bombing of targets in North Vietnam would increase the pressure on the regime in Hanoi to withdraw its support from the National Liberation Front in South Vietnam.

When assumptions based on U.S. decision rationality are not supported by experience, leaders sometimes cling to the assumptions or to their supporting logic and blame the other side for "irrational" or illogical behavior. Khrushchev's deployment of missiles in Cuba in the face of U.S. warnings against doing so has been described as irrational by many American, and even some Soviet, sources. Yet in his memoirs Khrushchev gives two reasons, equalizing the balance of nuclear power and deterring U.S. attack on Cuba, which make plain sense from his political and military vantage point. Similarly, the North Vietnamese reaction to U.S. bombing from 1965 to 1968 was to increase their support to the NLF and their commitment to ultimate victory over the government of South Vietnam and its American supporters. The U.S. bombing could destroy valued targets in North Vietnam, but it could not remove from Hanoi its capability to support insurgency in the south. Nor could bombing impose any unacceptable cost to North Vietnamese military capabilities for large-scale, conventional ground warfare, later put to use in the final push by Hanoi against Saigon in 1975.

United States policymakers assumed in July 1990 that it would not be prudent for Saddam Hussein to attack and occupy Kuwait. The Iraqi leader was thought by most American prewar assessments to be using coercive diplomacy against Kuwait because of its uncooperative oil-pricing behavior. Saddam Hussein also miscalculated Bush administration perceptions of U.S. and allied interests in the region, and he misestimated U.S. domestic politics as still being caught up in a Vietnam syndrome that would preclude President Bush from the actual use of force. Even after weeks of pounding from the U.S. and allied coalition air forces in January 1991, Saddam disbelieved that the United States would initiate a ground war because of fear of excessive numbers of American and allied casualties.

Looking inside the heads of enemy leaders, especially those of idiosyncratic and impulsive dictators, is never easy. But the preceding examples hold some pertinent social science lessons. Explanatory and predictive approaches that may suffice for such issue areas as welfare, urban development, education, and other largely domestic matters are not necessarily optimal for explaining behavior pertinent to war and peace. In these other issues with less than ultimate stakes, it makes sense to base predictions of future behavior on *typical* past behavior and on culturally shared norms and values. However, in international behavior related to war and peace, it is more important to be able to explain and predict *atypical* behaviors between states and leaders who do *not share* cultural norms and values. In other words, the marginal utility of being able to explain typical, as opposed to atypical, behavior declines as the situation moves from one of general to immediate deterrence (see the preceeding discussion). When leaders belly up to the bar of war, the smart bartender (international peacekeeper) will make few assumptions about their states of drunkenness; he or she will remove their drinks and drive them home as fast as possible.

NUCLEAR WEAPONS ARE NOT ALONE

The spread of nuclear weapons is not an isolated danger, but one heavily bound up with the proliferation of other weapons of mass destruction (chemical and biological) and of the means for their delivery. Arguments that the spread of nuclear weapons will contribute to military gridlock in East Asia or in the Middle East, as in Europe between 1946 and 1990, ignore the synergistic threat to stability brought about by the lethal combination of chemical, biological, and nuclear weapons, and improved air- and land-based delivery systems, among aspiring regional hegemons or dissatisfied states. In the case of nuclear weapons per se, the post–Cold War years have already added two states to the list of acknowledged nuclear powers, and one of these states (India) has expressed consistent skepticism about the Non-Proliferation Treaty and its impacts. Table 5.1 summarizes the available weapons of the seven declared or acknowledged nuclear armed states.

The status of North Korea has been mired in a complicated shell game of U.S. political relations with both Koreas, of bureaucratic politics on the American home front, and of a confrontationally oriented U.S. government approach to North Korea, up to the very edge of a near outbreak of war in 1994.[25] North Korea's standoff with the United States and the International Atomic Energy Agency (IAEA) over its nuclear production program, culminating in the Framework Agreement of 1994 intended to cap that program, is well known.[26] During the 1980s and 1990s, North Korea was able to develop a complete nuclear fuel cycle, including a capability for the production of plutonium at its Yongbyon nuclear research center. A plutonium production reactor became operational in 1986, with refueling in 1989, making available weapons-grade plutonium for at least one nuclear weapon. North Korea was

Table 5.1
Nuclear Proliferation: Status and Summary Indicators

Country	Delivery Systems	Warheads	Total Warheads
United States			
Deployed ICBMs and SLBMs	1165	6227	
Bombers (START I counting rules)	315	1731	
Other warheads estimated		4112	
Total Warheads			12,070
Russia			
Deployed ICBMs and SLBMs	1392	6454	
Bombers (START I counting rules)	117	908	
Other warheads estimated		15,138	
Total warheads			22,500
China			
ICBMs and SLBMs	~30	~30	
Other missiles	~80	~80	
Other warheads estimated			
Total warheads			>400
France			
Total Warheads			>450
United Kingdom			
Total warheads			260
India			
Total warheads			~70
Israel			
Total warheads			>100
Pakistan			
Total warheads			15 - 25

Supplementary Notes

1. India and Pakistan declared themselves nuclear powers after each completed a series of tests in May 1998. India is estimated to have 60 to 80 weapons and Pakistan 10 to 15. Neither state is a member of NPT.
2. Israel is thought to have between 70 and 125 weapons. Isreal is not a signatory of NPT.
3. North Korea's nuclear program is supposedly frozen under International Atomic Energy Agency (IAEA) safeguards. In 1994 Pyongyang signed the Agreed Framework with the United States calling for North Korea to freeze and subsequently give up all parts of its nuclear weapons program. In return, the United States promised to arrange for North Korea to receive two 1,000-megawatt lightwater reactors, plus annual allotments of

500,000 tons of heavy fuel oil until the first LWR is completed. Implementation of the Agreed Framework has been assigned to the Korean Peninsula Energy Development Organization (KEDO), also including South Korea, Japan, and the European Union.

4. Iran is a member of NPT. The United States suspects that Iran seeks a nuclear weapons program and has tried to prevent other states from providing Teheran with pertinent technology or know-how. Russia agreed in 1995 not to sell uranium enrichment technology to Iran, and China promised in 1997 to end civil nuclear cooperation with Iran.
5. According to UN Security Council Resolution 687, the UN Special Commission for Iraq (UNSCOM) and IAEA were to verify the complete elimination of Iraq's nuclear, chemical, and biological weapons, its ballistic missiles, and its means for producing these weapons and delivery systems. After U.S. bombing attacks on Iraq in late 1998, Iraqi head of state Saddam Hussein ejected UNSCOM from the country and it is unclear as of this writing when, or if inspections can resume.
6. Libya is a member of NPT, but the United States maintains that the regime nevertheless wants to acquire nuclear weapons.

Sources: Updated and adapted by authors from: David B. Thomson, *A Guide to the Nuclear Arms Control Treaties* (Los Alamos, N.M.: Los Alamos National Laboratory, LA-UR-31-73, July 1999), pp. 318–19; Arms Control Association, Fact Sheet, *The State of Nuclear Proliferation* (Washington, D.C: May 1998); Scott Ritter, *Endgame: Solving the Iraq Problem—Once and for All* (New York: Simon and Schuster, 1999), esp. pp. 217–24. See also Commission to Assess the Ballistic Missile Threat to the United States (Rumsfeld Commission), Report (Executive Summary) (Washington, D.C.: July 15, 1998).

also building a 50-megawatt reactor at Yongbyon and a 200-megawatt reactor at Taechon before construction was halted under the Framework Agreement. The 50-megawatt reactor could have produced enough plutonium for North Korea to make between seven and ten nuclear weapons *per year*.[27]

North Korea was also developing a diversified industry for the production of ballistic missiles of various ranges, including missiles for export. North Korea in 1996 deployed with its forces several hundred SCUD-B and SCUD-C ballistic missiles with maximum ranges of 300 and 500 kilometers respectively. Its Nodong-1 medium range (estimated 1,000 km with a 1,000 kg payload) ground mobile, liquid-propelled missile was first tested in 1990 and entered service in 1994. By December 1994, according to some reports, between twelve and eighteen Nodong-1 missiles were in service.[28] A follow-on Nodong-2 with increased range and reduced payload has been deployed; its estimated range is 1,300 to 1,500 km with a payload from 500 to 750 kg.[29] North Korea has reportedly also deployed the Taepodong 1 medium range ballistic missile with an estimated range of 2,000 km with a single conventional or nuclear warhead.[30]

During the summer of 1998 North Korea test fired a three-stage ballistic missile rocket over the Sea of Japan. The DPRK government described the test as an intended satellite launch that was less than completely successful, but some U.S. observers drew the conclusion that North Korea had demonstrated a prototype capability for missile attacks well beyond the tactical or theater range. According to the Commission to Assess the Ballistic Missile Threat to the United States in its 1998 report to Congress, a North Korean decision to rapidly deploy the Taepodong 2 ballistic missile might not be known to U.S. intelligence very far in advance of the decision to launch. The capabilities of Taepodong 2 once deployed, according to the Commission, are potentially strategic in reach and impact:

This missile could reach major cities and military bases in Alaska and the smaller, westernmost islands in the Hawaiian chain. Light-weight variations of the TD-2 could fly as far as 10,000 km, placing at risk western U.S. territory in an arc extending northwest from Phoenix, Arizona to Madison, Wisconsin.[31]

A summary of some attributes of North Korea's currently deployed ballistic missiles appears in Table 5.2.

An important aspect of North Korea's ballistic missile program is that it is designed for export as well as for Pyongyang's own defense needs. Hundreds of SCUD missiles have been provided by North Korea to countries in the Middle East, including Iran, and North Korea is already marketing the NODONG for export. The U.S. Department of Defense estimates that, thus

Table 5.2
North Korean Ballistic Missiles

Missile System	Range/Payload
SCUD B	300 km/single conventional or chemical warhead
SCUD C	550 km/single conventional warhead
Nodong - 1	1,300 km/single conventional chemical or nuclear warhead
Nodong - 2	1,500 km/single conventional chemical or nuclear warhead
Taepodong - 1	2,000 km/single conventional chemical or nuclear warhead

far, North Korea has not become an international supplier of nuclear, chemical, or biological weapons technology, despite its aggressive marketing of missiles and missile technology. Pyongyang has a substantial chemical weapons capability and limited facilities for producing biological weapons.[32]

North Korea's ballistic missile export program has enhanced the threat to stability in Southwest Asia. Iran acquired SCUD-B missiles from Libya and North Korea and SCUD-C missiles from the latter in the 1980s. During just three years of the Iran–Iraq war, between 1985 and 1988, Iran fired almost 100 SCUD-B missiles at Iraq. In addition to obtaining ballistic missiles from North Korea, Iran is attempting to set up its own missile production capability. Acquisition of the North Korean Nodong missile would permit Iran to attack targets in Israel, much of Saudi Arabia and the Trucial States, Turkey, Russia and other former Soviet states, Pakistan, and India.[33] Iran's original reason for acquiring ballistic missiles was to employ them in its protracted war against Iraq during the 1980s. Having acquired the taste for technology and having taken note of Iraq's post–Desert Storm weakness in the 1990s, Iran now reasonably aspires to the status of first among equals among Gulf states. In addition to its ballistic missile capabilities, Iran has Chinese-supplied cruise missiles, artillery, and aircraft capable of delivering chemical and biological weapons, and Russian-built SU-24 fighter-bombers that can deliver nuclear weapons.[34] Rumors of Russian–Iranian nuclear cooperation and of leakage of nuclear weapons experts from the former Soviet Union into Iran are frequent in U.S. and other media sources.

The nuclear coming-out parties in Islamabad and New Delhi, added to Israel's de facto but unacknowledged nuclear status, add to the uncertainty regarding the relationship between nuclear weapons and regional conflicts. Pakistan and India have had several diplomatic crises growing out of their disagreements over the political status of Kashmir. This conflict is not likely to deescalate in the near term, although there is some evidence that the two sides have begun to discuss some rules of the road related to crisis management (e.g., mutual guarantees that neither will strike at the other's nuclear forces or facilities at the outset of an otherwise conventional war). Israel's nuclear deterrent also exists in a regional hot spot, and a Middle Eastern nuclear arms race between Israel and Iraq (or a possible war) was postponed by the latter's defeat in the Gulf war of 1991. Both Iran and Iraq still seek to become nuclear powers and Tehran is building toward a long-range ballistic missile force. Both Iran and Iraq consider the United States and Israel as enemies of first resort; on the other hand, each distrusts the other and aspires to regional hegemony. Life could get interesting in the Middle East/South Asia region during the next decade or two.

The U.S. inability or unwillingness to deter Iraq's invasion of Kuwait in 1990 contains another warning about realist optimism and proliferation. The basic maxims of deterrence learned during the Cold War years may have to be rethought, or in some cases rejected outright, in the remainder of the century and thereafter. Nuclear weapons and war avoidance worked together during the Cold War because U.S.–Soviet strategic nuclear bipolarity enforced a *connection between general and immediate deterrence*. One could make many reliable guesses about the outcome of any particular challenge to the international status quo on the basis of the superpower relationship and the ability of Washington and Moscow to dominate allies and deter third parties.

The collapse of bipolarity after the Cold War diminishes the link between general and immediate deterrence; one can make fewer reliable predictions about states' behaviors on the basis of "system" variables. The significance of this theoretical construct for the practical problem of nonproliferation is illustrated by then Secretary of Defense William J. Perry's comment that future terrorists or rogue regimes "may not buy into our deterrence theory. Indeed, they may be madder than MAD."[35] Deterrence theory a la the Cold War, based on realist premises that assume risk-averse and cost-benefit sensitive leaders, may no longer hold tenable for leaders armed with weapons of mass destruction and motivated by "irrational" or "illogical" objectives by at least U.S. standards. As Keith B. Payne has explained,

Assuming that deterrence will "work" because the opponent will behave sensibly is bound to be the basis for a future surprise. I do not know whether our expectations of a generically sensible opponent will next be dashed by a so-called rogue state, such as North Korea, or by another challenger. That they will be dashed, however, is near certain. As we move into the second nuclear age and confront opponents with whom we are relatively unfamiliar, assumptions of a generically sensible foe almost certainly will ensure surprises.[36]

CONFLICT TERMINATION AND NUCLEAR WEAPONS SPREAD

Most discussions of deterrence seem to assume that it will fail all at once or not at all. This all-or-nothing perspective on deterrence reflects the daunting size of U.S. and Soviet nuclear arsenals during the Cold War and the evident hopelessness of limiting any nuclear exchange between them to politically acceptable limits. However, in a post–Cold War world of nuclear arsenals of diverse sizes, vulnerabilities, and doctrines, deterrence might fail in stages. The question of how to stop a war between nuclear armed states prior to nuclear first use by either side would be important. So too, although obviously more intimidating, would be the problem of bringing the fighting to an end even after some nuclear weapons had been fired in anger.

The first requirement for war termination is the accurate and timely communication of an interest in cease-fire. Unless and until most forces in any war can be made to cease their fire, policymakers' desire to stop a war is more theory than reality. In a conventional war fought mostly or entirely between professional armed forces accountable to civil authorities, this should be a comparatively simple matter of communication between heads of state. Even in this case, however, there are many variables to consider. Armies may or may not be promptly responsive to directives from their superiors to stop shooting. Disengagement of forces and virtual disarmament of troops on both sides may be necessary before serious negotiations over policy issues can begin. The problem is exacerbated if, within the country of one or more combatants, there exist factions opposed to any peace settlement short of victory or death. For example, in World War II a diehard faction in the Imperial Japanese military leadership resisted surrender even after Hiroshima and Nagasaki. Germany's surrender in World War II was made more difficult because the "diehard" was Hitler himself, who preferred to see his country destroyed along with his own life rather than agree to terms.[37]

A nuclear conflict between major powers would have aspects of both conventional and unconventional warfare. It would in all likelihood be fought between states, with militaries supposedly under the operational control of duly constituted civil authorities. However, once a nuclear war had begun, the empowered nuclear commanders have been converted into potential nuclear ministates. This is especially so in the case of nuclear force commanders in a state without a democratic tradition of political accountability of the armed forces. More will be said about the problem of politico-military control, but the present point is about the ability to communicate a timely and accurate sense of one side's willingness to stop fighting. If there are plural instead of singular effective fighting forces in the field with whom to communicate, cease-fire becomes harder to obtain. Russia's frustration in attempting to negotiate a cease-fire with rebels in Chechnya, and not only in this century, makes the point.

Therefore, a second requirement for war termination is military compliance with the terms of armistice and, ultimately, the peace settlement. If disarmament and peace can be imposed on the losers by the victors, as in World War II, then the issue of military compliance is solved by diktat. Under somewhat different conditions, the issue of military compliance may be solved for the defeated military of the loser, but may remain as a sore point among one or more military elements of the winning side. Militaries bound by an alliance agreement may find their commanders straining at the leashes in advocacy of their preferred strategies for victory as the war nears its termination and the writing of history is anticipated. In World War II, the allied armies from Normandy to the Rhine were marked by contention, caused both by personality differences and serious differences in operational appreciations of the situation. These differences were not only apparent in the field, but in Whitehall and in Washington. Only Eisenhower's brief to deal with Churchill as something approaching a military proconsul for Europe (pro tem, and with occasional intrusive oversight) was able to resolve the differences that sparked disagreements among highstrung field commanders and allied chiefs of service in Europe.

The U.S. and allied militaries did comply with the terms of settlement in Europe, of course, in part because everyone had had enough of fighting by this time and because the last symbol of Hitler's resistance had been crushed by the Soviets in Berlin. Also, Japan remained to be dealt with, and U.S. leaders assumed that Soviet cooperation would be needed to finish the war against Japan. Therefore, issues that might have been provocative of immediate postwar disagreement, as between the Western allies and the Soviets, were papered over for later argument. However, a good historian could easily concoct a "counterfactual" scenario in which U.S. and Soviet forces fought at the Elbe instead of shaking hands across it. Where that would have led is speculative. If Field Marshal Montgomery's preference for a sudden and spectacular thrust into Germany's vital regions in late 1944 had been followed, instead of Eisenhower's preference for a slower and surer pushing of Germany's defenses across a broad front, would faster moving U.S. and British forces have threatened Stalin's plans for an east–west dividing line? And if they had, what would Stalin have done about it?

The termination of World War II in Europe did not involve military noncompliance with civil authority. The latter stages of World War I are another story. The mutinies of the French army in 1917 forced a change to a less aggressive and casualty intensive operational art on the Western front, and a reshuffling of the French military high command.[38] The widely politicized and demoralized Russian army walked away from the field of battle and many soldiers joined workers in Russia's cities in revolt against the provisional government. The soldiers' and workers' soviets that seized power in Petrograd in November 1917 prolonged the war by withdrawing the Soviet Union from the confict in the spring of 1918, according to the terms of Brest-Litovsk. This defection from the entente almost dealt a mortal blow to

Germany's enemies. Russia's willingness to sue for peace counted as a rationale for later British, U.S., and Japanese intervention in the Russian civil war, prolonging and exacerbating that conflict and poisoning U.S.–Soviet relations for more than a decade.[39]

An even more interesting case is the situation in Germany after the armistice. Since Germany's military had not been annihilated in the field, many Germans believed that a dishonorable peace had been agreed to by an insufficiently patriotic civil government. Germany's military leadership played this "undefeated in battle" card effectively in the period between the two world wars. The German army became a state within a state even within a supposedly liberal-democratic political order. In the 1920s the army and the social democrats proved to be the pillars on which a reconstructed state could be built: The army had respect, and the social democrats, more or less, could govern under the constraints of the Versailles peace treaty. Ironically, the military combined this institutional autonomy with ideological neutrality. They would serve any duly elected or appointed civil masters, including Hitler, but not as his political enforcers. Thus, Hitler was, before and during World War II, forced to turn to paramilitaries other than the Wehrmacht for the suppression of his political enemies.

The preceding cases are not historical excursions. They illustrate the significance of the second requirement for nuclear, or other, war termination: military compliance. The contrast between the first and second world wars shows that, whereas a more ambitious war aim (unconditional surrender) may be harder to impose in battle, it leaves fewer ambiguities both during and after the fighting. Disarmed and dead troops and deposed cabinets can no longer resist. On the other hand, the proclamation of unconditional surrender as a wartime policy objective may cut the ground out from under peace proponents within the government or military of the other side.

In the case of a nuclear conflict between powers in possession of large arsenals and ample numbers of delivery systems, conditional surrender may be difficult if not impossible to arrange. Nuclear weapons not yet fired must be rounded up and cantoned. Troops capable of firing those weapons will have to stand down. Commanders will have to yield their weapons and codes to some representatives of the other side or to neutral arbiters, despite less than complete knowledge of the degree of disarmament and compliance by their opposite numbers in uniform. One of the most death-defying scenarios to challenge creative "counterfactual" historians is this: the regathering of nuclear weapons among Cold War NATO forces in Europe, after they had been given out during a crisis that led to conventional fighting, but before nuclear escalation had taken place, once governments had decided to cease fire.

Nor should this problem be assumed as easily manageable for nuclear arsenals much smaller than those of the United States and other large nuclear powers. The nuclear tests by India and Pakistan in May 1998 added two states to the ranks of acknowledged nuclear powers and created the potential for a race in weapons of mass destruction on the Asian subcontinent. Experts feared that a conventional war between India and Pakistan (say, over Kashmir) might easily escalate into nuclear first use by one side, followed by an equivalent or worse response from its opponent. The concern is realistic; the two states' armed forces clashed on three different occasions during the Cold War, and one of those Indo-Pakistani wars created Bangladesh out of a dismembered Pakistan. Therefore, Islamabad, facing apparent defeat in a conventional war, might be prompted by bitter memories and available nuclear weapons into first use.[40] A nuclear response by India would be almost certain. What would happen next is conjectural. At least one U.S. unified command has apparently already tested a "game" scenario in which India and Pakistan were preparing for nuclear use against one another. According to the unified commander, "I said to the group, as a matter of policy, do you want to alter their command and control capability to the point where neither side has a clear picture of the battlefield, thereby preempting their use of nuclear weapons?"[41] The assumption that blind screens will induce restraint is interesting, but possibly wrong.

Once India and Pakisan had begun firing nuclear weapons at one another, the immediate priority of the world community, and especially of other states in South Asia, would be to stop the war. Control over postnuclear attack militaries could be part of the problem for the governments of both India and Pakistan, especially the latter. Pakistan's nuclear program has been more or less under tight military control from its inception. Political leaders in both states are probably unfamiliar with the details of nuclear force alerting or operations. Military leaders themselves have almost certainly never rehearsed a nuclear standdown, and they may not even understand fully the process of alerting nuclear forces. For these and other reasons, military noncompliance with de-alerting and cease fire orders might be impossible to obtain due to deliberate resistance or because the problem was simply not in the institutional repertoire of standard or expected behavior.

The reliability of the military machine might also break down because the abject horror of the effects of nuclear strikes would shock the human decency of observers and create dysfunctional psychological effects. The behavioral syndrome of combat exhaustion has been well documented for troops taking part in conventional conflicts. Something like this or like "post-traumatic stress disorder" might similarly influence the behavior of soldiers in contact with urban areas that had been subjected to nuclear attacks. Even in the case of limited counterforce strikes on the military forces and assets of the other side, the numbers of casualties would be without historical precedent in the society affected. For example, one projection of the effects of "limited" attacks on the military centers of India and Pakistan gave the estimates shown in Tables 5.3 and 5.4.

Related to the second requirement for war termination, military compliance with settlement, is the third: stable command and control during war. There are at least two aspects to this requirement: stability of central control, and preservation of continuing control over widely dispersed forces on the periphery of the command, control, and communications links. Of course, if central control falls apart, so too will control over the peripheral actions of armed forces engaged in combat. Central control could fail due to destroyed command posts or communications, or both, among other possibilities. Peripheral control might fail if embattled commanders and troops were cut off from central authority, as is quite conceivable under many cir-

Table 5.3
Casualties in Limited Military Attack on Pakistan

Target Cantonments	Population of City (1990)	Deaths (Estimated)	Injuries (Estimated)
Karachi	8,337,100	128,900	211,541
Lahore	4,599,900	66,100	10,800
Rawalpindi	1,427,100	68,300	11,200
Hyderabad	1,088,000	44,600	73,200
Peshawar	383,100	27,500	45,100
Sialkot	283,200	20,400	33,400
Quetta	282,600	35,500	58.300
Bhawalpur	261,900	18,800	30,900
Wah	222,100	148,000	74,000
Gujrat	212,500	15,300	25,100
Sahiwal	51,600	3,700	6,100
Total	**17,149,100**	**577,100**	**579,641**

Source: J. Rashid Naim, "Asia's Day After: Nuclear War Between India and Pakistan," in Stephen P. Cohen, ed., *The Security of South Asia: American and Asian Perspectives* (Urbana: University of Illinois Press, 1987), pp. 251–82, citation p. 271. The method used to estimate deaths and injuries is explained in the text; population figures are projections.

cumstances in war and has occurred more than once in military history. In addition, it has happened more than once in a military crisis or war that command, control, and communications failures occur in previously unseen, and therefore unpredicted, patterns.

The case of the present-day Russian nuclear arsenal is instructive in this regard. Prior to the collapse of the former Soviet Union, Russian and allied Soviet nuclear weapons were subject to multiple and redundant checks and balances in order to ensure political reliability and prevent accidents or unauthorized uses. The assumption of reliable and safe Russian nuclear weap-

Table 5.4
Casualties in Limited Military Attack on India

Target Cantonments	Population of City (1990)	Deaths (Estimated)	Injuries (Estimated)
Bombay	11,914,900	136,900	224,600
Delhi	9,118,600	40.700	66,900
Ahmedabad	3,164,100	153,500	251,900
Agra	1,041,800	91,100	149,400
Gowaliar	944,300	18,000	25,400
Baroda	821,400	4,200	6,900
Amritsar	813,500	15,500	21,900
Ludhiana	775,800	14,800	20,900
Jullandhar	590,900	11,300	15,900
Rajkot	529,100	10,100	14,200
Meerut	528,400	10,100	14,200
Jamnagar	408,400	79,300	13,000
Jhansi	337,300	6,400	9,100
Ajmer	334,300	6,400	9,000
Jammu	273,400	5,200	7,400
Total	**31,596,200**	**603,500**	**850,700**

Source: J. Rashid Naim, "Asia's Day After: Nuclear War Between India and Pakistan," in Stephen P. Cohen, ed., *The Security of South Asia: American and Asian Perspectives* (Urbana: University of Illinois Press, 1987), pp. 251–82, citation p. 272. The method used to estimate deaths and injuries is explained in the text; population figures are projections.

ons, including those assigned to intercontinental launchers, can no longer be made with confidence.[42] For example, former Russian Defense Minister Igor Rodionov warned in 1996 and 1997 that, due to lack of funds and poor administration, Russia's nuclear forces were dangerously "unmanageable."[43] And the CIA contended in 1997 that outdated Russian missile-control systems had accidentally gone into full combat mode on several occasions since 1991.[44] General Rodionov's successor as Russian Defense Minister, General Igor Sergeev, has denied allegations of any problems in the Russian nuclear command system.[45] General Eugene Habiger, Commander in Chief of U.S. Strategic Command, visited Russian strategic missile installations and troops in June 1998 and averred that Russia's nuclear combat control system "is as safe as the U.S." according to Russian media reports.[46] Meanwhile, Russia continues the trend adumbrated in its 1993 military doctrine toward increased reliance on its nuclear forces for operational and tactical as well as strategic missions, in order to compensate for its conventional military weaknesses.[47] Russia's current military planning guidance may include the option of nuclear use to preempt a conventional land or missile attack from states bordering Russian territory, including those on Russia's turbulent southern periphery.[48]

The possible combination of a conventional war begun on Russia's periphery with raised levels of military alert could lead to political misjudgments clouded by failures in nuclear warning, communications, and command/control equipment. According to recent U.S. government reports, Russia's space warning system can no longer guarantee twenty-four hour coverage of American missile fields, and Russian warning systems failed to detect the September 1998 North Korean missile launch in the direction of Japan. Russia's missile tests are experiencing repeated failures, funds to pay scientific and technical personnel are lacking, and its production base for modern military hardware was in a state of disintegration for most of 1998. Continued arrears in funds to pay military service personnel could lead to walkouts from nuclear installations or unwillingness to respond to authorized commands. In sum, even without the stimulus of information warfare designed to confuse Russian radar screens, computers, or communications, Russia's insufficiently modernized and accident prone early warning and C4 (command, control, communications, and computers) system has the potential to disinform itself into accidental or inadvertent nuclear war or escalation.[49]

There is a mistaken assumption that, with the plethora of communication links that exist today, forces of great powers on one side of the globe could not be disconnected from their owners and operators on the other side. This view assumes incorrectly that only simple messages need to get through from center to periphery, and vice versa. To the contrary, for central and regional commands to make intelligent decisions about fighting or war termination, they would need to exchange with field commanders highly precise and often technical information about status of forces and other variables. In addition, it might be prudent or even necessary for these kinds of information exchanges to take place between or among opposed field commanders, and between each of them and their respective central commands. Sorting out confusion within the same chain of command is difficult enough as a war nears its presumed end. For example, the timing of the cease-fire in the Gulf war of 1991 caught the commanders of the U.S. XVIII Airborne Corps and VII Corps off balance. Deputy CENTCOM Lieutenant General Calvin Waller regarded the decision as premature on operational grounds.[50] CENTCOM General Norman Schwartzkopf, according to one account, was prepared "to subordinate the final destruction of the Republican Guard to the administration's political goals" such as avoiding images of U.S. brutality and avoiding American and Iraqi casualties.[51] Some Washington policymakers were operating under the mistaken assumption that the crack Republican Guard Iraqi armoured divisions had in essence been destroyed by the time the cease-fire took place.

Intelligence failures can contribute to wartime confusion between center and periphery in the latter stages of a war. The Battle of the Bulge beginning in December 1944 is an example. Neither field commanders nor allied command Europe anticipated that seemingly exhausted and virtually defeated German forces would attempt one final, desperate offensive that prolonged the war and shook allied confidence. Initial reports from forward units suddenly caught off guard and committed to furious firefights were at first disbelieved or misconstrued by army intelligence as a result of preconceptions about German capabilities, based on recent performance.[52] The assumption that Germany was down to its shoe leather was correct; what was missed was that resources remained to be called out, including previously untapped manpower both old and young, for Hitler's final throw of the dice.[53]

A fourth requirement for war termination can be deduced easily from what has been argued so far: verification of behavior in compliance with a cease-fire and subsequent peace settlement. In conventional wars this is done by exchanges of military observers. Doubtless this would be difficult to accomplish in a fast-paced and highly destructive nuclear conflict. Substitutes for observers, especially in the early stages of any war termination, would have to be found. Overhead reconnaissance by satellites and aircraft, if any satellites remained functional and aircraft could count on flying safely, would provide some necessary verification of compliance with agreed cease-fire protocols. However, any reconnaissance or surveillance is highly selective. One must have a conceptual roadmap for what to look at, and in wartime this is all the more significant than in peace. Just as moving targets are harder to hit than stationary ones, so, too are mobile and movable missiles and command posts harder to verify than fixed forces or sites. In addition, some platforms used for nuclear launch might not be locatable at all; the virtue of submarines in time of peace, stealthy defiance of location detection, could become an obstacle to locking down a truce or cease-fire in war.

Illustrative of the overlap between the requirements for war termination is the essential nature of reliable and uncorrupted communications links for sending a message of intent to terminate, and for monitoring compliance with termination agreements. Quite obviously, each side would have to be able to verify that its own communication links were operating with fidelity and fully under its own control at the endgame of negotiation as well as when negotiation feelers are first put out. Ghosts in the machine that spoofed or distorted information could slow down or bring to a halt the process of arranging cease-fire.

CONCLUSIONS

The spread of nuclear weapons will be even more dangerous to international stability in the dynamic post–Cold War world than it was during the Cold War. The U.S.–Soviet bipolarity and global competition between 1945 and 1990 helped to prevent nuclear proliferation in two ways. First, the superpowers' nuclear umbrellas made it unnecessary for their allies to seek independent nuclear forces. Second, the U.S. and Soviet Union monopolized second-strike capability, the sine qua non of nuclear deterrence, due to their large and diverse arsenals and vast territories. These exceptional conditions are now gone. Inferences based on United States and Soviet Cold War experience cannot be extrapolated into the new world order as reliable predictions of future state behavior. Indeed, it would be dangerous to do so. Contrary to the assertions of pro-proliferation realists, "system" level variables do not suggest a rosy future for stability based on nuclear weapons spread.

The United States, now left alone as the world's sole military superpower, finds that nuclear weapons are the great equalizer of the weak against the strong. Nuclear weapons in the hands of regional antagonists have the potential to negate U.S. defense guidance calling for capability to fight two nearly simultaneous conventional theater wars. Nonstate actors may acquire nuclear weapons, including terrorists, whose behavior has never been the subject of reliable prediction by social science models. Even the leaders in India and Pakistan, after having officially joined the nuclear club in May 1998, have already recognized the need to discuss mutual arms limitation and confidence-building measures against accidental or inadvertent nuclear war or escalation. Nuclear weapons will, if ever again used in anger, falsify the expectation by some theorists that more is better; however, at that stage it will be too late for argument.

NOTES

1. Bernard E. Trainor, "War by Miscalculation," Ch. 8 in Joseph S. Nye, Jr. and Roger K. Smith, eds., *After the Storm: Lessons from the Gulf War* (Lanham, Md.: Madison Books/Aspen Institute, 1992), p. 216.

2. Realists contend that power is based on tangible resources, such as population, economic capacity, and territory, and the most influential among them also believe that power is both a means and an end in international politics. See Hans J. Morgenthau, *Politics among Nations: The Struggle for Power and Peace* (New York: Alfred A. Knopf, 1948). Neorealists hold, as do realists, that the structure of the international system, especially system polarity, is the most important determinant of the context for state decision-making. Neorealists, in contrast to realists, are more likely to acknowledge sources of power other than tangible ones, and to treat power as a means but not as an end in itself. Paul R. Viotti and Mark V. Kauppi divide international political theories into realist, pluralist, and globalist schools, a taxonomy similar to that offered by Kalevi J. Holsti. See Viotti and Kauppi, eds., *International Relations Theory: Realism, Pluralism, Globalism* (New York: Macmillan, 1993), esp. Ch. 1, pp. 61—227, and Holsti, *Peace and War: Armed Conflicts and International Order* (Cambridge: Cambridge University Press, 1991), p. 328. See also Holsti's comments on the roots of realism and neorealism, pp. 329–30. An excellent summary and critique of neorealist views is provided by Robert O. Keohane, "Theory of World Politics: Structural Realism and Beyond," in Ada W. Finifter, ed., *Political Science: The State of the Discipline* (Washington, D.C.: American Political Science Association, 1983), and reprinted in Viotti and Kauppi, eds., *International Relations Theory*, pp. 186–227.

3. The point is emphasized in Joseph S. Nye, Jr., *Bound to Lead: The Changing Nature of American Power* (New York: Basic Books, 1990), esp. pp. 193–195, which emphasizes the importance of soft power as a potential power resource.

4. Paul Kennedy, *Preparing for the Twenty-First Century* (New York: Random House, 1993).

5. Some experts argue that the most important international conflicts of the future will be rooted in cultures and civilizations. See Samuel P. Huntington, "The Clash of Civilizations?" *Foreign Affairs*, Summer 1993, pp. 22–49.

6. Here we concede to realists and neorealists more than some of their stronger critics might. Read literally, some realists argue that states are bound to *maximize* their power or power potential. However, taken to its logical endpoint, this assumption cannot permit the existence of a stable international order; all states attempting power maximization will sooner or later corrupt the balance of power on which strategic realism actually depends. Therefore, we prefer to give realists the benefit

of the doubt on this issue, allowing that they would, in their right minds, acknowledge the need for autolimitation of objectives in the interest of system stability.

7. Kenneth N. Waltz, *Theory of International Politics* (Reading, Mass.: Addison-Wesley, 1979). See also, and more specifically on Waltz's views of the relationship between nuclear weapons and stability, two of his other works: *The Spread of Nuclear Weapons: More May Be Better*, Adelphi Papers No. 171 (London: International Institute of Strategic Studies, 1981), and "Nuclear Myths and Political Realities," *American Political Science Review*, No. 3 (September, 1990), pp. 731–745. See also Scott D. Sagan, "More Will Be Worse," Ch. 2 in Sagan and Kenneth N. Waltz, *The Spread of Nuclear Weapons: A Debate* (New York: W.W. Norton, 1995), pp. 47–92.

8. John J. Mearsheimer, "Back to the Future: Instability in Europe after the Cold War," *International Security*, XV (Summer 1990), pp. 5–56.

9. For the distinction between general and immediate deterrence, see Patrick M. Morgan, *Deterrence: A Conceptual Approach* (Beverly Hills, Calif.: Sage Publications, 1983).

10. The distinctions between assertive and delegative control are explained in Peter Douglas Feaver, *Guarding the Guardians: Civilian Control of Nuclear Weapons in the United States* (Ithaca, N.Y.: Cornell University Press, 1992), pp. 3–28 and passim. On U.S. nuclear predelegation during the Cold War, see Bruce G. Blair, *The Logic of Accidental Nuclear War* (Washington, D.C.: Brookings Institution, 1993), pp. 46–52.

11. Lewis A. Dunn, Sarah A. Mullen, Gregory F. Giles, Joseph A. Yager, and James S. Tomashoff, *The Next Nuclear-Weapon States?* (McLean, Va.: Science Applications International Corporation, 1991), pp. 2–51.

12. The term "system" has many uses in international politics and political science. Structural realist theories of international politics emphasize the causal importance of system *structure*: numbers and types of units in the system and the distribution of military and other capabilities among those units. Other variations of systems theory emphasize the *interactions* among components of the system, including the *interdependence* of the actors or units. For a concise discussion of systemic theories of international politics, see James E. Dougherty and Robert L. Pfaltzgraff, Jr., *Contending Theories of International Politics*, 4th ed. (New York: Longman, 1997), pp. 100–134.

13. Bruce Bueno de Mesquita and David Lalman, *War and Reason: Domestic and International Imperatives* (New Haven, Conn.: Yale University Press, 1992).

14. *Ibid.*, p. 267.

15. *Ibid.*, pp. 267–68.

16. Kenneth N. Waltz, *Man, the State and War* (New York: Columbia University Press, 1959). The first image includes human nature and individual psychological attributes pertinent to decision-making. The second image refers to state level decisions and behaviors.

17. Bueno de Mesquita and Lalman, *War and Reason*, p. 269. The authors acknowledge that, under conditions of imperfect information, states might mistak-

enly stumble into war as a result of misjudgments based on inaccurate information. But in a domestically constrained as opposed to a realist model of strategic rationality, leaders may also "mistakenly" avoid war and "stumble into negotiation or other peaceful solutions to their differences"(idem, p. 269).

18. Or, as Hobbes explained it, it is a precept or general rule of reason that "every man, ought to endeavour Peace, as farre as he has hope of obtaining it; and when he cannot obtain it, that he may seek, and use, all helps, and advantages of Warre." Thomas Hobbes, *Leviathan* (New York: Washington Square Press, 1964), p. 88. See also Hedley Bull, *The Anarchical Society: A Study of Order in World Politics* (New York: Columbia University Press, 1977).

19. For a more complete definition of immediate deterrence, see Morgan, *Deterrence: A Conceptual Analysis*.

20. As Jervis explains, rationality assumptions are not necessarily falsified by cases in which leaders have chosen poorly. But, in many other instances, "the beliefs and policies are so removed from what a careful and disinterested analysis of the situation reveals that the failure is hard to fit into the framework generated by rationality." Jervis, introduction in Jervis, Richard Ned Lebow, and Janice Gross Stein, *Psychology and Deterrence* (Baltimore: Johns Hopkins University Press, 1985), p. 6. In addition, leaders' beliefs about deterrence and credibility are interactive with the probability that particular strategies will succeed or fail. As Jervis acknowledges, "there is no objective answer to the question of which nuclear postures and doctrines are destabilizing, apart from the highly subjective beliefs that decision makers hold about this question . . . Not only do each side's beliefs constitute an important part of the reality with which the other has to contend, but also states can collude or contend on the constructions of reality that frame these judgments" (Jervis, *The Meaning of the Nuclear Revolution*, p. 183).

21. See Raymond L. Garthoff, *Reflections on the Cuban Missile Crisis* (Washington, D.C.: Brookings Institution, 1989, rev. ed.), pp. 6–42.

22. U.S. officials at the time of the Cuban missile crisis underestimated significantly the size of the Soviets' conventional forces deployed on that island (actually some 40,000). Nor did they realize that, in addition to warheads for medium and intermediate range missiles deployed in Cuba, the Soviets also deployed nuclear warheads for tactical weapons launchers. At the time of the crisis, U.S. leaders were uncertain whether *any* Soviet warheads actually arrived in Cuba. Raymond L. Garthoff, "The Havana Conference on the Cuban Missile Crisis," *Cold War International History Project Bulletin* (Washington, D.C.: Woodrow Wilson Center, Spring 1992), pp. 1–4. According to Bruce Blair, actual orders to the senior Soviet commander in Cuba specifically precluded the use of any nuclear weapons without prior approval from Moscow (Blair, *The Logic of Accidental Nuclear War*, p. 109).

23. U.S. leaders were not well informed about the actual Soviet nuclear force deployments in Cuba in October 1962. With regard to nuclear force loadings, Soviet *tactical* nuclear weapons (in addition to those intended for SS-4 and SS-5 launchers) numbered between 98 and 104: 80 for two regiments of *front* cruise

missiles; 12 for Luna surface-to-surface, short-range missiles; 6 for gravity bombs for IL-28 bombers; and possible additional charges for nuclear armed naval mines. The approximate maximum range for the cruise missiles, fired from Cuban shore points nearest to U.S. territory, was 90 miles; warheads for these cruise missiles were in the 5–12 kiloton range. The sixty warheads deployed for SS-4 and SS-5 launchers in Cuba (the latter never actually reached Cuba, having been turned back by the U.S. quarantine) were in addition to these tactical weapons; all but the SS-5 warheads apparently reached Cuba in a single shipment on October 4. The existence of a Soviet tactical nuclear force of this size, unknown to U.S. invasion planners, indicates that for Moscow the psychological investment in defense of Cuba was apparently much higher than Americans, then and subsequently during the Cold War, believed. The potential for inadvertent escalation was obviously much greater than crisis participants could have known. We are very grateful to Raymond Garthoff, Brookings Institution, for updated information on Cuba, based on his extensive discussions with Russian defense experts and many years of study devoted to this issue.

24. Gaddis, "The Essential Relevance of Nuclear Weapons," Ch. 6 in his *The United States and the End of the Cold War* (New York: Oxford University Press, 1992), pp. 105–32.

25. Leon V. Sigal, *Disarming Strangers: Nuclear Diplomacy with North Korea* (Princeton, N.J.: Princeton University Press, 1998), esp. pp. 3–14.

26. See Michael J. Mazarr, *North Korea and the Bomb* (New York: St. Martin's Press, 1995), passim.

27. Office of the Secretary of Defense, *Proliferation: Threat and Response* (Washington, D.C.: U.S. Government Printing Office, 1996), pp. 6–7 provides background on the North Korean nuclear program.

28. Jane's Strategic Weapons Systems, September 30, 1998. http://janes.ismc.sgov.gov/egi-bin . . . h_janes/.

29. Ibid.

30. Patrick M. O'Donogue, *Theater Missile Defense in Japan: Implications for the U.S.–China–Japan Strategic Relationship* (Carlisle Barracks, Pa.: U.S. Army War College, Strategic Studies Institute, September 2000), p. 6.

31. Commission to Assess the Ballistic Missile Threat to the United States (Rumsfeld Commission), *Report* (Executive Summary) (Washington, D.C.: July 15, 1998), p. 9. Pagination may be inexact due to variations in electronic transmission.

32. Ibid.

33. See map, *Ranges of Current and Future Ballistic Missile Systems* (Iran), in Office of the Secretary of Defense, *Proliferation: Threat and Response*, p. 17.

34. Ibid., p. 16.

35. Secretary of Defense William J. Perry, *On Ballistic Missile Defense: Excerpt from a Speech to the Chicago Council on Foreign Relations*, March 8, 1995, p. 1 (mimeo), cited in Keith B. Payne, *Deterrence in the Second Nuclear Age* (Lexington,: University Press of Kentucky, 1996), p. 58.

36. Payne, *Deterrence in the Second Nuclear Age*, pp. 57–58.

37. For these and other World War II cases, see Paul Kecskemeti, *Strategic Surrender: The Politics of Victory and Defeat* (Stanford, Calif.: Stanford University Press, 1958).

38. Douglas Porch, "The French Army in the First World War," Ch. 6 in Allan R. Millet and Williamson Murray, eds., *Military Effectiveness, Vol. I: The First World War* (Boston: Unwin Hyman, 1988), pp. 190–229, esp. p. 201 and pp. 216–217.

39. George F. Kennan, *Russia and the West Under Lenin and Stalin* (New York: Mentor Books/New American Library, 1960, 1961), esp. Ch. 7–8.

40. Military planners in India and Pakistan cannot discount the possibility of conventional preemption by the other side. The Indian Air Force, while withholding at least ninety strike aircraft designated for nuclear missions, could easily attack all of Pakistan's main air bases and other vital military targets. In turn, a potential threat to Pakistan's nuclear armed bombers in a crisis could lead to a decision for preemptive attack on Indian airfields: Pakistan did so in the wars of 1965 and 1971. See Dunn et al., *The Next Nuclear-Weapon States?*, 2–56, 2–57.

41. Graham, "Cyberwar," p. 10.

42. For extensive documentation, see Peter Vincent Pry, *War Scare: Russia and America on the Nuclear Brink* (Westport, Conn.: Praeger Publishers, 1999), passim.

43. International Institute for Strategic Studies, "Nuclear Weapons First in Russia's Defence Policy: Gambling on a Dangerous Reform Plan," *Strategic Comments: Russia*, No. 1 (January, 1998), p. 1.

44. Ibid.

45. Ibid.

46. Mikhail Shevtsov, "Russian, U.S. Missile Force Chiefs Discuss Security Issues," Moscow ITAR-TASS in English, June 6, 1998.

47. See, in particular: Col. V.V. Kruglov and Col. M. Ye Sosnovskiy, "On the Role of Nonstrategic Nuclear Weapons in Nuclear Deterrence," *Voennaya mysl,'* No. 6 (September, 1997), pp. 11–14, FBIS translation.

48. Thomas Woodrow, Defense Intelligence Agency, *Russian Nuclear Strategy: A Policy in Change*, paper presented at conference in Washington, D.C. on "New Frontiers in Arms Control," March 30–31, 1995, p. 9.

49. *The Washington Post*, September 18, 1998, pp. A25 and A26. See also AFIO *Weekly Intelligence Notes*, September 22, 1998, afio@his.com.

50. Michael R. Gordon and General Bernard E. Trainor, *The Generals' War: The Inside Story of the Conflict in the Gulf* (Boston: Little, Brown, 1995), pp. 419–423.

51. Ibid., p. 423.

52. John S. D. Eisenhower, *The Bitter Woods* (New York: G.P. Putnam's Sons, 1969), pp. 172–174.

53. Allied and German order of battle data for the Ardennes (Battle of the Bulge) campaign from December 16, 1944, to January 16, 1945, are given in Trevor N. Dupuy, David L. Bongard, and Richard C. Anderson, Jr., *Hitler's Last Gamble: The Battle of the Bulge, December 1944–January 1945* (New York: HarperCollins, 1994), Appendix D, pp. 424–57.

CONCLUSION

THE BROADER CONTEXT

There are old and new issues with respect to nuclear arms control and U.S. policy in the twenty-first century. The end of the Cold War and the dawn of the twenty-first century have left behind the certainty of bipolar competition between the United States and the Soviet Union. Instead, the arrival of a multipolar world with diffuse threats of uncertain origin has left U.S. and allied policymakers without a menu-driven answer sheet for many questions, including those dealing with nuclear strategy and arms control. During the 1990s, the Clinton administration emphasized nonproliferation and arms control over the formulation of nuclear strategy for deterrence. As the decade drew to a close, U.S. nuclear strategic doctrine still contained echoes of the 1980s and earlier: a triad of nuclear forces; a requirement for targeting nuclear counterforce, command system and other target classes inherited from war plans of the Cold War; and a priority emphasis on the nuclear deterrent relationship between the United States and Russia, with the latter standing in for the now defunct Soviet Union and its remaining nuclear arsenal.

During the 1990s, the United States and Russia engaged in a process involving both structural and operational arms control. Structural arms control was focused on START nuclear force reductions. START II was signed in 1993 and finally ratified by Russia under the administration of Vladimir Putin eight years later. START II called for both sides to reduce their total warheads carried on strategic nuclear delivery systems to some

3,000–3,500 by 2007. Even before ratification was completed for START II, the two states had begun serious discussions pertinent to concluding a START III or other follow-on agreement. Notional numbers discussed between Russian and American representatives during the Clinton administration called for a START III upper limit of 2,000–2,500 warheads for each side. As the pages turned from the Clinton to the Bush administration, the Putin government indicated it might prefer an even lower ceiling for START III, perhaps as low as 1,500. This reflected Russia's economic constraints in maintaining its forces and the obstacles it anticipated in modernizing all three legs of its strategic nuclear triad. In November 2001 President Bush and Putin met in Washington, D.C., and announced that both the United States and Russia would reduce strategic weapons by at least two-thirds within ten years.

President Clinton had made the Russians nervous with his research and development program for National Missile Defenses (NMD) designed to intercept rogue or "states of concern" attacks or accidental nuclear launches. Clinton said that his program posed no threat to Russia since it was intended to deflect only small attacks. Under Yeltsin Russia remained skeptical, worried that a smaller U.S. system might eventually be expanded into a larger one. When George W. Bush was elected president in 2000, he indicated he would press ahead with NMD and probably expand upon the Clinton program. Russia's reaction from the Putin administration was delphic. The most frequent official line was that the ABM Treaty of 1972, which limited both U.S. and Soviet (and therefore Russian) national missile defense systems in size and character, would have to be amended to permit American NMD. And Russia was not in favor of doing this. On the other hand, Putin also indicated that he might be receptive to amending the treaty by mutual U.S.–Russian agreement, in return for concessions on the size and character of U.S. offensive forces. Bush settled the missile defense issue in December 2001 by announcing the U.S. intent to withdraw from the ABM Treaty.

The U.S. plans and decisions with respect to NMD and for nuclear force modernization also held implications for the control of nuclear proliferation. The United States and Russia were declared supporters of the Comprehensive Test Ban (CTB) treaty and President Clinton was among the treaty's most assertive proponents in the international community. However, the U.S. Congress failed to ratify the treaty during Clinton's second term. Clinton was more successful in achieving indefinite extension of the Nonproliferation Treaty. In the debates surrounding both treaties, some nonnuclear states argued that the United States and Russia had not lived up to their own self-imposed mandates for drastic reductions in strategic nuclear weapons (vertical disarmament) even as Washington and Moscow steadfastly insisted on the need to prevent the spread of nuclear weapons to new owners and/or to roll back some cases of previously acquired nuclear status (horizontal disarmament).

The U.S. national missile defenses might further complicate the relationship between strategic arms reductions and nuclear proliferation. Other states might react to American NMD by increasing the sizes of existing strategic nuclear arsenals; Russia and China both indicated a possible need to do so in 2001. A U.S. national missile defense system might also spur additional interest in the military uses of space, including the weaponizing of space by satellite killers or space-to-earth weapons. Or, for those states that could not compete head to head with U.S. military space technology, asymmetrical responses to missile defenses could include terrorist attacks on American national territory or against U.S. allies, including attacks with weapons of mass destruction (WMD) of the nuclear, chemical, or biological variety. National missile defenses for the United States also raised tricky diplomatic issues. Among these was the question whether a U.S. system would also provide any protection to American allies in NATO. The North Atlantic Treaty provides that an armed attack on any member state is an attack against all. Would a U.S. territorial national missile defense system "decouple" the defense of the American homeland from that of NATO Europe? And if so, would it encourage some European states to rely more on their own national nuclear deterrents, or, in cases of nonnuclear European powers, develop their own nuclear forces?

Within this broader context for the consideration of U.S. and others' nuclear strategy and arms control options, we offer the following conclusions.

SPECIFIC CONCLUSIONS AND ARGUMENTS

First, the question of *strategic stability* lends itself to misconstruction and confusion, with implications for theory and policy. The bipolar rivalry between the United States and the Soviet Union during the Cold War created a fixation on the U.S.–Soviet strategic nuclear balance as the rising and setting sun of international politics. Stability was, during this time, not infrequently measured in a comparably static manner. There was an excessive emphasis on measuring static stability: that is, comparing the various numbers of delivery vehicles (missiles and bombers) and warheads on each side, and calculating from this comparison the "first-strike advantage" available to either side. Although this *first strike stability* was a useful indicator, it left out of the stability equation the larger behavioral and doctrinal issues that drive policymakers and military planners toward or away from war. In addition, we have shown that two new concepts with appropriate measures of effectiveness, *generation stability* and *prompt launch stability*, improve upon the conceptual clarity and methodological validity of first-strike stability.

In addition to first-strike stability, generation stability, and prompt launch stability, *crisis stability* is also an important dimension of the larger concept. Crisis stability includes not only the quantitative attributes of military forces, but also their operational characteristics that might influence leaders to make a hasty or delayed decision for or against war. Further, crisis stability also includes the nonmeasurable attributes that contribute to the development and termination of a crisis: personalities of leaders; group decision-making processes; standard operating procedures and routines of organizations; and command and communication channels that determine who talks to whom, about what, and when. Measures of generation stability and prompt launch stability capture some aspects, but not all, of the more inclusive problem of crisis stability. A summary of the different types of stability appears in Table C.1.

Why is this issue of "deepening" the concept of stability and measuring that deeper concept significant? Part of the answer is that, based on first-strike stability measures alone, one might be complacent about the U.S.–Russian arms control relationship after the turn of the century. In fact, first-strike stability measures might suggest complacency about the entire Cold War period, since no calculation of "relative advantage" for a first striker could have held good once both the Americans and Soviets deployed survivable, diverse, and redundant missile forces. On the other hand, once first-strike stability is supplemented by the concept of crisis stability and an attempt to provide operational definitions and measurements for that concept, otherwise inexplicable events become less mysterious. To take one example from the past: Khrushchev's willingness in 1962 to run the risk of placing Soviet missiles in Cuba makes no sense—indeed is "irrational"—from the standpoint of first-strike stability. Even a "successful" Soviet nuclear first-strike on U.S. national territory would have accomplished only the one-sided destruction of the Soviet Union, which was operating at a seventeen-to-one disadvantage in survivable strategic nuclear power. On the other hand, when we also take into account the behavioral and psychological factors which are important constituents of crisis stability, then the Cuban missile crisis seems less anomalous. Khrushchev's perceived political predicaments in 1962, his risk-acceptant personality, and his expectation that Kennedy might yield in Cuba as the U.S. president had appeared to do over the Berlin Wall in 1961 make his singular attempt to upset the strate-

Table C.1
Types of Stability

Type of Stability	Definition
First Strike Stability	A calculated coefficient or index, based on the cost of striking first compared to the cost of striking second for two states.
Generation Stability	The ratio of arriving retaliatory warheads under conditions of day-to-day alert compared to generated alert
Prompt Launch Stability	The ratio of arriving retaliatory warheads under conditions of delayed launch compared to prompt launch
Crisis Stability	All of the above, plus: The extent to which nuclear command and control, warning and communications systems, including the behavior of leaders, is shock resistant to the possibility of an accidental launch or to an erroneously taken launch decision

Source: Authors. See also: Jerome Wiesner, Philip Morrison, and Kosta Tsipis, *Beyond the Looking Glass: The United States Military in 2000 and Later* (Cambridge, Mass.: Program in Science and Technology for International Security, 1993); Committee on International Security and Arms Control, National Academy of Sciences, *The Future of the U.S.–Soviet Nuclear Relationship* (Washington, D.C.: National Academy Press, 1991), pp. 40–44; Glenn A. Kent and David E. Thaler, *First-Strike Stability: A Methodology for Evaluating Strategic Forces* (Santa Monica, Calif.: RAND, August 1989), pp. 24–29; and Desmond Ball, Hans A. Bethe, Bruce G. Blair, Paul Bracken, Ashton B. Carter, et al., *Crisis Stability and Nuclear War* (Ithaca, N.Y: American Academy of Arts and Sciences and the Cornell University Peace Studies Program, January 1987), pp. 1–25.

gic nuclear balance and deter further American attacks on Castro less at variance with accepted definitions of political rationality.

Second, nuclear deterrence is not self-enforcing, and it may be considerably weaker in the "new world order" than it was during the Cold War. The reasons for this are several. First, new actors will acquire nuclear or other weapons of mass destruction and suitable delivery systems. Second, some of these new nuclear nations will live in the same neighborhoods and dislike each other (Israel and Iran, Iran and Iraq, India and Pakistan, India and China). Third, those recently empowered post-Cold War nuclear states may have fragile or politically irresponsible military command and control systems, including their nuclear ones. Fourth, some of the forces deployed by new nuclear states may be relatively untested under realistic training conditions, dependent on primitive early warning networks, and prone to "assumption failure" as a trigger for war. Fifth, the nuclear forces of regional atomic powers are likely to be compared to those of the Americans, Russians, and other major powers, small and potentially first-strike vulnerable. If so, regional powers will be tempted to operate their forces at higher alert levels and to adopt firing doctrines that emphasize prompt instead of delayed launch.

Third, the reader has by now noticed that some of the preceding descriptors of the likely attributes of new nuclear powers also fit some of the old ones. Russia is the most interesting case in point. Russia's nuclear attack warning and communications system deteriorated in the first decade after the breakup of the Soviet Union. Its economy also went into near receivership for the better part of the 1990s, making possible little in the way of force modernization and investment in improved warning and control systems. Financial distress also meant delayed or denied pay for officers and enlisted personnel, including some of those responsible for the custody of nuclear weapons or for the operation of nuclear forces under normal conditions and during alerts. President Boris Yeltsin's autocratic decision-making, supported by the Russian Federation Constitution, purportedly concentrated the authority for nuclear retaliation in the hands of the Russian president. On the other hand, practical authority was also shared with the Defense Minister and Chief of the General Staff, and the actual ability to launch nuclear forces probably also resided in the General Staff and in the various nuclear forces commands in the missile and air forces. The United States and its nuclear allies in NATO have similar arrangements for delegation of nuclear authority and/or devolution of command. But Russia's delegation and devolution are highly dependent on the personalities who hold the various power ministries, including the Presidency, Defense Ministry, and Chief of the General Staff portfolios.

Russian delegation of authority and devolution of command are also dependent on the condition of the military in Russian society. This condition was arguably not good for the better part of the 1990s. In addition to having been cash starved and losing many of its Cold War level personnel and equipments, the post–Cold War Russian military establishment had a rundown, déclassé look about it. It began to disbelieve in itself from top to bottom. It did not help that underfed troops had to work off hours in fields or factories to purchase food. Nor did the Russian tolerance for *dedovshchina*, the brutal and systematic hazing of new recruits by senior enlisted men, improve matters of morale in the military or its standing in society. Russian men of eligible age avoided military service in record numbers. Those who could not, and survived, returned home with harrowing tales of abuse and neglect on the part of their own officers and enlisted colleagues. The Soldiers' Mothers of St. Petersburg organization became world famous for its investigations into hazing and other brutality inflicted on Russia's young men by its armed forces. Despite their best efforts, there is little evidence of a willingness on the part of Russia's high command to insist on changed personnel policies.

This willingness of Russia's military chiefs to tolerate a deplorable quality of human life in the daily routine of the ordinary soldier has two somewhat broader implications. First, it means that Russia's military is weakest at the sharp end of the spear: in the cohesion necessary for rifle squads, platoons, and companies to come to grips with the enemy in close quarters. The effects of lost military morale and esprit were all too apparent during Russia's military debacle in Chechnya from 1994 through 1996. Even some Russian generals, in Moscow and in Mozdok, publicly expressed dissatisfaction with the entire effort to pacify Chechnya. Further down in the trenches, the dissatisfaction was even more pronounced, and more self-defeating. Russia's own 2001 version of its military doctrine acknowledges that it needs to be better able to deal with internal conflicts and small wars in its "near abroad" of contiguous former Soviet republics. Russia appeared to do somewhat better in Chechnya in 1999 and 2001, if only because Acting President and then President Vladimir Putin was careful to build up popular support in Russia for military escalation. And Russia did improve upon its field performances of 1994–1996 by emphasizing firepower and brutal occupation of devastated and cleared areas outside of the mountainous parts of Chechnya.

On the other hand, Russia's apparent success in the latter Chechen war revealed its conventional military weakness compared to the United States or NATO. Without its nuclear weapons, Russia by 2000 had clearly fallen into the category of a regional military power and not a global one. Whereas during the Cold War it was NATO that pleaded an inferiority in conventional military power and therefore adopted a declaratory policy of nuclear first use, it is now Russia that had adopted an official policy permissive of first use in case of conventional attacks on vital assets in Russia, or in cases of attack on its neighbors posing a strategic threat to Russia. This doctrinal formulation of Russia's nuclear possibilities, undoubtedly the work of its General Staff, reflects the impact on Russian military thinking of two trends. The first, adumbrated by the U.S. use of high-technology, conventional weapons in the Gulf War of 1991, is the "revolution in military affairs" and its possible consignment of Russia to a status of permanent military-technical inferiority relative to the United States and NATO. The second force pushing Russia toward adoption of nuclear first use was NATO enlargement. NATO's expansion to include former Warsaw Pact members Poland, Hungary, and the Czech Republic, made official in the spring of 1999, coincided with NATO's air war against Yugoslavia. Russia felt humiliated in its inability to deter NATO's seventy-eight–day air campaign (Operation Allied Force) or to intervene with more than token diplomatic influence to bring about a cease-fire and war termination. Russia's share of the postwar peace operation did little to console its military establishment, which faced the reality that NATO had gone to war for the first time in its half-century of existence without concurrence from Russia and without bothering to obtain blessing from the UN Security Council.

Fourth, however bad the situation with respect to Russia's nuclear command and control system, and however much its military posture is now dependent on nuclear first use, Russia's situation poses less of an intelligence puzzle (and therefore less of a deterrence puzzle) than does the situation in rogue "states of concern" that may be expected to join the nuclear club in the next decade or two. This list includes Iran, North Korea, Iraq, and other states whose decision-making processes and military operational command systems, compared to those of Russia, are opaque or even unknown. Deterrence, when all is said and done, depends on the assumption that both the "deterrer" and the "deterree" are rational decision-makers. This decision rationality implies that each side in a deterrence relationship can be expected to calculate its relative costs and benefits, or gains and losses, associated with each "move" in a bargaining situation, including nuclear crisis management. But this notion of decision rationality is a Western, not a universal, one, and even in the West it has been subject to occasional amendment by a forceful or aberrant personality.

Faced with nuclear proliferation into the hands of state leaders who are politically unaccountable and perhaps criminally insane, or whose decision proclivities are unknown to U.S. intelligence assessment, deterrence becomes undependable. There is no assumption here that non-Western leaders are any more prone to nuclear risk taking or clinically detached decision methods than their Western counterparts: Hitler, after all, was a product of European culture. What is at issue here is culture combined with: (1), the experience or lack thereof in operating nuclear forces in periods of high political tension; (2), the accountability, or lack thereof, of armed forces' commanders to political authorities, especially those commanders who have custody or control of assembled nuclear weapons. Where culture is highly inflamed by nationalist, religious, or ethnic rivalry, and where these primordial disagreements combine with slack command and control and politically unaccountable brass hats, a recipe for at least regional nuclear war has been brewed. And, once regional, who can guarantee that a "local" nuclear war will not spread further?

There is another disquieting implication of regional cultural hatred, combined with nuclear command-control disability and political irresponsibility. Not only might new nuclear powers be "beyond deterrence" of the cost-benefit sort. They might also seek nuclear weapons to offer an asymmetrical challenge to the U.S. primacy in high-technology, conventional weapons. Combined with ballistic missiles of medium and longer ranges, nuclear or biological weapons could pose deadly threats to deploying or deployed American troops in the Pacific basin or around the rim of Eurasia. Current U.S. strategy, compared to Cold War strategy, envisions the stationing of fewer troops overseas on a permanent basis and more rapid deployment to trouble spots from forces based in the continental United States. Ballistic missiles armed with weapons of mass destruction could pose viable threats to the supply lines and logistics bases of American and allied forces intervening outside of Europe, in addition to their deadly consequences for those forces first tasked to execute forcible entry against hostile defenders.

Fifth, the possible use of asymmetric strategies to deter or defeat U.S. policy planning guidance for being able to fight two, nearly simultaneous, major regional conflicts or theater wars calls for a comprehensive assessment of U.S. national military strategy and its required force composition. This assessment must include the numbers and kinds of strategic nuclear forces that future challenges to deterrence will require. The Cold War gold standard of "assured destruction," conveying the requirement to destroy the Soviet Union as a functioning society, has obviously been superseded by Soviet collapse and the officially nonhostile political relationship between the United States and Russia. The two "superpowers" of the Cold War no longer seriously contemplate the possibility of a deliberate nuclear attack on one another's homelands, or the likelihood that a large-scale, conventional war in Europe would promptly escalate into a world war. The entire question of U.S. nuclear targeting is up for debate and U.S. nuclear planning guidance still required, during the second term of the Clinton administration, preplanned major attack options against Russian nuclear forces, command and control, conventional military forces and their supporting assets (OMT), and Russia's economic base capable of supporting war. Additional attack options were included for strikes against China and probably against regional states of concern.

The outcomes of START II and START III negotiations, assuming they are concluded favorably, will be among the determinants that require rethinking of nuclear strategic targeting. Whether the United States needs a singular, all-encompassing and tightly knitted operational nuclear war plan such as the SIOP, on the assumption that war may come "out of the blue" like a nuclear Pearl Harbor, is a matter already in considerable dispute among military experts. Another issue of contention is the relative balance among weapons and delivery systems set aside for intercontinental nuclear missions, compared to conventional ones. There are also difficult issues about launch platforms that the United States and Russia will have to face. The strategic nuclear "triads" of both are Cold War leftovers, but nonetheless fiercely defended by their partisans for that. There *are* cogent military arguments for preserving the U.S. nuclear triad (for Russia, the question is more urgently one of slack resources), but there are also some persuasive arms control arguments in favor of a U.S. "dyad" of bombers and submarines. Russia, for its part, will be faced with a necessity between 2001 and 2010 to apply Occam's razor to the modernization of its intercontinental nuclear forces. Therefore, it is not impossible that Russia will prefer to settle for a START III agreement that reduces each side to a maximum 1,500 warheads and allows Russia to concentrate its modernization on the ICBM leg of its nuclear forces.

Another issue for considerable debate in the post-START environment is the question of national missile defenses. The Bush administration in January 2001 declared its intention to deploy an American NMD system and Russia's reaction was equivocal: in theory, unalterably opposed; in practice, maybe we'll make a deal. One possible bargain would be an agreement to permit each state to deploy a mixture of offenses and defenses ("freedom to mix") within certain broad ceilings of offensive and defensive capability. Such a bargain might appeal to Russia for reasons both economic and strategic. Russia cannot compete with the United States either in offensive force modernization or in developing and deploying antinuclear defenses. And even if Russia could so compete, Putin's first military priority must be the rebuilding of Russia's conventional armies, fleets, and air forces, for all the reasons discussed earlier. Nuclear weapons can deter a nuclear or major conventional (à la NATO) attack on Mother Russia; after that, they have little practical use, regardless of the inventiveness of overwrought General Staff officers with too much time on their hands. Nuclear weapons are politically useful under very specific conditions, but not militarily useful unless against a nonnuclear state (and, even then, strikes by Russia against a nonnuclear state risk international condemnation and loss of economic aid from the West judged vital by Russia's own economic planners).

The defense planning review conducted by the Bush administration, already under way in February 2001, offered some hope of answering these larger issues of U.S. nuclear arms control and other relationships with Russia, with allies, with potential U.S. adversaries, and with other state and nonstate actors. There were some early indications that Bush and his defense secretary Donald Rumsfeld would opt for selective modernization that emphasized next-generation high-technology weapons for C4ISR (command, control, communications, computers, intelligence, surveillance, and reconnaissance) together with precision strike and stealth. Such a perspective would mandate more selectivity in procurement and purchase among weapons systems already in the services' and contractors' pipelines, including three different types of advanced fighter aircraft. Nuclear weapons could be cut too, but nuclear weapons are inexpensive relative to advanced conventional weapons that require "smart" eyes, ears, and brains. Dumb and cheap as they are, nuclear weapons remain dangerous and appealing to possible opponents of the United States. Therefore it seems unlikely that Bush or his successors will opt for fewer or less capable nuclear weapons than the numbers and quality to maintain American nuclear standing at the head of the pack. This can be done with fewer weapons than we have now—in fact, with many fewer if Russia and China cooperate, as in the Putin-Bush declarations of November 2001 on force reductions. Symbols of power but also of risk and of catastrophe during the Cold War, nuclear weapons remain as necessary evils into the twenty-first century. This is for understandable reasons of no comfort to ethicists or theologians, but politicians and military planners are trapped in a Clausewitzian universe, where the road test for weapons and deterrence is the successful outcome that advances the national interest.

HYPOTHESES AND SPECULATIONS

The Russian Enigma

From the perspective of some expert analysts and policymakers, the changed international environment for security issues in the twenty-first century, compared to that of the Cold War, requires drastic rethinking of arms control and nuclear strategy too. The arguments for paradigm change in the U.S. approach to security have deduced certain military expectations from geopolitical and operational assumptions. The first, or geopolitical, argument is that Europe is essentially pacified or, at least, debellicized. The probability of major interstate war in the next decade involving Russia or any other European state, including the member states of NATO, is so low as to pass below the radar of major threat assessment. Therefore, according to the second, or operational-strategic line of argument, American and allied NATO threat assessments should focus on the more diffuse, chaotic, and asymmetrical threats to U.S. and allied security. These threats include: ballistic missiles and WMD in the hands of rogue states; unconventional warfare, low-intensity conflict and terrorism, including the urban varieties of each; cyberwar and netwar; and the possibility that humanitarian crises and failing states' civil wars will grow into security challenges calling for military peace support or other armed intervention by outside powers.

If these geopolitical and military-strategic arguments about a new security landscape are credible, what are their implications for arms control and U.S. nuclear strategy? Not all of that subject can be addressed here, but we offer some food for thought pertinent to the future international security environment and U.S. nuclear arms control options.

First, the United States must decide which Russia it prefers to deal with. Two antithetical images of Russia's future compete for validity in the minds of U.S. policymakers and policy-attentive publics. The first perspective on Russia is the one that exists in the minds of some high-level civilian and military leaders in the Putin government, shared with some disgruntled Russian parliamentarians and media pundits. This view assumes that Russia is the former Soviet Union temporarily down on its luck, combined with the national character and potential greatness of pre-Soviet imperial Russia. Russia's emphasis in foreign and security policy, from this perspective, should be on restoration of its former Russian-Soviet grandeur and international influence. Russia's military should be rebuilt so that it is eventually capable of remaining first among equals in Europe, if not a peer competitor for the United States. Further NATO enlargement should be rebuffed. And U.S. plans to deploy a national missile defense system should be deflected unless the Bush administration agrees to make major concessions on offensive arms limitations to Russia's liking. Meanwhile, so long as Russia's economic condition precludes serious military improvement, especially of its conventional forces, Russia must act the role of a major diplomatic player on the international stage and make no gratuitous concessions in nuclear arms control or on proliferation. We might refer to this perspective as the "pessimistic-unilateralist" view of future Russia and its perceived security dilemmas and options.

Assuming a second perspective on Russia offers a different set of opportunities and constraints for U.S. policymakers. This second perspective assumes that Russia is in a state of flux, feeling diplomatically and strategically weakened and embarrassed by the demise of the Soviet Union and the economic collapse of the 1990s. But this state of flux does not necessarily have to lead to U.S.–Russia conflict on nuclear arms control or on other important security issues. Russia, from this perspective, needs time to construct a new relationship with the international community, including the definition of a more inclusive security space that embraces Russia as well as NATO Europe. Therefore, it follows that further NATO enlargement should be delayed until Russia can be offered membership in NATO or in some NATO-plus-Russia grand security glacis from Vancouver to Vladivostok. The object of such a Northern Security Pact would be to diminish Russia's feelings of backwardness and isolation vis-à-vis the United States and NATO. It might also serve to bring Russia into peace operations and other taskings already shared among NATO and its Partnership for Peace collaborators. The Northern Security Pact or its equivalent (an OSCE with organic military muscle, or a European regional pillar of NATO including Russia) might also expedite the further reduction of U.S., NATO, and Russian strategic and nonstrategic nuclear weapons. National missile defenses, within this larger security space more permissive of agreement, could be multilateralized to include West and East Central Europe as well as European Russia. This view of Russia's security possibilities and constraints might be termed the "optimistic-multilateralist" view of Russia's perceived security dilemmas and responsive options.

From both perspectives, admittedly exaggerated for the purpose of bringing out contrasting views, we have stressed the significance of Russia's *perceived* security dilemmas and responses. The United States, in formulating its diplomatic and strategic options, has all too often indulged in "mirror imaging" of another state's international intentions and foreign policy proclivities. This mirror imaging happened too frequently during the Cold War, and it resulted in reading Russians wrong because we read them as somewhat backward Americans. Thus, it was assumed that the Soviet military and political leadership, including their representatives in nuclear arms limitation talks, would eventually learn from their U.S. counterparts the "correct" way to think about deterrence and the prevention of nuclear war. Of course, the Soviets were sometimes guilty of making the same mistake: assuming that the Americans had to reason about deterrence and arms control just as Russians did. When the Americans did not, some Soviet leaders and their advisors assumed that Washington must be lying or tricking Moscow.

If the United States is to adjust to the new world order with Russia as a security partner instead of an implacable adversary, then the Russians' view of their own international security dilemmas and possibilities must remain uppermost in the minds of American policymakers. It need not be the case that Americans acquiesce to the Russian view as authoritative; nor should the United States make concessions, in nuclear arms or in any other area, that leave Russia or any other state in doubt about American military power and our willingness to use it on behalf of vital or other interests.

That having been said, as a singular global military superpower, the United States can afford to take into account Russia's present and understandable feeling of military inferiority and not necessarily paranoid fears of falling out of the ranks of great powers. Nuclear weapons keep Russia in the club of great powers for the moment, but they cannot keep Russia at the table forever unless Russia rebuilds its economy, improves its conventional forces, and repairs the ruts in its society created by seventy-odd years of communism and another decade of Yeltsin-esque escapism. A Russia that feels insecure is more, not less, dangerous to Europe and North America.

It follows that, with regard to nuclear arms control and antimissile defenses, U.S. dealings with Russia require a balance between *reassurance* and *dissuasion*.[1] Reassurance takes into account Russia's actual weaknesses and its perceived sensitivities about them. Dissuasion resembles deterrence, old style, but it also includes a component of military persuasion: using force not only to threaten, but also to encourage the other side to see that it is in the best interest of both not to escalate a crisis or war. Dissuasion adds the idea of de-escalation to deterrence. If, for example, a crisis should erupt in Europe over NATO enlargement and Russian counterdeployment of tactical nuclear weapons into Kaliningrad or Belarus, the United States would not only want to *deter* Russia from actual military attack. It might also want to *reassure* Russia that NATO planned no hasty military moves, and it might want to *dissuade* Russia from precipitate action by taking steps to dampen or de-escalate a looming crisis (e.g., by not deploying nuclear weapons or delivery systems capable of reaching Russia in East Central Europe or the Baltics). Applying the same combination of tools to the problem of antmissile defenses and the ABM Treaty, the United States should not have walked out of the treaty by unilateral decree in order to justify deployment of a missile defense system. Instead, the United States should have worked with Russia to define a perceived win–win solution and "multilateralize" the solution to include NATO as well as Russia.

We acknowledge that the preceding forecasts and arguments involve speculation about great uncertainties. But policymakers and their military advisors will be engaged in speculation and guesstimation too. The question is how they will approach the task. We are arguing for open-minded and nonjudgmental approaches to U.S.–Russian nuclear arms control and U.S. nuclear strategy in the belief that such approaches will maximize the likelihood of strategic partnership instead of security deadlock.

Defenses and Proliferation

Advocates and opponents of missile defenses now contend for center stage in the new great debates over nuclear deterrence. The administration of President George W. Bush is determined to move forward with National Missile Defense (NMD), come what may. The United States says that Russia should not be concerned about such limited defenses and that Russia's leadership and military are still locked into Cold War thinking. Russia recognizes that the United States is years away from being able to deploy a reliable system that can shoot down even a handful of warheads, and further still from deploying a system that can threaten Russia's retaliatory force. Nevertheless, Russia's view is less driven by technological possibility, as in the U.S. case, as it is motivated by its international threat perceptions and internal politics.

How good can missile defense technology get in the next decade or two? Undoubtedly better than it is now. Whether it will be good enough to overturn deterrence based on offensive retaliation, even with greatly reduced U.S. and Russian offenses, is doubtful. But even partial defenses, mutually deployed under an agreed arms control regime, might help to preserve the balance of terror in the twenty-first century instead of undermining it. The Cold War balance of terror was supported by a unique international distribution of military power. The Americans and Soviets towered over everyone else. The major issue for Cold War arms race and crisis stability was stabilizing the U.S.–Soviet nuclear strategic balance and, along with that, qualitative measures of reassurance to reduce the risk of accidental or inadvertent war. If Washington and Moscow were nuclear-pacified, the remainder of the system was probably safe.

Not so in the next several decades. When India and Pakistan went public in 1998 with their de facto nuclear status, a fault line was crossed. Previously declared nuclear powers, with the possible exception of China (on again, off again) during the Cold War, were those who more or less favored the international system status quo. The United States, Britain, France, the Soviet Union, and China were the original or successor Big Five members of the UN Security Council and this came to coincide with their eventual leadership in the development and deployment of nuclear weapons. Although the United States regarded the Soviet Union as an anti-system state and the Soviet Union similarly regarded the capitalist powers, the superpowers' strategic nuclear supremacy over other states held back tensions and outbreaks of war that might otherwise have resulted in a more diffuse nuclear system. We are heading into that more diffuse system now. As nuclear weapons and ballistic missiles spread to more states and perhaps to nonstate actors as well, the U.S. Cold War approach of pristine containment against proliferation will need to be rethought. Some of the "oldthink" about nuclear proliferation is still official policy: No proliferation is good, and less is better. No new states should acquire nuclear weapons, and those who do should be encouraged toward nuclear disarmament as soon as possible.

The sentiment for nuclear disarmament is as laudable as it is improbable of realization.[2] The established nuclear powers have "taught" the nonnuclear states the value of nuclear weapons as weapons of last resort against military coercion. Consider, in this regard, the currently prevailing nuclear doctrine of Russia. Russian military doctrine now holds that there are a variety of threats to Russia, in addition to the possibility of nuclear attack against Russian or allied territory, that would justify nuclear first use in self-defense. This is an obvious concession by Russia to its weakness in conventional military power.[3] But it also reflects the unwillingness of Russia, of the United States, and of the other acknowledged major nuclear powers to make drastic reductions in their strategic nuclear forces. This might change if the United States and Russia decided to use START III as an opportunity to reduce drastically their current numbers of warheads and launchers, say to 1,000 or fewer. Indications are that professional militaries in both countries would be loath to go that low because: (1) current targeting plans would have to be greatly revised and many hitherto targeted objectives would be deleted from their war plans; and (2) the willingness of Britain, France, and especially China to reduce their inventories of strategic nuclear warheads and delivery systems in proportion to American and Russian START III reductions has not been ascertained, and some experts are pessimistic. So, if the United States and Russia wish to preserve their status as first and second among nuclear powers, then there is a limit below which they cannot go, say 1,500 warheads or so. Interestingly this is the preferred benchmark proposed by some Russians for START III.

So, if the major nuclear powers cannot or will not set an example of drastic "vertical" disarmament, then their ability to influence or coerce others into a "horizontal" disarmament of contained proliferation is probably weaker. That being the case, the additional spread of nuclear weapons and long-range delivery systems outside of the currently acknowledged nuclear Club of Seven (with Israel generally regarded as a de facto, but unacknowledged, nuclear power) is inevitable. Accepted as inevitable, proliferation invites some very different predictions as to its consequences. Some international relations theorists argue that the spread of nuclear weapons is not necessarily dysfunctional for stability.[4] This school of thought judges that nuclear-armed states in the present century will be as risk averse as were the Cold War nuclear powers. Other experts contend that it is futile for the United States to object to any and all nuclear and missile proliferation. Instead, they contend, the United States should selectively oppose proliferation in so-called rogue states or "states of concern" that pose a serious security threat to the United States, its allies, and their military forces.

We might refer to these pro-proliferation positions as the pandemic and the pick-and-choose arguments. On the other side, various schools of thought argue against any additional nuclear proliferation, and some argue as well for the rolling back or even the elimination of all existing weapons until a virtual or actual nuclear disarmament has taken place. Those arguing for nuclear disarmament include not only academic or other analysts, but also former policymakers and strategic force commanders (Robert McNamara, secretary of defense under Kennedy and Johnson, and Lee Butler, former commander in chief of U.S. Strategic Command). Those against proliferation might be divided into antiproliferation incrementalists and antiproliferation systemists. The incrementalists want to prevent any additional states from going nuclear and to create additional disincentives for nuclear first use and prompt launch doctrines. The antiproliferation systemists are not content to stop where we are with respect to the numbers of weapons, or with regard to existing habits of operating nuclear forces. The systemists want to roll back the number of nuclear powers by moving to "virtual" nuclear weapons (disassembled in peacetime and capable of being reconstituted in the event of a threat of war) or to complete nuclear disarmament. Incrementalists emphasize what can be accomplished in the here-and-now and under the existing constraints imposed by state sovereignty. Systemists emphasize the continuing risk of a nuclear shot fired in anger so long as nuclear weapons remain deployed and armed for ready firing.

A summary chart for the various positions on proliferation already identified above appears in Table C.2.

What are the implications of these diverse perspectives on proliferation for defenses? Defenses might help to restrain proliferation if they discouraged aspiring small powers, including rogues, from deploying warheads and ballistic missiles—on the grounds that defense by denial was available to the attacked state in addition to the possibility of retaliation. On the other hand, if U.S. defenses moved beyond the capability to defeat small attacks (tens of warheads) toward a capacity for deflecting larger attacks (hundreds of warheads), then American defenses might encourage "vertical proliferation" on the part of Russia and China. Russia and China might respond to U.S. defenses by increasing the numbers of their delivery systems and deployed warheads and by MIRVing their ballistic missile systems.

It seems, therefore, that defenses have to find a *zone of imperturbability* such that they are good enough to deter bad actors with small arsenals, but not good enough to deter bad actors with big nuclear inventories. And if

Table C.2
Nuclear Proliferation Perspectives

Position	Definition
Pro-proliferation "pandemicists"	The spread of nuclear weapons can be controlled and made compatible with international stability. Under some foreseeable conditions, "more" is actually "better." Nuclear weapons are no more dangerous after the Cold War than they were during it. New nuclear powers are not necessarily more accident prone or risk averse than older ones.
Pro-proliferation "selectivists"	Proliferation is dangerous if weapons and delivery systems spread to rogue regimes, terrorists, and those with grudges against the existing order. But in the hands of states that support peaceful resolution of disputes and among whom a stable security community exists, nuclear weapons do no harm and may reinforce stability.
Anti-proliferation "systemists"	No nuclear weapons spread is good. Efforts should be made to prevent any additional non-nuclear states from going nuclear, and opportunities to roll back existing nuclear arsenals should be taken advantage of. "Fewer" is better.
Anti-proliferation "incrementalists"	Despite the best of intentions, nuclear weapons, other WMD and missile delivery systems are fated to spread beyond the circle of present holders. U.S. policy should aim to check those aspiring nuclear powers who might pose security risks to U.S. allies, to the American homeland or to U.S. capabilities for military deployment overseas.

technology takes U.S. missile defenses beyond current limitations into another generation, in which space-based, speed-of-light weapons can actually be deployed, then these weapons will become the new dominators of the arms race. For if such weapons can be moved from the drawing board and laboratory into outer space and parked there without being shot down by opposed antisatellite weapons, then the United States will have at least temporarily seized the "high ground" of military supremacy with regard to nuclear deterrence and defenses. On the other hand, these space-based weapons will have offensive as well as defensive capabilities; they can themselves serve as ASATs in order to attack another state's communications, navigation, reconnaissance, and command-control systems. In other words, "defensive" space based weapons can be used to make first strikes against the eyes and ears of another state, opening the door to strategic coercion or military defeat.

The relationship between twenty-first century antimissile technology and nuclear proliferation is therefore a complicated one, with pathways and relationships not as yet determined. There is the further complication that deterrence itself is at risk in an international order where bipolarity no longer reinforces the ordering effects of nuclear fear, as it did during the Cold War. The very structure of international politics is now a bidding game for which the anodyne term "multipolarity" is much too linear a word. Chaos would be a better term. No one is in charge, not even the United States; American military power, strong as it is, was hard put by the end of the 1990s to conduct several simultaneous peace operations, never mind to carry on two nearly simultaneous major wars as called for in official policy. Whether necessary modernization of U.S. conventional forces between now and 2020 can be afforded while antimissile defenses are also developed and deployed is a matter of some contention inside, and outside, the Pentagon. The existence of a chaotic world of diffuse and uncertain threats outside American borders, combined with the resource constraints that even a budget-busting "surplus" must impose, call for nuclear strategy planners and arms controllers to consider all possible choices, including policies and programs previously regarded as too drastic for polite discussion. The world is moving fast and it may not wait for the usual pace of bureaucratic "options" to catch up with it. The real "Revolution in Military Affairs" that is now called for is not only about technology, it is also, and more fundamentally, about our thinking.

NOTES

1. See Stephen J. Cimbala, *The Past and Future of Nuclear Deterrence* (Westport, Conn.: Praeger Publishers, 1998), pp. 19–31 and 61–84, and Cimbala, *Nuclear Strategy in the Twenty-first Century* (Westport, Conn.: Praeger Publishers, 2000), pp. 93–128 and 181–202.

2. For diverse perspectives on this topic, see Michael McGwire, "The Elimination of Nuclear Weapons," Ch. 9, pp. 144–166, and Michael Quinlan, "Aspiration, Realism and Practical Policy," Ch. 3, pp. 45–55, both in John Baylis and Robert O'Neill, eds., *Alternative Nuclear Futures: The Role of Nuclear Weapons in the Post-Cold War World* (Oxford: Oxford University Press, 2000).

3. Both the October 1999 draft and April 2000 official versions of Russia's military doctrine were expansive, but deliberately open-ended, on the circum-

stances under which Russia might resort to nuclear first use. See Dr. S. J. Main, *Russia's Military Doctrine*, Occasional Brief 77 (Camberley, Surrey: Royal Military Academy Sandhurst, Conflict Studies Research Centre, April 2000), for additional perspective.

4. The case for this position is argued by Kenneth N. Waltz. See his chapters in Scott D. Sagan and Kenneth N. Waltz, *The Spread of Nuclear Weapons: A Debate* (New York: W.W. Norton, 1995). Sagan's chapters in the same volume offer counterarguments to optimists about controlled proliferation.

FURTHER READING

Blair, Bruce G. *The Logic of Accidental Nuclear War.* Washington, D.C.: Brookings Institution, 1993.
Cimbala, Stephen J. *Nuclear Strategy in the Twenty-first Century.* Westport, Conn.: Praeger Publishers, 2000.
Clausewitz, Carl von. *On War.* Edited and translated by Michael Howard and Peter Paret. Princeton, N.J.: Princeton University Press, 1976.
Feaver, Peter Douglas. *Guarding the Guardians: Civilian Control of Nuclear Weapons in the United States.* Ithaca, N.Y.: Cornell University Press, 1992.
Gray, Colin S. *Modern Strategy.* Oxford: Oxford University Press, 1999.
Jervis, Robert, Richard Ned Lebow, and Janice Gross Stein. *Psychology and Deterrence.* Baltimore: Johns Hopkins University Press, 1985.
Kent, Glenn A., and David E. Thaler. *First-Strike Stability: A Methodology for Evaluating Strategic Forces.* Santa Monica, Calif.: The Rand Corporation, R-3765-AF, August 1989.
Payne, Keith B. *Deterrence in the Second Nuclear Age.* Lexington: University Press of Kentucky, 1996.
Pry, Peter Vincent. *War Scare: Russia and America on the Nuclear Brink.* Westport, Conn.: Praeger, 1999.
Sagan, Scott D., and Kenneth N. Waltz. *The Spread of Nuclear Weapons: A Debate.* New York: W.W. Norton, 1995.
Scouras, James. "Post–Cold War Nuclear Scenarios: Implications for a New Strategic Calculus." In Stephen J. Cimbala (ed.). *Deterrence and Nuclear Proliferation in the Twenty-First Century.* Westport, Conn.: Praeger, 2001.

INDEX

ABM Treaty, 25, 30, 79, 108; modification of, 28–29, 122, 124; and national missile defense, 27, 47, 162
Accidental launches, 96; and newly acquired arsenals, 133
Agadir crisis, 78
Alert state: day-to-day, 10, 37, 94; failures of equipment and operator errors, 92–93; generated, 6, 9–10, 38, 94; and sending messages, 92–93
Alert strategic weapons, 35–36
Antinuclear strategic defense, 79–80
Arms control perspective, 79; and rejection of defense, 80
Arms race stability, 32
Assured retaliation, 54, 57, 58–60, 68; and arms control, 80; as nuclear strategy, 82
Asymmetric threats, 169, 172
Attack: advantage in, 19–20; order of, 8; preemptive, 9–10

Balance of power, 128–132
Bay of Pigs invasion, 88
Berlin crises, 88

Bipolarity, 130–31, 138; collapse of, 145, 161
BMD (ballistic missile defenses), 98, 122–23
Bombers, 8, 40, 43, 45, 108–9; and verification, 43
Bonaparte, Napoleon, 135
Brezhnev, Leonid, 90, 92
Brodie, Bernard, 82
Bueno de Mesquita, Bruce, 135–36
Bush administration, 162, 170–71
Bush, George, 139
Bush, George W., 26, 30, 105, 162, 171, 175; and National Missile Defense system, 98, 99
Butler, Lee, 177

Capability, 77
Carter administration, 85
Central deterrence, 80
Chaos, 179
Chechnya, 167
China, 122, 123, 124
Churchill, Winston, 147
Cities, 11

Clausewitz, Karl von, 75–76, 87, 88; war by algebra, 93, 95
Client states, 92
Clinton administration, 161; and National Missile Defense system, 98, 99, 124, 162
Clinton, Bill, 28–29, 107, 162
Clinton-Yeltsin summit in Helsinki, 1997, 29, 41
Coercive diplomacy, 91–92, 139
Cold War: characterizations of strategic stability, 31–32; crazy mathematics of, 1–22; and deterrence, 75; end of, 161; flexible response strategy, 77; and polarity, 131; and realism, 132–34
Combat exhaustion, 149
Compellence, 77
Comprehensive Nuclear Test Ban Treaty, 29, 123, 162
Conflict termination: and cease fire orders, 149, 153; and communication, 146; and conditional surrender, 148; and military compliance, 146–51; and nuclear weapons spread, 145–54; political and military control, 150–53; verification of behavior, 153–54
Conventional deterrence, 76
Costs, 14–17; and deterrence stability, 33; manageable, 129–30
Counterforce targets, 4–5
Countervailing strategy, 84–85
Countervalue targets, 4–5, 7–9; power-projection forces, 11–13
Crazy mathematics, 1–22
Credibility, 77
Crisis management, 88–93
Crisis stability, 31–32, 164–65
Cruise missiles, 42
Cuban missile crisis, 77, 88–91, 93, 136–38, 139, 164–65
Cultural symbolism, 11
Cyberwar, 81

Day-to-day alert, 6, 10, 36, 37, 38; and friction, 94
Decision trees, 17–18
Defense: and friction, 98–101; and proliferation, 174–79; rejection of, 80; and zone of imperturbability, 177
Defense emphasis, 82
Destabilizing tactics, 66
Deterrence, 2, 31, 33–35, 52–60, 165–66; and arms control perspective, 79; capability, 77; central, 80; chink in armor of, 22; compellence, 77; credibility, 77; friction and, 75–101; general and immediate, 136–38; latent, 78; manifest, 78; and mirror imaging, 56, 173; misread, 78; in the next century, 122; and proliferation, 168–69; realist premises of, 145; strategic orientation, 79; types of, 76–81
Diehard factions, 146
Diplomacy: coercive, 91–92, 139; shuttle, 91
Dissuasion, 174
Dominant battlespace awareness, 80
Drawdown curves, 6–10

Economics, 107; and international politics, 134–36; and modernization, 108–9, 121, 162
Economic targets, 11
Egypt, 90
Eisenhower, Dwight D., 147
Ellsberg, Daniel, 3

First-strike stability, 1–22, 31, 34, 163–64; assessments of, 10; and central deterrence, 80
First-use option, 33, 86, 176; contingent authority for, 87, 93
Flexible response strategy, 77, 85–87
Force reduction: and friction, 94–95; general goal of, 105

Force structures, 30, 38–47; and modernization, 106–9. *See also* Strategic forces
Friction: and crisis management, 88–93; and defenses, 98–101; and failures of equipment, 92–93; and force reduction, 94–95; and human behavior, 75, 87, 92–93; and nuclear deterrence, 75–101; and offensive force operations, 93–98; in policy and operations, 81–101

Gaddis, John Lewis, 138
General and immediate deterrence, 136–40
Generated alert, 6, 9–10, 35, 38; and friction, 94
Generating forces, as crisis decision option, 18
Generation stability, 32–33, 60–65; and friction, 94–95
Germany, between world wars, 148
Global Terrorism, 123
Gorbachev, Mikhail, coup attempt against, 37
Gray, Colin, 82
Gromyko, Andrei, 89
Gulf War, 153, 167

Hitler, Adolf, 135, 146, 148
Human behavior, 75, 87
Hussein, Saddam, 139

Impossible conditions, 1–2
Increased combat readiness, 6
Index of stability, 19–20
India: crises over Kashmir, 140, 144; nuclear detonations, 127, 175
Indo-Pakistani war scenario, 149–51
INF (Intermediate Nuclear Forces) Treaty, 25
Information technology, 80–81
Inputs, unknowable, 2
International politics, 134–36

Iran, 124; missiles acquired by, 144; rumors of Russian-Iranian nuclear cooperation, 144
Iraq, invasion of Kuwait, 139, 145
Israel, 90; nuclear weapons of, 92

Japan, 147
Joint defense deployments, 98
Joint statements, 28–29

Keegan, John, 87
Kennedy administration, 88–91, 137, 139, 164
Kennedy, John, 77, 89, 91, 137, 164
Kent, Glenn A., 3
Kent/Thaler methodology, 2–22; cost of nuclear war, 14–17; decision trees, 17–18; drawdown curves, 6–10; index of stability, 19–20; philosophy of, 22; results, 20–21; target damage curves, 10–14
Khrushchev, Nikita, 89, 91, 93, 136–37, 139, 164
Kissinger, Henry A., 90–91
Kuwait, invasion of, 139, 145

Lalman, David, 135–36
Lawrence Livermore National Laboratory, 133–34
Limits of realism, 132–40; economics and international politics, 134–36; exceptional cases, 132–34; general and immediate deterrence, 136–38; rational decision making, 138–40

Malinovskiy, Rodion, 89–90
Marshall, S. L. A., 87
Maximum retaliation, 50, 54, 57, 112
McNamara, Robert, 85–86, 177
Mearsheimer, John J., 131
Measures of effectiveness, 35–38
Mikoyan, Anastas, 89
Military compliance, 146–51

Military strategy, nuclear weapons and, 75
Minimum deterrence, 82
Mirror imaging, 54, 173
Missiles, 8, 44–45, 108; cruise, 42; North Korean, 143–44; rail mobile, 108; silos, 8, 44–45, 108; and weapons of mass destruction, 169. *See also* Cuban missile crisis; Submarines
Modernization, force structures and, 106–9, 120, 162
Moltke, Field Marshal von, 78
Montgomery, Field Marshal, 147
Morgan, Patrick M., 136
Multipolarity, 130–31, 161; and chaos, 179

National Defense Authorization Act (NDAA), 30
National missile defense, 98, 99, 108, 123–24, 162–63, 170, 175; and the ABM Treaty, 27, 47; and instability, 67; and NATO, 163
NATO: enlargement of, 27, 100, 107–8, 123, 168, 172–73, 174; flexible response strategy of, 77, 85–87; and national missile defense, 163; threat assessments, 171–72
Nixon administration, 90–92
Nixon, Richard M., 90–92
Nonproliferation Treaty, 29; Article VI of, 49; skepticism about, 140
Northern Security Pact, 173
North Korea, 145; status of, 140, 142–44; ballistic missiles of, 142–44
North Vietnam, bombing of, 139
Norwegian missile incident, 10, 37
Nuclear arsenals, control of, 133–34, 146, 150–53
Nuclear deterrence. *See* Deterrence
Nuclear disarmament: sentiment for, 176; virtual or actual, 177

Nuclear doctrine: first-use option, 33; of Russia, 176
Nuclear parity, and China, 122
Nuclear war: cost of, 14–17, 34; index of stability, 19–20
Nuclear weapons: Club of Seven, 176; increasing importance of, 27, 47; influence of, 138; and information technology, 80–81; Israeli, 92; and military strategy, 75; and peace, 128; quantity and quality of, 35–36; tactical, 77, 87, 174; targets for, 4–22

Ocean areas, 8
October war of 1973, 88, 90–92
Offensive force operations, 93–98
On-line strategic weapons, 35
On-site inspection, 26
Operator errors, 92–93
Order of attack, 8

Pakistan: crises over Kashmir, 144; Indo-Pakistani war scenario, 149–51; nuclear detonations, 127, 175
Payne, Keith B., 145
Perry, William J., 145
Pli'yev, General, 87, 89–90
Polarity, 130–315
Political legitimacy and military control, 133–34, 146, 150–53
Politics: economics and, 134–36; and triad of forces, 106–7
Power: balance of, 128–31; latent, 132
Power-projection forces, 11–13; Russian, 26
Preemptive attack, 9–10; generating strategic forces, 33
Probability domain, 19
Proliferation, 127–54; and antimissile technology, 179; conflict termination and, 145–54; defenses and, 174–79; and deterrence, 168–69;

incrementalists, 177–78; Nonproliferation Treaty, 29, 52, 140; pandemicists, 177–78; perspectives on, 176–77; and realism, 128–32; selectivists, 177–78; systemists, 177–78; weapons of mass destruction, 140–45
Prompt launch, dependence on, 115
Prompt launch stability, 33, 60–65, 67; and friction, 94–95
Putin, Vladimir, 27, 30, 105, 161

Rail mobile missiles, 108
Rand Corporation, 3
Rationality, 131, 138–40
Reagan administration, 85
Reagan, Ronald, 80, 99
Realism: limits of, 132–40; proliferation and, 128–32
Reassurance, 174
Regional cultural hatred, 169
Regional hegemons, and nuclear weapons, 122, 123, 127
Resolve, message of, 33
Retaliation scenarios, 36–38, 58, 80; and friction, 94; maximum, 50, 54, 57, 112
Revolution in military affairs, 167–68, 179
Rodionov, Igor, 152
Rogue nations, 67, 98, 145, 168–69, 177
Rumsfeld, Donald, 171
Russian Federation, 25; arms race and, 125; assured retaliation, 58, 60, 68; condition of the military in, 166–67; conventional forces of, 123; economic reform and democratization, 27, 122, 174; enigma of, 171–74; and first use, 168, 176; and former Soviet republics, 27; generation stability, 60–65, 95, importance of nuclear weapons for, 27, 47, 174; inclusive security space, 173; maximum retaliation, 54, 57; modernization of forces, 108–9, 120, 162; and NMD system, 124, 175; nuclear command system of, 151–52, 166–68; offensive force operations, 93–98; "optimistic multilateralist" view of, 172–73; "pessimistic-unilateralist" view of, 172; power projection capability of, 26, 34; prevailing nuclear doctrine of, 176; prompt launch stability, 33, 60–65, 95, 98 125; state of flux in, 172–73; strategic forces of, 45–49, 68; threat perception of, 107–8, 124; triad of forces, 54, 105, 108–9, 112, 115, 120, 125; U.S./Russian nuclear confrontation, 27–28

SALT Treaties, 25
Schlesinger doctrine, 84
Schwartzkopf, Norman, 153
Sergeev, Igor, 152
Shuttle diplomacy, 91
Silos, 8, 44–45, 108
South Vietnam, 139
Soviet Union: Cuban missile crisis, 88, 91, 93, 136–37, 139, 164; demise of, 75, 82, 107; and first use, 86–87; October war of 1973, 90–92; war plans of, 83–88
Space-based weapons, 178–79
Stalin, Joseph, 147
START I Treaty, 25–26; lapse of, 49; and offensive for operations, 94; Preamble to, 28; Russian force structure under, 47
START II Treaty, 26–27, 43; and offensive force operations, 93–94; Preamble to, 28; ratification of, 105, 107, 161–62; Russian force structure under, 47
START III Treaty, 26, 162, 176; and the ABM Treaty, 28–29; alternative force structures under, 43–44; anticipated as bilateral, 39; dura-

tion of, 42–43; negotiations, 27, 42; and offensive force operations, 93–98; Russian force structure, 44–45; strategic stability implications of, 30, 66, 68; and survivable warheads, 120,; and triad of forces, 43, 117, 120, 124–25; weapon limit under, 67

Strategic Defense Initiative, 98

Strategic forces, 38–47; alert weapons, 35, alternative structures, 34–44; arriving weapons, 36; asymmetry in, 67; inherent value of, 11; lack of parity in, 47; on-line weapons, 35; surviving weapons, 36; total weapons, 35, 47–50; triad of, 43, 45, 54, 105–25, 170

Strategic stability, 25–69, 163–65; assessments of, 10; Cold War characterizations of, 31–32; defining, 30–35; deterrence stability, 33–35, 50–60; first-strike modeling, 1–22; generation stability, 32–33, 60–65; greatest source of instability, 67; measures of effectiveness, 35–38; perceptions of meaning of, 30; prompt launch stability, 33, 60–65, 67; relevance of, 26–30; total strategic weapons, 47–49, 50

Strategic weapon system planning factors, 49–50

Strategy: asymmetric, 169, 172; and policy, 123–25

Submarines, 8, 46, 108; and verification, 45

Subsystemic dominance, 134–35

Surviving strategic weapons, 36

Syria, 90

System determinism, 135

Tactical nuclear weapons, 77, 87, 174

Tactical warning, 9–10; launch on, 38; quality of, 33

Targeting, 4–9; damage curves, 10–14; economic, 11; rethinking of, 170

Technology: information, 80–81; space-based weapons, 178–79

Thaler, David, 3

Theory of International Politics (Waltz), 130

Total strategic weapons, 35, 47–49

Triad of strategic forces, 43, 45, 105–25, 170; and maximum retaliation, 54; and politics, 106–7; rationales for, 106

United States: assured retaliation, 57, 58, 68; and asymmetry in strategic forces, 67; Cuban missile crisis, 88–91, 93, 136–37, 139, 164–65; first-use option, 34; force structure of, 39, 40–44; generation stability, 60–65, 95–98; and information technology, 80; maximum retaliation, 54, 57; and modernization of forces, 109, 120, 171, 179; and NATO, 77, 85–87; offensive force operations, 93–98; perspectives on Russia, 172–73; prompt launch stability, 60–65, 67, 95; as sole military superpower, 154, 174; threat assessments, 171–72; triad of forces, 43, 54, 105–7, 109–10, 117, 120, 125; war plans of, 83–88

Unknowable or unquantifiable inputs, 2

UN Security Council, 175

U.S./Russian joint statements, 28–29

U.S./Russian nuclear confrontation, 27–28

U.S./Russian relations: as exceptional case, 132–34; and strategic stability, 31

U-2 spy plane, 93

Verification, 26; and bombers, 43; and de-tubing, 44

Waiting, 18; advantage in, 19

Waltz, Kenneth N., 130–31, 134, 135

War by algebra, 93, 95

War plans, 83–88, 170
Weapons of mass destruction, 140–45, 163, 169
World War I, 129–30, 147–48

World War II, 146–47; Battle of the Bulge, 153

Yeltsin, Boris, 28–29, 96, 166

About the Authors

STEPHEN J. CIMBALA is Distinguished Professor of Political Science at Penn State University, Delaware County Campus. His most recent books include *Nuclear Strategy in the Twenty-first Century* (Praeger, 2000) and *Clausewitz and Chaos: Friction in War and Military Policy* (Praeger, 2001)

JAMES SCOURAS is a Principal Scientist at DynCorp National Security Programs.